American Home Life, 1880—1930

AMERICAN HOME LIFE, 1880–1930

A SOCIAL HISTORY

OF SPACES AND SERVICES

EDITED BY JESSICA H. FOY AND

THOMAS J. SCHLERETH

THE UNIVERSITY OF TENNESSEE PRESS
KNOXVILLE

The paper in this book meets the minimum requirements of the
American National Standard for Permanence of Paper for Printed
Library Materials. The binding materials have been chosen
for strength and durability.
Printed on recycled paper.

Library of Congress Cataloging in Publication Data

American home life, 1880–1930: a social history of spaces and
services / edited by Jessica H. Foy and Thomas J. Schlereth.
p.   cm.
Includes bibliographical references and index.
ISBN 0-87049-759-6 (cl.: alk. paper)
ISBN 0-87049-855-X (pbk.: alk. paper)
1. United States—Social life and customs—1865–1918.
2. Dwellings—United States—History. 3. Vernacular architecture—
United States—History. I. Foy, Jessica H., 1960–   .
II. Schlereth, Thomas J.
E168.A513   1992
304.2'3'0973—dc20   92-10425

Contents

Illustrations

Preface

In 1987 the McFaddin-Ward House began an annual series of symposia focusing on the American home in the decades just before and after the turn of the twentieth century. After focusing on that period as a transitional age and then on its consumer culture, the museum decided that the more ordinary aspects of domestic life deserved attention. This study would entail an examination of the physical environment and basic functions of the home: its rooms (public and, especially, private), its housekeeping practices (inside and out, machine-powered and manual), and its residents' activities (entertaining and edifying). To address these issues, eleven scholars gathered in Beaumont, Texas, for the museum's 1989 conference. This volume is an outgrowth of that event.

For putting this project within the realm of possibility, we thank the Mamie McFaddin Ward Heritage Foundation, which generously provided funding for the conference. The support of the foundation, the museum's board of directors, and museum director Gary N. Smith is evidence of their continuing dedication to promoting quality educational resources and opportunities. And to Carol Orr, former director of the University of Tennessee Press, we offer sincere thanks for recognizing the potential of the presentations collectively as a published work and for enthusiastically encouraging its development.

The decision to publish the carefully researched, interrelated body of work presented at the conference was easy. Transforming it from a group of oral presentations into publishable form required much more effort. For their diligence, we are deeply grateful to the authors themselves, whose dedication to the project helped make it an enjoyable one for the editors. Despite the fact that the authors were scattered around the country and swamped with other tasks, our work proceeded smoothly. It was our extremely good fortune to be involved with such an amiable, qualified, and cooperative group.

INTRODUCTION

American Homes and American Scholars

Thomas J. Schlereth

The household is, in itself, the condensed history of a nation's
past, the center of its present, and the cradle of its future.
—A. E. Kelly, "Electricity in the Household," *Scribner's*,
January 1890, p. 115

The American residence has been the focus of extraordinary personal and
scholarly attention throughout American history. It has been an inspiration for the literary imagination, a subject of artistic creativity, a metaphor
for social reform, and an icon of social and economic status.[1] For both professional scholars and ordinary citizens, the American home has been, and
continues to be, a site, a space, and a symbol of enormous importance—a
key artifact for studying the nation's past and present.

How have American scholars interpreted American homes in the past?
Why have they been especially fascinated with a particular period, namely,
the fifty years from the 1880s to the 1930s?[2]

In order to answer the first question, if only in schematic form, I divide
American house historiography into three phrases. Each has a dominant
attitude toward the material culture of the home, a disciplinary focus for its
investigation, and an interpretive perspective on American domestic life.
While the phases' ascendencies follow each other in a rough chronology,
each also has its supporters in the present. To be sure, the three typologies
overlap; there are interstices among them, and none applies to all scholars
in its time segment. To formulate them at all requires that I survey (and
fence) a large field over a long time at an abstract level. In so doing, one runs
the risk of oversimplifying and overgeneralizing. I will label three eras and
their approaches as: (1) collecting and authenticating; (2) describing and
classifying; (3) analyzing and explaining.[3]

A Brief House History Historiography

American interest in home history originated within an eclectic cadre of Victorian antiquarians, museum founders, literati, antique collectors, and local gentry.[4] These enthusiasts saw their task primarily as one of "find and save"; their principal objective was collecting, authenticating, and preserving (1) the American homes of the rich and famous, the literary and the literate; and (2) the colonial (particularly Georgian and Federal) residences of the nation's revolutionary generation. Their crusades drew upon the work of one of the country's early architectural historians, Ellen Terry, author of *A History of Architecture in Europe and America,* published in 1848, and were led by the first outstanding American historic preservationist, Ann Pamela Cunningham of South Carolina, and her Mount Vernon Ladies Association, which saved George Washington's home as a national shrine.[5] Similar ladies' voluntary organizations, in addition to addressing various women's issues of their time (a subject that deserves additional research), rescued the homes of great white men such as Jefferson's Monticello (Virginia) and Andrew Jackson's Hermitage (Tennessee).

The late-nineteenth-century Colonial Revival—a design style that would never go out of style in the twentieth century—provided an important catalyst to many of these students of the American home by the last quarter of the nineteenth century. Publications on the topic—for example, James Corner's *Examples of Colonial Architecture in New England* (1892) and two studies by Norman M. Isham and Albert Brown, *Early Rhode Island Houses* (1895) and *Early Connecticut Houses* (1900)—focused on the oldest and most picturesque American homes because their authors valued these buildings for their historical and patriotic associations with great personalities and national events.[6] To them, house history primarily meant the relics of the lives and ideals of the first Euro-Americans; facade and family, site and symbol served as sufficient rationales for their reverent and, in one sense, political interest.[7]

In the historical context of their collecting between the Civil War and World War I, a period of massive non–Anglo-Saxon immigration and widespread labor and political unrest, of religious and racial intolerance and much debate about the national identity, many sought to establish what was truly "American" about American residentiality. These scholars, curators, and collectors often thought "New England" when they wrote or said "American." Hence much early house history was done by New Englanders using examples from the northeastern United States.

Despite their political agenda, their regionalism, and their object fetish-
ism, these early students of the American home contributed significantly to
research on the American residence. They salvaged much material culture
that would have been lost to the juggernauts of progress and modernity.
They also established several of the major institutional formats—historic
house museum, connoisseur periodical, period room, and outdoor history
museum—wherein many of us still do house history.[8]

Art history, with its usual triad of fine, architectural, and decorative art
history, emerged as an important disciplinary perspective in the period just
described. It dominated the second era of writing on the American residence, a period from the beginning to the middle of the twentieth century.
This approach concentrated primarily on issues of form, style, and structure, encouraging connoisseurship (figure 1) and taxonomy.[9]

The art history approach tended to segregate and separate aspects of
home life, emphasizing the public as opposed to the private, downstairs
rather than upstairs, front over back. Much attention was lavished on the
study of facade formats, elevation details, and architectural ornament.
However, some innovators began studying the house as an interior space as
well as an exterior environment.[10] The few that ventured into the house's
interior most often remained content to explore the aesthetic decor and
stylistic accoutrements of a home's formal spaces: usually parlors and dining areas. The new fascination that art historians brought to American
home history was especially evident in the detailed attention they gave to
home furnishings.[11]

Beginning with popular studies such as Frank E. Wallis, *Old Colonial
Architecture and Furniture* (1887); Wallace Nutting, *Furniture of the Pil-
grim Century, 1620–1720* (1921); and Fiske Kimball, *American Architecture* (1924), and extending through well-known surveys such as Wayne Andrew, *Architecture, Ambition and Americans* (1947), and Alan Gowans,
*Images of American Living: Four Centuries of Architecture and Furniture as
Cultural Expression* (1964), these researchers, while their first allegiance
was to who *designed* a house, took a growing interest in who *lived* in it.
Although this art history orientation neglected an increasingly large spectrum of multi-occupancy housing types that had developed in Victorian
America—the boarding house, the apartment, the model tenement, and
the speculation tenement—it did teach us much about the detached single-
family, middle- and upper-class dwelling.[12] We are also indebted to these
scholars for organizations such as William Summer Appleton's Society for
the Preservation of New England Antiquities and its imitators; the Historic

Fig. 1. Sanford Thayer, *The Connoisseurs*, 1845, oil on canvas. Courtesy of the Onondaga Historical Association, Syracuse, N.Y.

American Buildings Survey (figure 2), the National Trust for Historic Preservation; and the Society of Architectural Historians. As the first coterie of students of the American home were predominantly women, members of the second grouping,[13] like the high-style architects and designers they so admired, were mostly male.

In the past two decades, a third approach has emerged, one I would characterize as social history. By no means have the other two major traditions disappeared. But, in addition to those who view American residential history as a select collection of opulent manses of the local/regional Medici or as an edifice gallery of architectural and decorative arts masterpieces created by American masters, we now have a large and diverse coalition of scholars who investigate home history as a complicated environment of social behavior—a complex artifact of artifacts embodying interactions between genders, classes, and generations.[14]

The social history orientation aspires to understand domestic routine as well as design scheme. It is concerned with housing as well as houses; often its researchers are more interested in a home's inhabitants—parents, boarders, servants, in-laws, children, guests—than in its physical habitat. In such scholarship, a home's actors and activities loom larger than its architecture and artifacts.[15]

A Social History of Spaces and Services

The authors in this volume research and write in this social history perspective. Their work here took first form at the third annual conference on house history sponsored by the McFaddin-Ward Historic House Museum in Beaumont, Texas, in November 1989. The objective of that scholarly meeting, titled "Life at Home, 1880–1930," was to "explore household routine and family life at the turn of the century, as revealed through the social and material environment of the home." This book has the same rationale. We concentrate our efforts on three large social history topics identified as "Room Life," "Home Life," and "Keeping House."

A common theme running throughout each chapter is how special rooms, some for special people (for example, children, boarders) and often requiring special furnishings, conditioned or were conditioned by special behaviors. The essays also provide analyses of several interior home spaces, some (such as the parlor) familiar to us, others (such as the bedroom) still largely unexamined by house historians.

As a preface to this focused social history, Candace Volz surveys the styl-

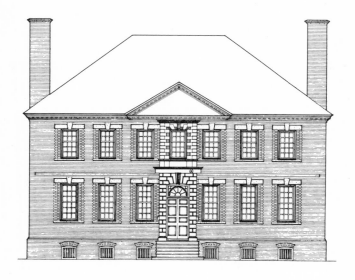

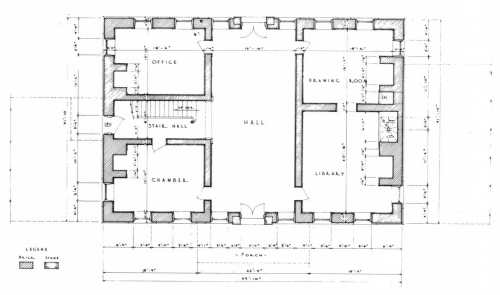

Fig. 2. Sabine Hall, Richmond County, Va., ca. 1735: a) Front elevation; b) First floor plan. U.S. Department of the Interior, Historic American Buildings Survey.

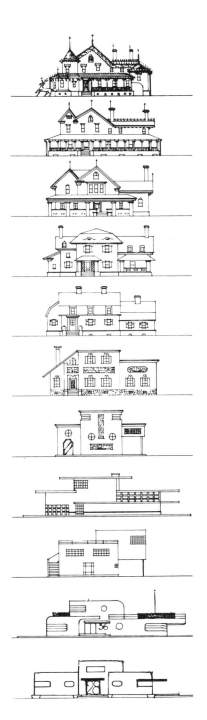

Fig. 3. Raymond Loewy, detail, "Evolution of Design—Housing." From Raymond Loewy, *Industrial Design* (Woodstock, N.Y.: Overlook Press, 1979). Used courtesy of Overlook Press.

Fig. 4a. Interior of residence of Mr. and Mrs. R.A. Acheson and daughter, Watertown, Neb., 1903. Photograph by Solomon D. Butcher; used courtesy of Solomon D. Butcher Collections, Nebraska State Historical Society, Lincoln, Neb.

istic shifts in what was considered "new" or "modern" (figure 3) in early twentieth-century domestic design, from the Colonial Revival to the Swedish Modern. As she chronicles this aesthetic typology, she connects changes in floor plans with shifts in decor preferences.

The room that Volz monitors most frequently is the formal, public space that changed in nomenclature, size, location, furnishings, and function from parlor to living room (figures 4a, 4b) over the period 1880–1930. This specific shift Katherine Grier examines (chapter 2) by demonstrating how the ambience and artifacts of the middle-class parlor expressed a dynamic tension in Victorian home life, a tension she designates by the shorthand terms *Culture* and *Comfort*.[16] Grier explains why the parlor, as a domestic ideal, a family museum, a consumer display, and a memory palace, went into eclipse. She attempts something not frequently undertaken in material culture studies: documenting and interpreting the *decline* of a complex artifact assemblage, while also assessing the surrounding cultural

Fig. 4b. Open-plan combined living-dining room and furnishings. Model bungalow, Sears, Roebuck and Co., Illinois State Fair, 1912. Photograph courtesy of Sears, Roebuck Archives, Chicago.

factors that encouraged such a declension. Since so much of artifact research champions winners, studies that probe why and how things are misused, abused, or abandoned are valuable correctives to the typical Whig interpretation of past objects to which we are all prone.[17]

With the research of Karin Calvert, we begin opening doors into various interior spaces where, to paraphrase Virginia Woolf slightly, middle-class house denizens could have "a room of one's own" for a special purpose or a particular privacy. The nursery (figure 5) and its accoutrements were spaces new to the American home. Calvert tells why and how this rise of the nursery came about and what it meant in terms of gender and generational relations.[18] Linda Kruger does the same for the middle-class home library.

Elizabeth Cromley concludes the book's house tour of turn-of-the-century "new" rooms with a fresh look at an old one (figure 6), the bedroom—a space used daily, yet one about which most house histories say little and of which most historic house museums show less. Cromley,

Fig. 5. Nursery in the home of A.C. Cronin, ca. 1915. Photograph by Joseph Byron; used courtesy of the Byron Collection, Museum of the City of New York.

Fig. 6. Piano Bed. U.S. Patent Office Presentation Drawing, Patent 56413, Charles Hess, Inventor, Filed 17 July 1866.

like Grier, is also intrigued by a cultural tension. She finds a gap between the functional way architects (and sometimes architectural historians) often employ (or interpret) the term *bedroom* on a floor plan and the actual uses and meanings of the bedroom for family members, boarders, and guests. Cromley finds not one but several functions and associations for the domestic space she investigates.

The complexity and diversity of house history as social history is further explored in part II's articles on "Home Life." Under this generic title, the authors are concerned with people acting and interacting—specifically in the activities of playing, praying, and planting—in the home, topics appropriately expressed with gerunds.

Donna Braden proposes a tripartite analysis of how family pastimes and indoor home amusements became increasingly distinct from work-related play carried on at home. She also shows that, just as in public recreation—where leisure pursuits shifted from informal, ostensibly educational experiences (for example, church picnics or nature walks in urban pleasure parks) to commercial, mass-media activities (e.g., attending motion pictures or amusement parks)—in home play, by the 1930s, fun and entertainment came to be emphasized over instruction and uplift.

In surveying parlor piety, Colleen McDannell traces how middle-class Protestants—particularly ministers, reformers, architects, and novelists—promoted an ecumenical, nondenominational religion of the home, wherein family devotions, Bible-reading, and a wide range of religious objects (needlepoint biblical scenes, wax crosses, chromolithographs of scripture verses) established the residence as a sacred space appropriate for religious practice. This domestic sanctuary, like the parlor of which it frequently was a part, however, underwent dramatic social and cultural changes in the early twentieth century. By the 1930s, domestic religion was no longer a unifying force in the pan-Protestantism Martin Marty calls "the righteous empire"; rather, it demarcated the conservative fundamentalist from the liberal modernist within the Protestant faith tradition.[19]

McDannell's comprehensive use of religious artifacts, objects ubiquitous in all of America's liturgical faith traditions and yet strangely ignored by most American material culture scholars, parallels Patricia Tice's work with physical evidence similarly neglected until recently, namely, the artifacts (figure 7) of the home lawn and garden. In addition to providing a typology of garden design (an interpretive scheme the reader might compare to Volz's chronology for furniture design over the same time period), Tice relates gardening, another form of home recreation (and hence com-

Fig. 7. Advertisement, Excelsior Lawnmower, Chadborn and Coldwell Manufacturing Company, Newburgh, New York, ca. 1890.

parable to Braden's games people played), to popular interest in the natural sciences, new botanical discoveries, and the expanding consumerism and specialization of turn-of-the-century home life.

By the book's part III ("Keeping House"), the essayists will have taken the reader practically all over the house, exploring its history, from inside to outside, backstairs to front stairs, routine activities to special events—with two exceptions, that of major new spaces such as the bathroom (a topic I attempt to summarize in chapter 10) and the important shifts in house maintenance that occurred between 1880 and 1930. Such changes involved transformations in *services* (for example, the home utilities of power, heat, light, water, and waste removal), in *servicing* (for example, the impact of home appliances such as gas and electric ranges, washing machines, and refrigerators), and in *serving* (for example, changes in domestic servants' duties, hours of work, racial and ethnic backgrounds).

Ruth Schwartz Cowan, a scholar who, in her study, *More Work For Mother* (1978), has set the research agenda for all future students interested in the interconnections of household technology, housework, housewives, and house servants, argues persuasively that many so-called "labor-saving devices" were not necessarily labor saving.[20] In fact, Cowan demonstrates the opposite of what advertisements (figure 8) for many "innovative" and "modern" household appliances claimed, showing that middle-class housewives were likely to be spending more time doing housework in 1930 than their mothers had in 1890.

Daniel Sutherland assesses another change in keeping house: how several factors—the alterations in household technology that Cowan describes, the changes in domestic interior design that Volz traces, and changing relationships (figure 9) between servants and employers and among paid household workers themselves—nudged domestic service toward some semblance of a "modern" twentieth-century occupation.

American Home Life, 1880–1930

Readers, after completing the essays below, should come away with greater insight as to why many house historians, particularly in the last two decades, have been especially fascinated with American residential life in the period 1880–1930. They should also have ideas as to what topics in the period deserve further study. Here, at the outset, let me summarize a few specific ways in which these chapters in domestic history are simultaneously studies in American intellectual history and in American house history.

Why are we so intrigued by the domestic history of the era 1880–1930? I think a partial answer is that various cultural phenomena were undergoing dramatic *transformation* or transition in that period, as they are in our own. In *Culture as History: The Transformation of American Society in the Twentieth Century,* Warren Susman suggested that *transformation* acted "as a key word in the late nineteenth and early twentieth centuries, becoming significant not only in the worlds of physics and biology but also in the worlds of history and social science as well." For example, writing on Vic-

Fig. 8. Advertisement, Western Electric Vacuum Cleaner. *McClure's Magazine,*
1904.

Fig. 9. "The Maid and Her Mistresses." *Harper's Magazine,* 1874.

torian America, Susman continues, "History increasingly had to confront the changing of forms in which experience was expressed—often rapid change because of technological innovation. Such transformations created the need for still others." In addition to Susman, other historians, using the idea of transformation as their interpretive key, have analyzed changes in housing preferences, consumer choices, recreational innovations, eating habits, and demographic patterns between the Civil War and World War I.[21]

Then, as now, issues of *gender* were in flux. While such issues were publicly manifested in the suffragette, reform, and feminist movements of the time, the most serious debates took place close to home. In our time it has been women scholars who have pioneered in analyzing gender's vital role in the human past.[22] It is no accident that the roster of this book's contributors includes who it does, since it is these women scholars and others who have produced some of the most innovative research on gender's significance in domestic life. We find this focus, for example, in Calvert's observations on male and female children's clothing. Kruger alludes to it in her reference to self-consciously masculine spaces such as dens, studies, and home libraries. For Grier, the Victorian parlor is one place where the woman of the house controlled its content and conduct as well as its culture and comfort. A feminine faith is essential to the domestic environment that McDannell describes. Finally, women's roles are crucial to Sutherland's study of domestic servants and Cowan's comparative work on the home life of middle-class and working-class women.

Ruth Cowan's essay, grounded as it is in the social history of domestic *technology*, identifies another theme of this volume. Each of part III's historians (Schlereth, Cowan, Sutherland) explores house technics, as do several others in earlier chapters: Volz on the introduction of central heating systems, Tice on the expansion of public water supply lines for lawn and garden, and Grier on the mechanisms of upholstery.

Technology—its products and promises—frightened and fascinated turn-of-the-century Americans. Its historical significance is equally compelling to those who probe one of technology's most dramatic half-century of expansion. Who creates technology? Who controls it? What is its impact within one's personal, domestic environment—a site, a space, a symbol that many Americans consider it their right to create and control?[23] In the studies that follow, several answers are provided to these questions, with particular attention paid to the impact of the steam heat radiator, the incandescent light, the gas range, and the family automobile.

Each of these items is, in addition to being a technological innovation, also a *consumer* product. While historians debate the exact origins of "the consumer revolution"—some date it as early as the eighteenth century in America—our authors all see it as a vital historical force shaping home life in the years 1880–1930.[24] Hence much of the graphic evidence by which they document their interpretations is the material culture of advertising. The visual portfolios that accompany their verbal arguments are largely composed of broadsides, posters, chromolithographs, and photographs. Such data has been extracted from the period's mail-order catalogs, mass-circulation magazines, metropolitan newspapers, or trade and promotional catalogs. Here there is considerable agreement with Marshall McLuhan, who wrote in *Understanding Media* (1964): "Historians and archaeologists will one day discover that the ads of our times are the richest and most faithful daily reflections that any society ever made of its entire range of activities."[25] To be sure, the authors recognize that advertising has its problems as historical evidence. An issue touched upon in Cowan's essay, for example, is how representative advertising is of different classes, regions, and racial and ethnic groups.

While advertising is not a particularly new or modern phenomena, its unprecedented proliferation is assuredly a characteristic of contemporary modernity. A final reason many of us are taken with house history between 1880 and the 1930s is that it is one tangible, physical context in which to study the perennial American enthusiasm for, and anxiety about, the meaning of *modernity*. Our first (Volz) and last (Sutherland) authors intone the "modern" in their titles. Several others address this issue more obliquely but no less seriously. They are struck by how many of that past era's crucial cultural questions—rapid demographic changes, increasing urban/suburban residentiality, expansion of a white-collar, managerial work force, the "discovery" of childhood and adolescence, consumerism, expanded leisure, and changes in family relations—still concern us.[26] They recognize that, in many ways, our times began in this time—in Home Life, 1880–1930.

House History: Future Questions to Explore

The chapters below probe the history of the American residence, 1880–1930, both as an assemblage of separate objects and as collective artifact ensembles—each undergoing changes in form and function, material and meaning. They also explore domestic life as an interaction of individual people and collective groups, one in which gender and generational, economic and social factors play important roles.

In this attempt to understand the domestic environment as an increasingly complex (also read "increasingly specialized") place, several authors analyze spaces that might be thought of as rooms within rooms, as "roomlets": inglenooks, playpens, sleeping rooms, breakfast nooks. Several of these types of space deserve additional research. We also need to know more about other such house spaces—basements and attics (storage areas vital in a consumer society), carriage houses and auto garages. The latter, in addition to being containers for consumer goods, have become—as in garage sales—sites for consumer buying and selling.

To speak of the home garage (an artifact that, like the privy, migrated from outside to inside the American residence) reminds us that historians still have much to explore concerning a house's relation to nature. Several chapters address this topic. There is Tice's on home and garden, certainly, but also Volz's brief discussion of sun rooms, Calvert's mention of the kindergarten, Cromley's attention to "the natural air movement" and sleeping tents, Grier's interest in "plants in the parlor," my reference to how home utilities technologies sought to master nature, and, finally, Braden's observation that certain outdoor home games (for instance, lawn tennis) moved indoors to become home entertainments such as ping-pong.

In addition to the outside-inside relation, this volume suggests research that might be done on the parallels between private domestic spaces and public institutional environments. To illustrate this point, we learn how the interior decor of railroad Pullman car, daguerreotypist studio, steamboat salon, and hotel lobby influenced home parlors. Many early public libraries had spacious hearths like those found in residential libraries. Catharine Beecher's chapter, "The Christian Home," in *The American Woman's Home* (1868), provides an analog (as well as floor plans) for the parlor as a sanctuary and the manse as a church. Other late Victorian institutional contexts deserve study as to their connections with their residential counterparts: orphanages and reformatories, botanical gardens and public conservatories, welfare agencies such as social settlement houses (recall that Hull House in Chicago eventually featured a New England Kitchen), and, of course, lodging and boarding houses.

While we include no extended discussion of multi-occupancy dwellings, much less public housing, in this book, Cromley connects sleeping spaces (different for male and female) in boarding homes with bedroom furnishings in the private residence.[27] House historians should follow this lead and research other homes-away-from-home: college dormitories, vacation cottages, motels, YMCA and YWCA residences, and mobile/motor homes.

Such a research agenda—one considerably wider than that of those scholars whom I earlier labeled political historians and art historians— moves us from the study of buildings to the study of behaviors. The essays below aspire to such a study, particularly the behaviors of those men, women, and children who peopled the middle-class, single-family, detached American home, in 1880–1930.

This social history orientation prompts me to conclude my recommendations for future house history by noting a group of individuals that I mention again in chapter 10. The "house people" I have in mind do not live in the American house but rather service it; they do so sometimes in ways similar to the work of those domestic servants described by Dan Sutherland, but at other times their tasks are different. Many of these "outside" house people have traditional occupations with important connections to residential life—house builders, movers, remodelers; delivery personnel (ice, coal, food, fuel); postal carriers, telegram and other messengers; peddlers and, of course, door-to-door salesmen of all types. How much do we know of the social history of such groups in the past? Did their relations with a house's inhabitants change over time? How? Why did some occupations (for example, home delivery) decline? How did such declension affect the quality of home life?

Victorian America also spawned new types of housework and home servicers: rural free delivery postal carriers, consumer salespeople (the Avon lady, 1896; the Fuller Brush man, 1905); mass-circulation magazine subscription promoters selling serials such as *Ladies' Home Journal, House Beautiful, House and Garden*; life, automobile, and home insurance agents; social service case workers, who began to visit lower-class homes; interior decorators, who called upon upper-class clients; building code inspectors and zoning ordinance officers, who evaluated everybody's residence. Finally, two occupations—real estate (agents, developers, building and loan officers) and service industries (appliance repair, meter reading) that parallel our dual concern with home life's social history of spaces and services—began to assume the roles they continue to play in twentieth-century residential life.

Notes

1. Alan Gowans, *Images of American Living: Four Centuries of Architecture and Furniture as Cultural Expression* (Philadelphia: J.B. Lippincott, 1964). Jean Mudge, *Emily Dickinson and the Image of Home* (Amherst: Univ. of Massachusetts Press, 1975). Vicki Halper Litman, "The Cottage and the Temple: Melville's Symbolic Use of Architecture," *American Quarterly* 21, no. 3 (1969):630–38. Kent C. Bloomer and Charles W. Moore, *Body, Memory, and Architecture* (New Haven, Conn.: Yale Univ. Press, 1977). Ellen Elizabeth Frances, "Progressivism and the American House: Architecture as an Agent of Social Reform" (M.A. thesis, Univ. of Oregon, 1982). Amos Rapoport, *House Form and Culture* (Englewood Cliffs, N.J.: Prentice Hall, 1969). Thomas J. Schlereth, *Historic Houses as Learning Laboratories: Seven Teaching Strategies* (Nashville, Tenn.: American Association for State and Local History (AASLH) Press, 1976).

2. See e.g., Gwendolyn Wright, *Moralism and the Model Home: Domestic Architecture and Cultural Conflict in Chicago, 1873–1913* (Chicago: Univ. of Chicago Press, 1980); Alan Gowans, *The Comfortable House: North American Suburban Architecture, 1890–1930* (Cambridge, Mass.: MIT Press, 1986); John R. Wunder, ed., *Home on the Range: Essays on the History of Western Social and Domestic Life* (Westport, Conn.: Greenwood, 1986); George Talbot, *At Home: Domestic Life in the Post-Centennial Era, 1876–1920* (Madison: State Historical Society of Wisconsin, 1976).

3. For a more detailed rationale for this periodization scheme, see Thomas J. Schlereth, "Material Culture Studies in America, 1876–1976," in *Material Culture Studies in America,* ed. Thomas J. Schlereth (Nashville, Tenn.: AASLH Press, 1982), 1–78. Peter Rider has applied the typology to Canadian scholarship in his essay, "Concrete Clio: Definition of a Field of History," *Material History Bulletin* 20 (Fall 1984):93–94.

4. Charles B. Hosmer, Jr., *Presence of the Past: A History of the Preservation Movement in the United States before Williamsburg* (New York: Putnam, 1965); Charles B. Hosmer, Jr., *Preservation Comes of Age,* vol. 1, *From Williamsburg to the National Trust, 1926–1948* (Charlottesville: Univ. Press of Virginia, 1981), 1–74; Claire Gilbridge Fox, "Henry Chapman Mercer (1856–1930); Tilemaker, Collector, and Builder Extraordinaire," *Antiques* 104 (Oct. 1973):678–85; Elizabeth Stillinger, *The Antiquers* (New York: Knopf, 1980).

5. Karal A. Marling, *George Washington Slept Here: Colonial Revivals and American Culture, 1876–1986* (Cambridge, Mass.: Harvard Univ. Press, 1988); John W. Tebbel, *George Washington's America* (New York: Dutton, 1954).

6. Dell Upton, "The Power of Things: Recent Studies in American Vernacular Architecture," in *Material Culture: A Research Guide,* ed. Thomas J. Schlereth (Lawrence: Univ. Press of Kansas, 1985), 59–60.

7. Harvey Green, "The Ironies of Style: Complexities and Contradictions in American Decorative Arts, 1850–1900," in *Victorian Furniture,* ed. Kenneth L. Ames (Philadelphia: Victorian Society, 1983), 23–29. Also see John Higham, *Strangers in the Land* (New Brunswick, N.J.: Rutgers Univ. Press, 1988); and Barbara Miller Solomon, "The Anglo-Saxon Cult," in *Intellectual History in America,* ed. Cushing Strout (New York: Harper and Row, 1968), 28–38.

8. Melinda Young Frye, "The Beginnings of the Period Room in American Museums: Charles P. Wilcomb's Colonial Kitchen, 1896, 1906, 1910," in *The Colonial Revival in America,* ed. Alan Axelrod (New York: Norton, for the Winterthur Museum, 1985), 217–40. Charles B. Hosmer, Jr., "William Sumner Appleton," in Hosmer, *Presence of the Past,* 237–59; Anne Farnam, "The Essex Institute of Salem," *Nineteenth Century* 5 (Summer 1979):76–81; Richard H. Saunders, "Collecting American Decorative Arts in New England," pt. 1, *Antiques* 109 (May 1976):996–1003; pt. 2, 110 (1976):754–63.

9. Charles Montgomery, "Some Remarks on the Practice and Science of Connoisseurship," *American Walpole Society Notebook* (1961):7–20; Neil Harris, "Museums, Merchandising, and Popular Taste: The Struggle for Influence," in *Material Culture and American Life,* ed. I.M.G. Quimby (New York: Norton, for the Winterthur Museum, 1978), 140–74.

10. Examples of broader house history studies include George B. Tatum, *Philadelphia Georgian: The City House of Samuel Powell and Some of Its Eighteenth-Century Neighbors* (Middletown, Conn.: Wesleyan Univ. Press, 1976); Samuel Chamberlain and Paul Hollister, *Beauport at Gloucester* (New York: Hastings House, 1980); and William Howard Adams, *Monticello* (New York: Abbeville, 1983).

11. Kenneth L. Ames and Gerald W.R. Ward, *Decorative Arts and Household Furnishings Used in America, 1650–1920: An Annotated Bibliography* (Winterthur, Del.: Winterthur Museum, 1989); Eileen Dubrow and Richard Dubrow, *Furniture Made in America, 1875–1905* (Exton, Pa.: Schiffer Publishing, 1982).

12. Other examples of resident-centered house history are J.B. Jackson, "The Westward-Moving House: Three American Houses and the People Who Lived in Them," in *Landscapes: Selected Writings of J.B. Jackson,* ed. Ervin H. Zube (Amherst: Univ. of Massachusetts Press, 1970), 10–42; Bernard Herman, "Theory and Artifact: An Interdisciplinary Approach Reshapes the Mendenhall Story," *History News* 30, no. 3 (Mar. 1983):32–35.

13. Mariana Griswold Van Rensselaer, a scholar who did pioneering research on the buildings of Henry Hobson Richardson, is an obvious exception to my masculine classification scheme.

14. Peter O'Connell, "Putting the Historic House into the Course of History," *Journal of Family History* 6 (Spring 1981):28–40; Patricia West, "The New Social History and Historic House Museums: The Lindewald Example," *Museum Studies Journal* 2, no. 3 (Fall 1986):22–26; Roger B. White, "Whither the Urban Row House Exhibit? The Peale Museum's 'Rowhouse,'" *Technology and Culture* 24, no. 1 (Jan. 1983):76–90.

15. Thomas J. Schlereth, "Social History Scholarship and Material Culture Research," *Journal of Social History* 16, no. 4 (June 1983):111–43.

16. An extensive discussion of these concepts is found in Katherine Grier, *Culture and Comfort: People, Parlors, and Upholstery, 1850–1930* (Rochester, N.Y.: Strong Museum, 1988).

17. On the Whig or Progressive interpretation of material culture evidence, see George Basalla, "Museums and Technological Utopianism," in *Technological Innovation and the Decorative Arts,* ed. Ian M.G. Quimby and Polly Anne Earl (Charlottesville: Univ. Press of Virginia, 1974), 360; Michael J. Ettema, "History, Nostalgia, and American Furniture," *Winterthur Portfolio* 17, nos. 2–3 (Summer-Autumn 1982);135–44; and Upton, "The Power of Things," 72.

18. In addition to Karin Calvert's forthcoming book-length study, *Children in the Home: A Social History of the Material Culture of Early Childhood, 1630 to 1900,* we have Mary Lynn Stevens Heininger, ed., *A Century of Childhood, 1820–1920* (Rochester, N.Y.: Strong Museum, 1984); Bernard Mergen, *Play and Playthings: A Reference Guide* (Westport, Conn.: Greenwood, 1982); Thomas J. Schlereth, "The Material Culture of Childhood: Research Problems and Possibilities," *Material History Bulletin* 21 (Sept. 1985);1–14; and Simon Bronner, *American Children's Folklore* (Little Rock, Ark.: August House, 1988).

19. Martin Marty, *Protestantism in the United States: Righteous Empire* (New York: Scribner's, 1986); Robert Handy, *A Christian America: Protestant Hopes and Historical Realities* (New York: Oxford Univ. Press, 1984).

20. Ruth Schwartz Cowan, *More Work for Mother: The Ironies of Household*

Technology from the Open Hearth to the Microwave (New York: Basic Books, 1983).

21. Warren I. Susman, *Culture as History: The Transformation of American Society in the Twentieth Century* (New York: Pantheon, 1984), 234; xxv–xxvii. On other aspects of transformation as an interpretive model, see Lawrence A. Cremin, *The Transformation of the School: Progressivism in American Education, 1876–1957* (New York: Knopf, 1961); Richard D. Brown, *Modernization: The Transformation of American Life, 1600–1865* (New York: Hill and Wang, 1976); Robert Higgs, *The Transformation of American Economy, 1865–1914: An Essay in Interpretation* (New York: Wiley, 1971); Karl Polanyi, *The Great Transformation: The Political and Economic Origins of Our Times* (New York: Farrar and Rinehart, 1944); Steven Hahn and Jonathan Prude, eds., *The Countryside in the Age of Capitalist Transformation: Essays in the Social History of Rural America* (Chapel Hill: Univ. of North Carolina Press, 1985).

22. For example, see Claudia Brush Kidwell and Valerie Steele, *Men and Women: Dressing the Part* (Washington, D.C.: Smithsonian Institution Press, 1989); and "The Material Culture of Gender/The Gender of Material Culture," a Winterthur Conference, Winterthur, Del., 9, 10, 11 Nov. 1989 (publication forthcoming).

23. George Basalla, *The Evolution of Technology* (Cambridge England: Cambridge Univ. Press, 1988); Siegfried Giedion, *Mechanization Takes Command: A Contribution to Anonymous History* (New York: Norton, 1969).

24. Simon Bronner, *Consuming Visions: Accumulation and Display in America, 1880–1920* (New York: Norton, for the Winterthur Museum, 1989); Susan Strasser, *Satisfaction Guaranteed: The Making of the American Mass Market* (New York: Pantheon, 1989).

25. As quoted in Robert Atwan et al., *Edsels, Luckies, and Frigidaires: Advertising the American Way* (New York: Dell, 1979), xiii.

26. On the diverse meanings of "the modern," "modernism," "modernity," and "modernization," see Douglas Tallack, "Introduction: Modernity," and Douglas Tallack, "From Victorianism to Modernism," ch. 4, both in Douglas Tallack, *Twentieth-Century America: The Intellectual and Cultural Context,* (White Plains, N.Y.: Longman, 1991); Richard D. Brown, *Modernization,* 3–22; Herbert G. Gutman, "Work, Culture, and Society in Industrializing America, 1815–1919," *American Historical Review* 78, no. 3 (June 1973):531–87; Alfred Chandler, *The Visible Hand: The Managerial Revolution in American Business* (Cambridge, Mass.: Harvard Univ. Press, 1977).

27. Cromley has done a study of early multi-occupancy residential life in her *Alone Together: A History of New York's Early Apartments* (Ithaca, N.Y.: Cornell Univ. Press, 1990).

PART I

ROOM LIFE

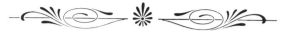

CHAPTER ONE

The Modern Look of the Early-Twentieth-Century House: A Mirror of Changing Lifestyles

Candace M. Volz

The first decades of the twentieth century were a time of tremendous change in America. The Spanish American War in 1898 and World War I both marked the emergence of the United States as a world power. The American economy was changing as well, with decreasing emphasis on farming and agricultural products, and more on manufacturing, factory production, and services. In response to the advent of the Industrial Revolution and the emergence of factory jobs in the first quarter of the nineteenth century, America's population was shifting from a rural agrarian base to an urban industrial one. With this transition came changes in the American family home and lifestyle. In seventeenth- and eighteenth-century America, the customary domestic arrangement was an extended family working the farm or running a business together and usually living adjacent to the shop. By the last quarter of the nineteenth century, however, with the coming of the Industrial Revolution, the American city had developed suburbs, residential enclaves where the typical middle-class family was headed by a husband who left home each day for a job in an office, shop, or factory. His wife stayed at home to raise the children and run the household. It is the purpose of this essay to examine how these profound domestic changes affected the floor plan, room use, and decoration of the American family home in the first decades of the twentieth century. Since the train, mail, telephone, and telegraph all provided rapid dissemination of ideas in turn-of-the-century America, this essay will focus on the nation as a whole rather than on regional variations. Home design and decoration books, household management guides, and catalogs of home furnishings, all from the period under study, have been used to analyze the dramatic changes which occurred in the American lifestyle.

In the second half of the nineteenth century, more affluent households took advantage of plentiful immigrant domestic help and engaged in a complex lifestyle that involved rooms for special uses, large flatware and china services with many specialized pieces, and numerous furnishings designed for special needs.[1] Previously the prerogative of only the wealthiest households, the ability to participate in this complex and formal lifestyle moved down the social ladder as the Industrial Revolution brought about widespread availability of inexpensive machine-made goods. The middle class welcomed the opportunity to fill its homes with textiles and furnishings which just a generation before had been available only in handmade, expensive versions. But by the early twentieth century, the new immigrants who filled the domestic service ranks found that factory work paid better and gave them more independence than working in a household. And in 1924, the United States virtually halted immigration from Europe, thus ending the supply of new immigrants willing to take the lowest entry-level positions. The result was that middle-class households increasingly had fewer servants, particularly of the live-in type, which in turn produced a predictable simplification of the American home and its furnishings. In addition to this necessary lifestyle simplification, a design reform movement emerged which rejected the plethora of overembellished goods which had filled American homes for so many decades. The demand for simplified designs more clearly expressing the function of the object was most eloquently expressed by reform movement leader Gustav Stickley: "I . . . tried to make furniture which would be simple, durable, comfortable and fitted for the place it was to occupy and the work it had to do . . . the only way to do this was to cut loose from all tradition and to do away with all needless ornamentation, returning to plain principles of construction."[2]

Because it is an important descriptive term for twentieth-century decorative arts, it would be well at this point to give some explanation of the use of the word *modern*. While the term *modern* has been used since the fifteenth century to describe ideas and objects which are up-to-date and/or current, it is most frequently used in Victorian design and decoration treatises as a descriptor for the new lifestyle fostered by numerous changes in an urbanized, industrial world and for the furniture and architecture produced in response to those innovations. *Modern* appears with increasing frequency in decorative arts literature starting in the mid-nineteenth century, and by the first decades of the twentieth century, it was being applied to all aspects of interior decoration. The "modern" home and its furnishings were seen as distinct improvements over their predecessors because of technological developments made possible by the Industrial Revolution. Modernity was viewed as a positive force; even the design reformers who demanded a return to simpler, more functional styles did not criticize the advantages to be offered by modern production techniques.[3] Manufacturers of traditional reproduction furniture also were enthusiastic about modern manufacturing methods, as a 1928 catalog of the Century Furniture Company of Grand Rapids shows: "Modern furniture draws its inspiration liberally from the past and adds the ingenuity of modern craftsmanship and modern machinery, together with all that modern designing has learned from the Golden Past."[4]

Interior Spaces: Changes in Function and Floor Plans

The early-twentieth-century house plan clearly reflected the changes in domestic life during this period. As early as 1909, Gustav Stickley commented on the servant problem in relation to the house plans he sold: "In these days of difficulties with servants and of inadequate and inexperienced help, more and more women are perforce learning to depend upon themselves to keep the household machinery running smoothly."[5] With fewer servants, a less formal lifestyle became the norm, and many of the rooms in a Victorian house that were related to formal entertaining and servants became obsolete. Music rooms, reception rooms, conservatories, sitting rooms, and butler's pantries were dropped from all but the most elaborate houses of the period 1910–30. A small bedroom or two for servants, a common feature of larger homes of the second half of the nineteenth century, is found in relatively few plans for early-twentieth-century houses. For example, in its 1908–1940 mail-order home series, Sears offered only four house plans with servants' quarters, one from 1912, two from 1913, and, in 1918, "The Magnolia, the grandest house Sears ever offered."[6] "The Magnolia" was clearly a holdover from the complex late Victorian lifestyle, with its butler's pantry, main stair hall, rear hall with a service stair, dressing rooms, and porte-cochere. But it also featured a number of "modern" twentieth-century additions to the house plan, including a sun room, two bathrooms and a downstairs lavatory, a breakfast nook opening off the kitchen for informal dining, a den or family room, and a sleeping porch.

All of these floor-plan additions can be related directly to changes in the American lifestyle: occupational, ideological, technological, and economic. For example, the breakfast nook as part of the kitchen was related

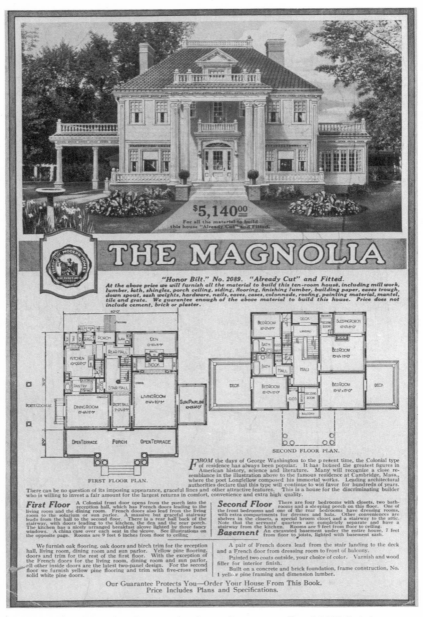

Fig. 10. "The Magnolia, the grandest house Sears ever offered." While it has a very traditional facade and many of the formal rooms of a Victorian house plan, "The Magnolia" also has a number of twentieth-century innovations, including a "sun parlor," a "den," a sleeping porch, two and a half bathrooms, and a breakfast nook. *Sears Modern Homes*, 1918. Courtesy of Sears, Roebuck and Co.

Fig. 11. "Modern Kitchen Equipment Gives Housewife More Leisure." In this advertisement, the potential home builder is urged to "include a modern, efficient kitchen, and a built-in breakfast or dining nook" to save hours of drudgery and make kitchen work easier and more pleasant. *Home Builders Catalog,* 1929, p. 363. Collection of Candace M. Volz.

to less formal dining habits requiring fewer servants, along with the new importance of the kitchen and its appliances, as the housewife increasingly became the principal cook. Sleeping porches were advocated by reformers such as Gustav Stickley as a healthy way to maintain a connection with the outdoors.[7] Looking back on this popular phenomena, social historian Alan Gowans sees sleeping porches as having been part of an early-twentieth-century "integration of space indoors and out . . . [which was] a nostalgic attempt to recapture the old American 'pioneer heritage' . . . where the sky is still the limit."[8] This desire for an indoor space which incorporated the outdoors was also responsible for the popularity of the sun room. The twentieth-century version of the conservatory, sun rooms were made more inviting for frequent use with less glass, fewer plants, and lots of comfortable seating. They were a very versatile secondary living area which could be screened in the summer and glazed in the winter. Located usually on the side of the house, sun rooms and closely related loggias and side porches also helped to replace the large Victorian front porch. As automobiles became the transportation of choice, the noise they generated caused the decline of the front porch as an outdoor living area.[9] With the advent of sun rooms and other indoor/outdoor living areas on the side of the house, only a token small entry porch remained at the front door. Eventually, by mid-twentieth century, porches had moved completely around to the back of the house, where outdoor patios and carports became popular.[10]

A detailed examination of the evolution of just one room in the Victorian house, the entrance hall, will illustrate the reasons for the dramatic floor plan changes found in twentieth-century houses. In Federal and Greek Revival houses of the first half of the nineteenth century, the main entrance corridor typically was a wide hall which completely bisected, and was the central axis of, a very symmetrical floor plan. If it was a two-story house, what was usually the only stair occupied a prominent location along one wall of this central hall. With the coming of the asymmetrical Victorian house design in the 1850s, the main stair hall generally continued to have a central position but rarely went completely from the front of the house to the back. The stair hall was smaller in house plans of the 1850s to the 1870s, and more elaborate homes had a secondary stair in a rear service hall for the servants. Popular builders' pattern books of the 1870s and 1880s, such as those by A.J. Bicknell and William T. Comstock, show that the central stair hall in stylish homes had evolved by that period into a large living space at the front of the house. This "living hall" type was advocated by the English design reform movement of the 1870s to the 1890s as a return to the medieval great hall. In this type of hall, the stair was treated in an elaborate, highly decorative manner, and in larger houses there frequently was a fireplace with a seating group. The Victorian "living hall" and the earlier central hall functioned not only as separators and connectors of rooms, but as entrance areas for the home. Both the center hall and the living hall plans worked well with servants because they allowed privacy for the homeowner and his peers, while social inferiors remained in the hall or were directed elsewhere, preventing intrusion on family and guests. Since the larger home of the late-nineteenth century usually included a back service hall with a secondary stair, it was possible to separate the ceremonial and utilitarian functions of life in a complex Victorian household. This ability to segregate the different aspects of domestic life was essential to the functioning of the late-nineteenth-century lifestyle. As decorative arts historian Kenneth Ames has noted in his essay on stair halls: "It is easy to forget the social realities of the nineteenth century. Victorian homes document a way of life which has largely disappeared."[11]

With the popularity of the Colonial Revival in the first decades of this century, Colonial-style houses returned to the traditional central stair hall plan. But many other less traditional house designs from this period, even for larger homes, had only a small vestibule entrance or simply opened directly into what was, by the first decade of the twentieth century, consistently called the living room. The living room, which had evolved from the Victorian living or stair hall, replaced both the parlor and the entrance hall; now the visitor entered directly into the life of the family. Because most new home construction was in the homogeneity of suburbia, there was not as much need to screen visitors to the household as there had been when people lived in a mixed commercial-residential area. In those houses without real entrance halls, the stairway generally opened immediately off of, or went up, one wall of the living room. If not associated with the living room, the stair occupied its own space in the center of the house plan, adjacent to the kitchen and any downstairs bedrooms. Either location was related to the increasing informality of early-twentieth-century lifestyles. The additional flight of service stairs leading to the second floor also succumbed to simplified lifestyles, all but disappearing by the 1920s except in very large, elaborate homes. Only five of the Sears 1908–1940 house plans, four from 1911 and one from 1918, had separate service stairs.[12] However, a compromise stair form appears in some early-twentieth-century two-story house plans (it is seen in the Sears plans by 1908 and as late as 1939[13]) which accomplished some of the same goals as the earlier separate service stair and front stair. This new form was the two-way stair which could be entered from either the front hall or the kitchen, both sets of risers meeting at a common landing and continuing as a single set of steps to the second floor. This combination stair form provided a degree of privacy for the homeowner who still had a cook or maid.

The dramatic changes between the Victorian decades and the early twentieth century were reflected in still other ways by residential interiors. Social and cultural historian Karen Halttunen has identified this as a shift from nineteenth-century interiors, designed to mold character, to twentieth-century interiors created as expressions of personality.[14] The American home of the 1850–90 period was viewed by contemporary pre-

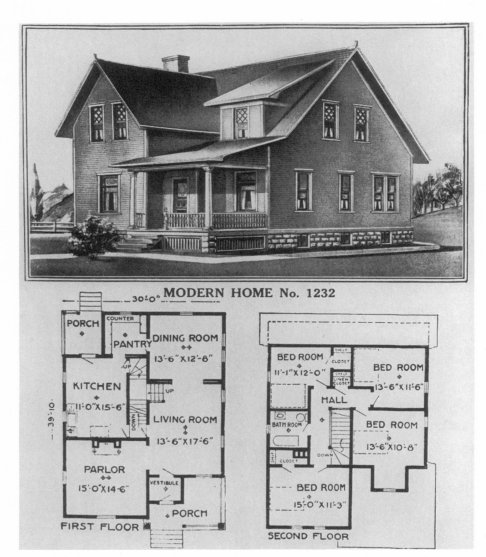

Fig. 12. Design No. 1232, *Sears Modern Homes,* 1911. Note the one set of stairs, which can be entered from either the kitchen or the living room. This house was clearly designed to appeal to a more traditional home buyer, as it retains the nineteenth-century parlor in addition to the twentieth-century living room. Courtesy of Sears, Roebuck and Co.

scriptive literature as a retreat from the demands of the workplace and as a moral haven for the proper nurturing of children and the transmission of traditional cultural values. Catharine Beecher and Harriet Beecher Stowe's 1869 treatise on domesticity, *The American Woman's Home,* draws on this concept in reference to the decoration of houses: "While the aesthetic element must be subordinate to the requirements of physical existence, and, as a matter of expense, should be held of inferior consequence to means of higher moral growth; it yet holds a place of great significance among the influences which make home happy and attractive, which give it a constant and wholesome power over the young, and contributes much to the education of the entire household in refinement, intellectual development, and moral sensibility."[15]

During the design reform movement of the 1870s and 1880s, women were encouraged to embellish their homes with their own handiwork, but even this apparent move toward creative expression and personalizing interiors was in essence a continuation of the effort to link home and its decoration to proper moral growth and the perpetuation of "gentility."[16] As the preface of a popular 1870s "how-to" household art book for ladies expressed it: "The beauties and attractions of Home can be none too pleasant or tasteful. Here gather the young to learn for all years to come. Here social life gains its lessons of utility and sense. And in these pages all may find a stimulus for new thoughts, more active work, with pretty fancies, and aesthetic beauty to gild the days for years to come—Bright moments shall still brighter grow/While Home becomes our heaven below."[17]

Warren Susman's basic text on the transformation of American life in the twentieth century, *Culture as History,* refers to the new consumer-oriented society as the "culture of abundance." He points out that the "original enthusiastic support . . . [for this new cultural ideal] was often Utopian. Many saw in the promise of the new culture a solution to fundamental human and social problems, a new world of fulfillment and even liberation."[18] In the field of decorative arts, the turn-of-the-century Arts and Crafts movement is the expression of utopian ideals which formed the transition into the twentieth-century consumer-oriented society. The advertising material and publications produced by leaders of the Arts and Crafts movement stressed a stripping away of superficiality and the return to a simplified lifestyle.[19] Following on the heels of exuberant Victorian embellishment, the starkly simple, functional Arts and Crafts furnishings exemplified the movement's belief in the ability of interiors to shape a new and better world. However, the popularity of the Arts and Crafts movement had begun to fade by 1915, when Gustav Stickley filed for bank-ruptcy. But the bungalow house form advocated by Stickley and others of the movement, along with Spanish and Tudor variations and Colonial Revival designs, continued to fill America's suburban developments.

As urbanization and the corresponding middle-class move to the look-alike houses of the suburbs brought an increased degree of impersonality, the need to "personalize" residential interiors grew. As Susman points out: "We live now constantly in a crowd; how can we distinguish ourselves from others in that crowd? . . . the question is clearly one of life in a mass society . . . it is important to develop one's self . . . those traits . . . that will enable us to think of ourselves and have others think of us as 'some-bodies'."[20] Simultaneously, the Industrial Revolution and the resulting plethora of consumer goods was producing a visible change in the American self-concept. When furnishings were handmade and society was still producer-oriented, self-denial was a virtue. Accordingly, the suppression of individual goals and desires was stressed in nineteenth-century prescriptive literature. Susman sees this as a lingering Puritan ethic and points out that, for the new salaried clerical/service/sales middle-class, created between 1870 and 1910 in response to the Industrial Revolution, "Puritan moralism and the Puritan social and political order so long admired became the enemy, enshrining an improper kind of moral elite and improper values for the new rationalized order."[21] As America was transformed into a consumer-oriented society, the economy revolved around acquisition rather than production. Now there was a need for consumers to be concerned with self-aggrandizement and fulfillment. "How-to" books, ladies' periodicals, and other popular literature that emphasized morality and self-denial were replaced by similar publications which linked success in life to the accumulation of consumer goods.[22]

For those who could afford it, the embellishment of the early-twentieth-century home was often left to an interior decorator. Interior decoration developed in the mid-nineteenth century as a profession assisting the very wealthy client with multiple homes to select furnishings from among the many available styles. As with so many trends which gradually filter down to lower socioeconomic levels, by the turn of the century, the interior decorator's services were being utilized by upper-middle-class households as well. The development of the interior decoration profession was related to the shift from an economy based on production to one revolving around acquisition. It was the job of the interior decorator to help the client sort through the quantities of available home furnishings and select those which filled the client's needs and best reflected her or his personality. That interiors from the first decades of the twentieth century were designed to express the personality of the owner (or his interior decorator) can be seen in this quote from a popular home decoration manual of the 1930s and 1940s, *The Book of Furniture and Decoration:* "It remains then to choose the manner and the materials. Shall it be gay? or restful? or studious? or frivolous? or monastic? This is the individual element. Let us not ask, 'Shall it be Louis XVI? or modern? or Turkish Cozy Corner?' Rather ask what or whom we want to express, and how to express it."[23]

An example of this transition from interiors that shaped character to interiors that expressed personality can be found in the residential library. Before the second quarter of the nineteenth century, residential libraries were limited to upper-class homes. Few people could read, and books were handmade and therefore expensive and rare. By 1830, machine-made paper had reduced the price of books so that they began to be published in series referred to as "libraries," bringing a wide range of literary material within reach of middle-class households.[24] With the middle class now able to participate in home education for the first time, the home library, as it developed in the Victorian era, was a room reserved for this new activity. It housed collections of plant and animal specimens, travel souvenirs, art prints, and pictures and busts of historical figures, in addition to books. The library was the room in the house where children were encouraged to look at books and be read to, to study the collections and look at the pictures. It functioned in a similar way for adults, and, in addition to being a place for family activities, the library was a signal to visitors that this household valued intellectual curiosity.

By the turn of the century, as the education of children increasingly moved out of the home and into the public school system, the library evolved into a room or part of the house, depending on the size of the residence, which was set apart solely for the enjoyment of books. This change is expressed by Edith Wharton and Ogden Codman in their well-known interior decoration manual, *The Decoration of Houses,* written in 1897. These arbiters of taste advocated libraries "of such character as to form a background or setting to the books, rather than to distract attention from them. The richly adorned room in which books are but a minor incident is, in fact, no library at all."[25] Bungalows, the most popular suburban house form of the first decades of the twentieth century, usually incorporated a nook with built-in bookcases or, in larger houses, a separate room as a library. The bungalow's subdued Arts and Crafts interior, with its simple, functional furnishings, is a good example of a space which enhanced rather than diminished the presence of books. Whatever style the house might be architecturally, the home library of the first decades of this century typically was a paneled room with built-in bookcases extending from floor to ceiling, sparse but comfortable furnishings, and a subdued decorative scheme based on the colors of the book bindings. The library was now viewed by various home decoration authorities as more than a place for serious study; it was also a retreat from the noise and cares of the household and the world outside. Within the dynamics of the early-twentieth-century family, it was the man of the house who had time to retreat from the distractions of the household and the need to retreat from the world after a day of business downtown. So the rather simple, masculine design of the library of this era was no accident.[26] The accessories used reflected not only this masculine focus, but a desire to make a statement about the owner's personality as well. Personal photographs, trophies, awards, and items related to leisure pursuits and sports were the symbols of a man's accomplishments which personalized the "modern" library and accentuated the change from its late-nineteenth-century counterpart. The home library is an excellent example of a room which evolved to reflect the shift from the nineteenth-century interior, designed to mold character, to the twentieth-century interior's focus on personality and personal fulfillment.

Technology and Its Effect on Interior Decoration

Changes in the placement of furniture and, to some degree, the floor plan of the early-twentieth-century house were a direct result of the domestic amenities which were becoming widespread after 1900. Throughout much of the nineteenth century, chairs were placed around a center table as needed to take advantage of the comparatively dim light from a central gas or oil fixture.[27] Task lighting was provided by oil lamps, which required constant maintenance, or rubber hoses carried gas from the central fixture to a not-too-distant gas portable lamp. Once electricity was introduced at the end of the nineteenth century, older homes were retrofitted with surface-mounted wiring. Often, portable task lamps were powered via electric cords plugged into the sockets of a central hanging electrical fixture. As electricity became more widely available, it was the preferred light source in new houses, and concealed wiring, baseboard outlets, and wall switches, all dictated the way furniture was arranged. Lamps were placed on tables beside sofas or between chairs around the perimeter of the room instead of the furniture's being grouped around a central oil or gas fixture. With the advent of this new power source, the dark corners of the house of preceding generations were a thing of the past.

The second amenity which altered floor plans and furniture arrangement was central heating. Forced-air heating systems were available only to the very wealthy in the later years of the nineteenth century, with coal- or wood-burning fireplaces or stoves still serving most homeowners' needs. Because these heat sources could warm only limited areas and were activated only when a room was in use, doors and *portiere* curtains were necessary to help contain the heat. The effort required to light, feed, and maintain a single-room heat source meant that, practically speaking, rooms had to be used by several people for different concurrent activities. When central heating was developed, radiators or, with a forced-air heating system, floor and wall registers, kept the entire house heated relatively uniformly. But the exposed floor or wall components required by these types of systems meant that rugs and furniture had to be placed, as today, to prevent blocking the heat source. And, even though the new central heating systems made fireplaces and mantels obsolete, these traditional architectural elements, long associated with the concept of "home," were retained in twentieth-century floor plans as the ceremonial focal point of major rooms.

Furnishing Styles and Changing Tastes

As electricity brightened rooms, furnishings and interior treatments also shifted to a lighter look, in reaction against what has been described as the Victorian "gilded age of decoration."[28] There was a general simplification of woodwork and hardware, and a removal of clutter and bric-a-brac. Instead of several different wallpapers in a room, the early-twentieth-century interior featured a deep paper border at the ceiling line above solid-color walls or striped wallpaper. Small, delicate "Colonial" print papers were also popular for bedrooms. By 1930, the popular use of wallpaper had narrowed to bathrooms, kitchens, and perhaps a "scenic" design in the hall or dining room. The favored wall finish instead was a pale pastel paint used with white ceilings. As the new century progressed, dark-stained woodwork was supplanted by a lighter natural finish, and, by 1930, trim was most often painted white.

Window treatments also followed the trend to lighter interiors, a shift which inspired comments in the home decorating literature such as the following:

National Two-Column pattern of American Radiators.

The Radiator is here placed under a window of this Colonial Bed Room and treated as a piece of furniture;
though if considered obtrusive, it could, to quite equal radiating advantage,
be hidden in corner back of the dresser.

Fig. 13. "National Two-Column Pattern of American Radiators." While locating radiators under windows was considered optimal so as to offset the radiant cold from the glass, this radiator catalog acknowledges that radiators could be visually and physically obtrusive. In "Radiation & Decoration," catalog of the American Radiator Co., 1905. Courtesy of Smithsonian Institution Libraries.

> It is a gratifying change after the voluminously enveloped window hang-
> ings of the Victorian period which were heavy and unhealthy, their mis-
> sion seeming to be to crowd out the last breath of fresh air that squeezed
> through the window. Befringed, betasseled, beroped, and valenced to the
> utmost, they acted as a dragon to the fresh wandering little
> breeze . . . Luckily, elaborately festooned and trimmed curtains have
> long since been relegated to the dust heap—and that without regret on
> the part of every sensible decorator and housewife.[29]

The elaborately layered window treatments of the Victorian period were gradually simplified to glass curtains which most often terminated at the window sill. These were accompanied by simple pleated floor-length side

Fig. 14. Dining room. The simple gathering of the glass curtains and the busy floral pattern of the chintz side panels are the predominant design features of this drapery treatment in a 1930s Tudor-style dining room. "How to Drape Your Windows," catalog of the Kirsch Co., 1930, plate 3, p. 18. Courtesy of Smithsonian Institution Libraries and the Kirsch Co., Sturgis, Mich.

draperies, and at the top, an ornamental rod or a simple, narrow fabric valance. Draperies were finished very plainly, with a minimum of the rich trimmings which had been so popular in the Victorian period. Development of the modern traverse rod in approximately 1905 produced the precision-pleated drapery look which has ever since characterized "modern" window treatments.[30]

Floorcoverings were also simplified early in the present century. Wall-to-wall carpeting had prevailed in American interiors for the entire last half of the nineteenth century.[31] By 1900, polished hardwood floors covered with bordered area rugs were popular. In the formal rooms of new homes, decorative parquet floors were installed, and these were partially covered with the most desirable floorcovering of the era, Oriental carpets. If genuine Orientals were too expensive, American copies were available in all qualities. Imported Chinese and Chinese-style rugs became popular in the 1920s and 1930s, as did solid-color area rugs. The reason for the popularity of the area rug is perhaps best expressed in an advertising brochure of the period entitled "The Passing of the Carpet": "In homes of all classes rugs are rapidly taking the place of carpets. It is fitting that they should. They are more healthful and more economical, they are easily taken up and quickly put down; they fit all floors without alteration, and to clean them and the floors under them is a simple matter."[32] Another easily maintained, economical floorcovering that was widely popular for kitchens, sun rooms and other informal areas was linoleum. First appearing as a luxury product in the 1870s, linoleum was originally available in simulated tile patterns. By the early twentieth century, it could be had in patterns which copied almost every other material that was used on floors as well as solid colors.

An additional change in early-twentieth-century interiors was not as obvious as new colors and designs, but it had a profound affect on the appearance of a room. After the turn of the century, bungalow and Prairie Style houses, with their low, horizontal lines, became popular. Gustav Stickley's monthly magazine *The Craftsman* has numerous illustrations of Craftsman bungalow interiors, featuring lowered ceilings, heavy, wide horizontal moldings, and low, wide windows, all of which pulled the focus of the rooms downward. This design aesthetic influenced more traditional interiors as well, with the result that pictures and paintings came down to eye level and even the horizontal lines of furniture were closer to the floor. Instead of the lofty verticality of Victorian interiors, rooms now were low and horizontal in orientation. While very much a part of a new design aesthetic, the change from high ceilings to low ceilings also worked well with the mass production of suburban houses after the turn of the century, and with the concomitant effort to reduce construction costs. This "tendency to lowness rather than height" is explained in a home decoration manual of 1936 as one of the characteristics of "modern" decoration and furniture: "Space is essential in a room and we can conserve it by not filling it with furniture. Low lines are restful, easy to live with."[33]

As interiors and their finishes were lightened and simplified, furniture designs followed suit. Although a glance through an early-twentieth-century furniture catalog suggests that there were numerous popular furniture styles, these really can be divided into just two basic types, "Historical Revival" and "Modern." European historical revival styles had been popular throughout the Victorian decades. To these were added in the 1870s an interest in America's colonial past. Sparked by an Early American kitchen exhibit at the Philadelphia Centennial Exposition of 1876, Colonial Revival reproductions also included the Federal and Empire styles which immediately followed this country's colonial period. The immense popularity of the Colonial Revival produced the first real interest in American antiques, and many of the better reproductions of period pieces were so exact that they cause problems in today's antique market. During the early decades of this century, the interest in the colonial period produced such great American decorative arts collections as those at Williamsburg and the Winterthur Museum. The fascination with colonial America is still a powerful influence on American interiors, as a visit to a furniture store will attest. Two major wars, a world shrinking through mass communications and a global economy, and the increasing complexity and fast pace of modern life have romanticized the virtues of the American colonial past and made that era a seemingly permanent part of our design vocabulary.

Along with Colonial Revival furnishings, European revival styles continued in popularity as well. Edith Wharton and Ogden Codman's 1897 book, *The Decoration of Houses,* popularized the light, elegant Louis XV or XVI styles for the reception rooms and bedrooms of wealthier families. Sometimes these were genuine French antiques, but more often they were good-quality reproductions. Noted early-twentieth-century interior designer Elsie de Wolfe perpetuated this style, with her emphasis on light-toned walls, Louis XVI furniture, and quantities of chintz fabric. For the less well-to-do, she suggested "improving" earlier furnishings by having them enameled in pale colors and painted with delicate French designs.

By the 1920s, the French Louis styles popular with wealthy Americans

A CRAFTSMAN FARM HOUSE. ILLUSTRATED AND DESCRIBED IN THE CRAFTSMAN FOR DECEMBER 1908.

LIVING ROOM IN THE CRAFTSMAN FARM HOUSE (SHOWN ABOVE). SHOWING INGLENOOK AND GLIMPSE OF HALLWAY.

Fig. 16. Parlor, house of D.H. Caswell, Austin, Texas, ca. 1914. The curves of the mirror over the mantel and of the golden oak rocker adjacent to the fireplace in this parlor are typical of the Art Nouveau influence seen in many moderately-priced, machine-made, turn-of-the-century American furnishings. Collection of Candace M. Volz.

Fig. 15. "A Craftsman Farmhouse & Living Room." *Craftsman Furniture Made by Gustav Stickley* (1909), p. 113. The dark line of the picture moulding just below the ceiling, the heavy ceiling beam, and the short windows set low in the wall all help emphasize the horizontal character of the interiors of this Craftsman home. Collection of Candace M. Volz.

had given way to an interest in Spanish and Italian Renaissance furnishings. This rather massive furniture worked well with the stuccoed Mediterranean villas popular in the 1920s and 1930s. For the half-timbered Tudor houses of the same period, Jacobean revival furniture was popular.

The other major design focus of the early years of this century was the "Modern" look which originated in the late-nineteenth-century English Aesthetic movement. Developing from criticism of the design excesses of typical Victorian manufactured furniture, this movement laid the groundwork for the American appearance in 1898 of Gustav Stickley's Arts and Crafts or "Mission" furniture. Functional, unembellished, and fabricated with simple exposed joinery, this furniture was an extreme change from the preceding elaborate Victorian designs. Popular in middle- and upper-middle-class households, "Mission" furniture "represented the advanced taste of the day." It was part of a lifestyle which included Stickley's magazine, *The Craftsman,* house designs in the "bungalow" style, and a full range of home furnishings, including light fixtures, table linens, metal wares, and draperies.[34] Arts and Crafts furniture was extremely popular and spawned many imitators, including the furniture businesses established by Gustav Stickley's three brothers. But competition and the decline in the style's popularity brought on Stickley's bankruptcy in 1915. In the American home, this sturdy, casual furniture was subsequently moved to a secondary room and eventually to the country house, where it is now commanding a second look.

At the same time, the European Art Nouveau style was also modestly popular in America. Early twentieth-century golden oak furniture of the type inexpensively mass-produced in Grand Rapids exhibited more Art Nouveau characteristics than did expensive American cabinetmaker pieces. But it was in smaller decorative accessories such as vases, desk sets, and lamps that the influence of the Art Nouveau was seen most often in the United States.

Another alternative to traditional reproductions was provided by European "Moderne" furniture, which came to the forefront when the Exposition Internationale des Arts Decoratifs opened in Paris in 1925. The exposition popularized modern decorative and industrial art; excluded from display were "copies, imitations, or counterfeits of ancient styles."[35] Although early Art Moderne pieces were often very extreme, the style as it evolved in America was streamlined and functional, with emphasis on the beauty of material and execution. Art Moderne furniture was America's precursor to the International Style and the German Bauhaus designs it

Fig. 17. Bedroom. The stair-step "ziggurat" shape so typical of Art Moderne furnishings can be seen on the dresser, headboard, dressing table, wardrobe, and floor lamp in this "Modernistic" bedroom. Other features representative of interiors from the first decades of the twentieth century are the solid-color floorcovering and a drapery treatment consisting of simple glass curtains with a narrow metal cornice that conceals the traverse rod for the side drapery panels. "How to Drape Your Windows," catalog of the Kirsch Co., 1930, plate 11, p. 64. Courtesy of Smithsonian Institution Libraries and the Kirsch Co., Sturgis, Mich.

fostered; although never widely popular in this country, the streamlined, functional International Style introduced Americans to the light-finished "modern" furniture of the 1930s and to the "Swedish Modern" designs of the 1940s and 50s.

Because the home is a stage upon which so much of daily life is lived, it has always been an accurate reflection of the lifestyles, technology, and cultural and social influences of its time. But while house design and furnishings have, over the centuries, generally followed a gradual, predictable evolution, the up-to-date American home of the first decades of the twentieth century was dramatically different from its late-nineteenth-century predecessor. This rapid change in domestic arrangements is one of the more obvious manifestations of the profound changes which reordered American life in the late nineteenth and first decades of the twentieth centuries. Technology produced so many dramatic innovations so rapidly that America's self-image was radically altered in an effort to assimilate the "progress." While the technological advances were welcomed because of the improved standard of living, better health, and increase in leisure time they provided, there was a need for Americans to cloak the rapid changes in traditional guise to ease the transition. Thus is explained the continuing popularity of Colonial Revival houses and furnishings, and the establishment of museums such as Williamsburg, Winterthur, and Greenfield Village, which glorify the agrarian and handcraft traditions of an earlier America. To study the domestic life of any era is to hold a mirror to its culture, and as a 1936 interior decoration manual put it, "The modern house is a compound of the servant problem and plywood and electricity, bridge and the rumba, the depression and high taxes and nursery schools, glass bricks and radio and rayon and insulating and automobiles, reading in bed, stainless steel, labor problems, transportation, amateur photography, oil burners and ten thousand other ingredients."[36]

Notes

1. Edgar deN. Mayhew and Minor Myers, Jr., *A Documentary History of American Interiors from the Colonial Era to 1915* (New York: Scribner's, 1980); this book is an excellent basic history of American interior design.

2. Gustav Stickley, *Catalogue of Craftsman Furniture* (Eastwood, N.Y.: Craftsman Workshops, 1909), 3.

3. L. and J.G. Stickley, *The Work of L. & J.G. Stickley* (Fayetteville, N.Y., ca. 1914), 3.

4. *Furniture: As Interpreted by the Century Furniture Company* (Grand Rapids, Mich.: Century Furniture Co., 1928), 10.

5. Gustav Stickley, *Catalogue of Craftsman Furniture,* 116.

6. Katherine Cole Stevenson and H. Ward Jandl, *Houses by Mail* (Washington, D.C.: Preservation Press, 1986), 24, 119, 170, and 171.

7. Gustav Stickley, *Catalogue of Craftsman Furniture,* 114.

8. Alan Gowans, *Images of American Living* (New York: Harper & Row, 1976), 424.

9. Clifford E. Clark, Jr., *The American Family Home* (Chapel Hill: Univ. of North Carolina Press, 1986), 228.

10. Gowans, *Images of American Living,* 424.

11. Kenneth L. Ames, "Meaning in Artifacts: Hall Furnishings in Victorian America," *Journal of Interdisciplinary History* 9, no. 1 (Summer 1978): 19–46; see 30.

12. Stevenson and Jandl, *Houses by Mail,* 232, 267, 270, 285, 312.

13. Ibid., 199, 311.

14. Karen Halttunen, "From Parlor to Living Room: Domestic Space, Interior Decoration, and the Culture of Personality," in *Consuming Visions,* ed. Simon J. Bronner (New York: Norton, for the Winterthur Museum, 1989), 172.

15. Catharine E. Beecher and Harriet Beecher Stowe, *The American Woman's Home* (Hartford, Conn.: Stowe-Day Foundation, 1975), 84.

16. Halttunen, "Parlor to Living Room," 172. Also see Katherine Grier's essay in this publication, with her analysis of how the cult of domesticity could be "signaled by . . . details in rooms that evinced nurturing feminine attention, [such as] . . . well-tended houseplants and feminine needlework."

17. Mrs. C.S. Jones and Henry T. Williams, *Household Elegancies: Suggestions in Household Art and Tasteful Home Decorations,* 2d ed. (New York: Henry T. Williams, 1875), iii.

18. Warren I. Susman, *Culture as History* (New York: Pantheon, 1984), xxix.

19. Gustav Stickley, *Catalogue of Craftsman Furniture,* 3–5.

20. Susman., *Culture as History,* 277.

21. Ibid., 46.

22. For a discussion of this "change in the American concept of the modal self," see Halttunen, "Parlor to Living Room," 187.

23. Joseph Aronson, *The Book of Furniture and Decoration: Period and Modern,* rev. ed. (New York: Crown, 1941), 17.

24. For more information on this topic, see Linda Kruger's essay in this volume, "Special Spaces, Reading Places: The Placement of Books in the American Home, 1890–1930," 4 and 22.

25. Edith Wharton and Ogden Codman, *The Decoration of Houses* (New York: Scribner's, 1897, rptd. 1919), 150.

26. Aronson, *Book of Furniture and Decoration,* 342.

27. Denys Peter Myers, *Gaslighting in America: A Guide for Historic Preservation* (Washington, D.C.: U.S., Department of the Interior, Heritage Conservation and Recreation Service, 1978).

28. Wharton and Codman, *Decoration of Houses,* 196.

29. Agnes Foster, *Making Curtains and Hangings* (New York: Robert M. McBride, 1915), 10–11.

30. Advertisement in the trade publication *Upholstery Dealer and Decorative Furnisher,* Oct. 1905, n.p.

31. Helene Von Rosenstiel, *American Rugs and Carpets from the Seventeenth Century to Modern Times* (New York: William Morrow, 1978); this book gives an excellent history of floorcovering use in the American interior.

32. Sanitary Manufacturing Co., "The Passing of the Carpet" (Philadelphia, 1902), 2.

33. Aronson, *Book of Furniture and Decoration,* 186.

34. Ibid., 191.

35. Louise Ade Boger, *Furniture Past and Present* (Garden City, N.Y.: Doubleday, 1966), 471.

36. Aronson, *Book of Furniture and Decoration,* 181.

CHAPTER TWO

The Decline of the Memory Palace: The Parlor after 1890

Katherine C. Grier

As anyone who works with historic houses will admit, "house history" has its own repertoire of informal lore which almost certainly predates the developing bibliography of scholarly accounts. This "houselore" exists because houses are so fundamentally familiar; everyone is an expert on the subject. The interpretation of domestic material culture—architecture, furnishings, and technology—is both enriched and obscured by this familiarity. Visitors to house museums, for example, keep in circulation a group of stories about rooms and their contents that resist eradication by trained guides as stoutly as any garden weed. These range from the story of the infamous "petticoat tables" (neoclassical pier tables with mirrors in their bases, popularly believed to have been used by women to check whether their petticoats showed beneath their skirts) to the suggestion that families were necessarily emotionally "closer then" because limited sources of artificial light and heat forced groups of people into physical proximity.

The parlor in Victorian house museums is the room that seems to prompt "houselore" most readily. Visitors explain to each other that parlors disappeared from modern houses because the rooms were "uncomfortable" and women got tired of taking care of the dirty curtains, the dust-catching fuzzy upholstery, and all that meaningless bric-a-brac (figure 18). As with much popular wisdom, there is truth to this explanation, and its clean simplicity tempts one not to look further. There must be a more complex story, however. Anecdotes from other visitors confirm this; they sometimes recall formal parlors of their childhoods, in the houses of relatives or neighbors in the 1920s and 1930s—sometimes even later.

These separate, apparently contradictory, bits of houselore suggest that there is indeed a complex story underlying the Victorian parlor. Why did people have parlors in their houses in the first place? Why did rooms that

Fig. 18. Parlor, "Castle Tucker," house of Richard Holbrook Tucker, Wiscasset, Maine, ca. 1895. Photographer unknown. Courtesy of Castle Tucker.

were obviously the focus of so much expenditure and care disappear? Did women simply get tired of parlors they had lovingly tended for several generations? And were women alone the arbiters who decreed the demise of the parlor? What changes occurred in the ways people lived in houses, and how they thought about those houses, that nudged the parlor into decline? Did its transformation into the modern "living room" take place everywhere in a short period of time (say, in the decade of the 1920s)? Finally, why should anyone care about a historical narrative with a room as its protagonist?

Answering these questions requires first considering the appearance and meaning of the middle-class parlor in its heyday during the second half of the nineteenth century, and then charting the array of changes underlying its replacement by the living room. The decline of the room I have christened "the memory palace" is more than a simple question of household dirt; it reflects the decline of Victorian culture itself, for the parlor was the quintessential Victorian room, where many of that culture's dynamics were most clearly expressed. Further, the history of the parlor is a good vehicle for addressing the methodological complexities of house history in documenting and explaining change over time.

The history of the parlor and the living room is a tale that, like all the stories in material culture study, interweaves the concrete and the intangible, a collection of images and objects and the realm of values and aspirations. Setting aside space and furnishing a parlor gave certain characteristically Victorian values and aspirations physical presence in the world. The actual character of the social life taking place in that parlor often seems to have been a consideration secondary to the simple fact of parlor making. Further, parlors actually persisted in twentieth-century households long after the culture that created them was in decline; they were the echo (or the fossilized remains) of a declining worldview.

The Parlor as Memory Palace

The middle-class parlor grew out of the conjunction of the multipurpose "parlor" of the pre-Georgian house and the gala "drawing room" of fashionable houses in the eighteenth century.[1] By the 1850s, what was considered a modern parlor (the old name remained in use) was a room intended for the purposes of formal social life as middle-class people understood it. It was like the gala drawing room in its emphasis on sociability and the decor to support it, although the ordinary houses that contained such parlors often did not also have the variety of other special-use rooms that grand houses did.

One important characteristic of Victorian house architecture, including modest plan-book houses in the second half of the nineteenth century, was that public and private spaces were clearly defined and separated from one another as much as possible. Ideally, public spaces were in the front and utilitarian rooms at the rear of the structures (figure 19). In small houses, differentiating special-use rooms often resulted in a warren of cramped, small spaces, as the plans in S.B. Reed's small, popular book *Modern House-plans for Everybody* (1878, 1900) demonstrate.[2] Setting aside a parlor represented a sacrifice of utilitarian space for everyday living. Further, parlor making reflected a set of spending priorities, with expenditure on special furnishings that were not designed to withstand heavy family use. Complaints about parlors, deploring both the waste of space and the consumption of family resources, began to appear as soon as the room became a truly middle-class convention of house building and furnishing. Clarence Cook, author of the 1878 volume *The House Beautiful*, called parlors "ceremonial deserts . . . useless and out of place in the houses of nine-tenths of our Americans," while another author decried the "stereo-

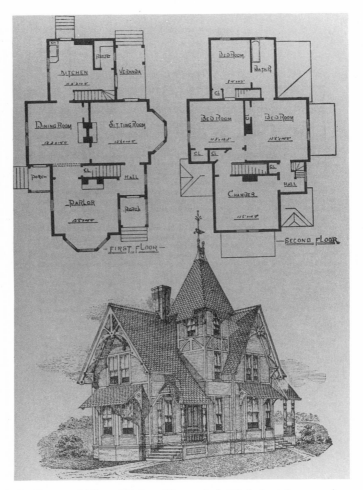

Fig. 19. Residence of Albert Trinler, Albany, Ind. Trinler's eight-room house plan exhibits the Victorian interest in separating public and private space in a front-to-back arrangement. The family had a sitting room for its daily use and a formal parlor whose functional importance was emphasized architecturally by its bay window and the overhanging shed roof on the front facade. The separate entry hall was a buffer zone, where outsiders were admitted to the front, public spaces of the house. Sliding doors are indicated between the parlor and dining room, allowing further segregation of space. Notice that the only entrance to the kitchen–service area is through the dining room. Even the bedrooms are hierarchically arranged, with the most important, the "chamber" (probably Mr. and Mrs. Trinler's bedroom), located at the front above the parlor. Unlike most of the new construction of the era, Trinler's house was plumbed. *Palliser's Model Homes* (Bridgeport, Conn.: Palliser, Palliser and Co., 1878), plate 6.

typed parlor, with its aspect of funereal gloom."[3] Harriet Beecher Stowe claimed that a too-fashionable, gala parlor in a middle-class house had the ability to crush family life "under a weight of upholstery."[4]

In the first half of the nineteenth century, gala parlors in the houses of urban or urbane people of wealth and position were the sites of elaborate and frequent social activities.[5] As the making of modern parlors seemed to spread across the entire spectrum of consumers in the decades after 1850, many people actually used their own "gala" rooms for fewer and different kinds of occasions. Some of these activities were new forms of middle-class social life, borrowed from elites—formal calling and theatricals, for example. Others were social rituals—weddings, funerals, visits from local dignitaries, and household celebrations—that had taken place in old-fashioned multipurpose parlors, but which now were given extra social weight by their being set in a room that was intended solely for such purposes.[6] What is significant about middle-class parlors—and, by the 1890s, parlors made by prosperous working-class people—is that there was such a powerful urge on the part of ordinary families to give social ceremony its due.[7]

Throughout most of the nineteenth century, the decor of middle-class parlors expressed a dynamic tension in Victorian culture. On one hand, their contents reflected the complex of ideas we now call *domesticity*. Domesticity encompassed a set of norms for family life, centered on a perceived dichotomy between the private household and the world beyond the boundaries of each family's private space. Women were, as Catharine Beecher noted, the "chief ministers" of the "family state," and to them fell the responsibility of making homes look like proper expressions of the domestic ideal.[8] Materially, domesticity could be signaled by many things, including the cleanliness of the space, but major signposts were those details in rooms that evinced nurturing feminine attention because they were symbolic representations of work that had long been assigned to women— well-tended houseplants and feminine needlework, for example. A specific few kinds of furniture also had strong domestic connotations. Center tables, practical when artificial lighting was expensive, became symbols of the family circle—a classic instance of necessity becoming a virtue.[9] Some objects symbolically completed the "family circle": for example, hair wreaths in glass frames, photo albums, and large family Bibles with decorative covers.

Along with domesticity, the furnishings of parlors signaled popular interest in being cosmopolitan, reflecting the nineteenth century's continuing fascination with the eighteenth-century European cultural ideal now called

"gentility." Gentility, a model of personal excellence originating in the up-
permost classes of society, stressed individual cultivation and social display, and it required rooms and furnishings designed for that purpose.
While few middle-class families could afford the kind of architecture that
made spaces truly gala, some mass-produced furnishings played an important role in commercializing gentility. For example, parlor suites of the
1860s and 1870s usually were concise catalogs of the kinds of formal seating furniture employed in eighteenth-century European salons or drawing
rooms, such as the chair type called the *fauteuil* (figure 20). Their design
was meant to encourage formality rather than relaxation; seated comfort,
as the concept is understood today, was of little concern. Even when furniture manufacturers began to produce suites that included rocking chairs,
they acknowledged the importance of formality in parlor decor by disguising the rocker, giving it a platform base and a frame and upholstery that
matched the forms of the other seats in the set.

Cosmopolitanism—being at home in the world, having wide knowledge
of its learning and high culture—also was signaled through specific objects
that referred to that outside world. Pianos and music corners in parlors are
a good example of this, as are the portfolios of prints that were placed
around parlors to serve as the focus of genteel conversation. The cultured
facade also was expressed through participation in what can be called the
"aesthetic of refinement," which translates loosely into the idea that more,
and more elaborate, possessions were evidence of civilization.

What the proper relationship between these two poles, designated by the
shorthand terms "Culture" (for cosmopolitanism and gentility) and
"Comfort" (the Victorian ideal of family-centered domestic life), should be
was the object of considerable debate until the end of the nineteenth century. And this debate was not trivial at the time, for it was an argument
about what constituted the good life. Middle-class families tried various
strategies to accommodate both visions, some by reserving space for separate parlors and sitting rooms, or by the dining room sometimes doing
double duty as the family's evening gathering space.

The contents of parlors were the medium for expressing a family's position in this web of values, and to understand the rich meaning possible in
such display, it is necessary to know how objects functioned as symbols.
Furnishings exist as fact, but, particularly in the rooms where others see
just "who we are," they also make rhetorical statements, that is, statements
meant to persuade others (and, it can be argued, also ourselves) that we
actually are what our possessions claim us to be. They do this by being tied

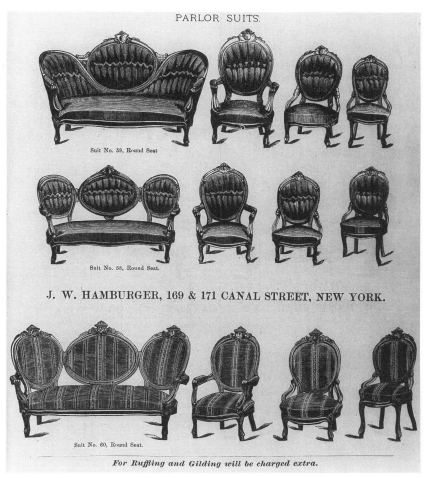

Fig. 20. "Parlor Suits." *Price List and Illustrated Catalogue*, J.W. Hamburger and Co., New York, N.Y., 1874. Courtesy the Strong Museum, Rochester, N.Y.

to chains of associative thought, both highly personal and conventional (commonly understood). Harnessing associations to objects can make even the most ordinary things into potent symbols, as when a pottery company decided to transfer-print George Washington's portrait onto pitchers in the early years of the Republic.

Symbols capitalize upon agreed-upon sets of associations with ideas. They can be created in many ways, but their meanings are reinforced through such channels as the popular media, informal learning through family and friends, or formal instruction in schools and other institutions. Many chains of association blend personal and commonly agreed-upon meanings. A photograph of a young woman holding a baby can be read as one's wife, daughter, or friend, but it can also be understood as a Madonna image, particularly if certain poses from the history of painting are mimicked in the photo.

In Victorian culture, ordinary people used objects to create dense webs of connections to their culture and society, so much so that these webs are almost difficult to credit today. In an analysis of Victorian mementos of mourning, Lawrence Taylor has used the subjects and imagery of sentimental mourning poetry in *Godey's Lady's Book* to demonstrate how series of symbolic associations were believed to work: "This increasing importance of ritual objects—from locks of hair and empty cradles to gravestones— was the natural outcome of the prevalent 'theory of associations.' Put simply, objects by virtue of their cultural form and/or specific history, were thought to be packed with meanings" for those individuals with "sensitive souls, or souls made sensitive by the impress of a properly ritual setting, whether church, cemetery, or museum."[10] The parlor was another ritual setting, dedicated to the secular rituals of social life as well as the occasional rites of passage with religious contents, such as funerals.

Taylor notes that women were considered more naturally sensitive to symbolic meanings, but a second category of the "symbolically sensitive" also existed. This was the cultivated person, whose personal gentility made her or him more attuned to the possibility of many levels of meaning in things. Emily Thornwell, author of *The Ladies' Guide to Perfect Gentility*, explained this sensitivity to associations in relation to the concept of "taste," noting that

Taste, there can be little doubt, depends, in great measure, upon association. . . . Our tastes and distastes proceed, for the most part, from the power that objects have to recall other ideas to the mind. And persons of superior cultivation have not only established for themselves a higher standard of grace, or excellence, to which they refer, but they have attained to a quicker perception of the relation of things to each other. They trace the connexion immediately, and, as it were, intuitively.[11]

The logic of the American democracy of manners, with its belief that gentility was accessible to all through etiquette books and other avenues of popular education, also implied that the ability to spin out chains of associations from the presence of things could be cultivated by almost anyone. Structured associative thinking, like knowledge of the rules of etiquette, made individuals more fully human because they were engaged with civilization in a deeper way. This kind of meaning-making was a highly self-conscious act on the part of the receiver, particularly at a time when public media were less insistent than their electronic descendents today.

This is where the concept of the parlor as memory palace becomes a useful aid for understanding the Victorian parlor. The term *memory palace* refers to a worldview and a philosophy of learning centuries old: the ancient, medieval, and Renaissance mnemonic theories and techniques that helped preserve information in societies where literacy still had not completely supplanted oral modes of learning. One of the most intriguing of these artificial memory devices actually was called the "memory palace." Here students were exhorted to create mental storage spaces in the form of rooms or entire buildings, with the knowledge they wished to preserve stored there in the form of images or furnishings. Renaissance teachers and students of memory drew inspiration from Quintilian (ca. 35 A.D.–c. 100 A.D.), whose *Institutio Oratoria* explained the memory palace concept thus:

> The first thought is placed, as it were, in the forecourt; the second, let us say, in the living room: the remainder are placed in due order all around the *impluvium* (the cistern in the center of Roman households) and entrusted not merely to bedrooms and parlours, but even to the care of statues and the like. This done, as soon as the memory of the facts requires to be revived, all these places are visited in turn and the various deposits are demanded from their custodians, as the sight of each recalls the respective details.[12]

In other words, the student walked through each room of the memory palace in his mind, seeing the contents and retrieving the ideas associated with each object. Quintilian was concerned with training pleaders for the Roman legal system; however, such mnemonic systems were used for many other kinds of learning as well. The world of formal knowledge was thus contained in a building or a room.

One wonders whether this longstanding pattern of thought may have contributed eventually to the habits of mind, well established by the eighteenth century, that found actual room decor suggestive as sites encoding formal knowledge. This line of speculation cannot be pursued further in this essay, but the image of the "memory palace" is a suitable metaphor for what decor could mean to properly susceptible and sensitive Victorians. Certainly the Victorian construction of meaning in the parlor, when most fully developed, was a highly artificial and convention-laden exercise—as full of artifice as the memory palace of Renaissance mnemonic theory.

How did the Victorian house function as a memory palace? The most significant rooms were those designated "public" by custom. Large houses had many single-purpose rooms that were appropriate for outsiders and which could be decorated to make rhetorical statements about their owners. Libraries were the site where, through their possession of books and bookcases, busts of famous authors, mineral specimens, globes, and the like, families presented themselves as participants in the worlds of literature and scientific learning. Even the patterns selected for the wallpaper could reflect this scholarly cast of mind; "Gothic" patterns were suitably serious. The contents of music rooms expressed their interest and accomplishment in the world of performing arts; conservatories, their relationship to the living natural world. Such a brief discussion fails to do justice to the potential complexity of this system of references and the long traditions underlying some of them. The sideboards in dining rooms alone incorporated a complex iconographical tradition relating to banqueting and the hunt.[13] The display of silver and silver plate on those sideboards descended from the ancient tradition of the cupboard, where the exhibition of objects made from precious metals was a symbol of power.[14] Still, the point holds; rooms were sites for certain kinds of conventionalized cultural information, which families could "own" in the form of possessions. Collections of natural specimens—shells and minerals—were not simply souvenirs but palpable connections to natural history. Prints of famous paintings joined their owners to the great traditions of art.

What if a family had only one or two rooms for "public" social purposes, a parlor and a dining room typically? Under such limitations, the occupants often displayed considerable ingenuity in making a wide, and not always compatible, range of rhetorical statements in a compressed way. Here, parlors alone had to become the "memory palaces" where formal social life and cultured learning and domesticity were *all* given their due. No wonder photographs of such parlors look like such a jumble to modern eyes—the rooms embodied the ideal family circle, the character of genteel social life, and, as we shall see, the cosmopolitan world of learning and high culture to which Victorian families aspired.

The height of the middle-class parlor as memory palace coincided with the decades of the great American expositions, the 1870s through the turn of the century, with the 1890s as its apex. Expositions claimed to offer visitors a summary of human achievement, at least as Victorian eyes saw it. Some of the constellations of objects in middle-class parlors reflected this same popular understanding of the structure and order of learning. In the Victorian world view, knowledge was still organized and categorized hierarchically with confidence, and judgments of quality made. The fine arts stood at the apex of human achievement, followed by the decorative arts, which combined art and utility. These were followed in turn by artifacts of technology (human artifice turned to purely practical purposes), exhibits from other lands (the more exotic the better), the products of agriculture, and specimens of natural history, which had been classified, *ergo* tamed, by humans.[15] Some exhibits, such as the New England Kitchen, encoded and popularized history itself.[16] Many Victorian Americans had themselves seen the expositions firsthand, or studied them through illustrated books. Further, popular compendia of exhibitions, as well as one-volume "family cyclopedias," preserved this hierarchy of human knowledge by the ways they organized their subject matter.[17]

Evidence of popular participation in this model of the world is present in the material culture of parlors. In keeping with their desire to be both cultivated and domestic, middle-class parlor denizens created complex "shrines into which is placed all that is most precious" in both the realm of education and high culture and the realm of sentiment and domesticity.[18] The Minneapolis parlor of Abbie and Samp, depicted in an 1878 stereo view inscribed to a friend, contains an etagere (display shelf) with sets of books (probably "classics" of literature) and a large bust of Shakespeare. Abbie and Samp try to depict themselves as exemplars of genteel ease. Their poses with books are a portrait convention that dates as far back as the Roman Empire.[19] Further, domesticity is represented by Abbie's needlework on the wall pocket and by the photographs of friends and family, which also personalize the references of high culture. The

Fig. 21. "Our Home./From Samp and Abbie To Fanny Rich/Minneapolis, Minn./October 8th 1878." Stereograph by M. Nowack, Minneapolis, Minn., 1878. Courtesy of the Division of Costume, National Museum of American History, Smithsonian Institution, Washington, D.C.

"shade," perhaps taxidermy birds under glass, and the seashell on the etagere represent natural history.

A memoir of growing up in a middling Buffalo, New York, household of the 1880s shows how two small parlors accomplished this complex work of cultural references through paraphrasing with a carefully selected sample of the family's best possessions. Alice Hughes Neupert recalled that "the front parlor was for state occasions only, and for entertaining priests, nuns, and important visitors such as Charles Deuther, organist at St. Patrick's Church." To this end, the room contained fancy drapery and chairs with upholstery too good to allow the children to sit on it. One shrine to high culture in the room was "a marble topped table in the center on which stood a carrara marble statue of 'winter' . . . another little silver dish for cards and a bound book of *Great Musicians*, that smelled sort of leathery." The front parlor also contained a piano, over which hung a large print of Beethoven.

If the Hughes family's front parlor was reserved for the world of art, the back parlor, which had older furniture and the heating stove for both rooms, contained a small display of international exotica in the form of "a table cornerwise with a cover made of scarlet flannel, black fringe, and black cut out dragons at each corner" with "a lamp and teakwood box which smelled like cinnamon and held a turtle that could move its legs" and "a Chinese ornament made with brown and yellow shells." References to tamed nature included a bird cage with a Kentucky cardinal and a bowl of goldfish. A "whatnot used as a bookcase" also contained "a piece of amethyst colored quartz that we were never allowed to touch" and the six-volume set of *Dr. Kane's Trip to the Arctic*.[20] Technology per se—celebrations of the machine for its own sake—are missing both in Abbie and Samp's picture and in the Neupert parlor, but both rooms were loaded with references to technology in the service of art, as in the use of the parlor stove or photography as decoration.

The look of parlor furnishings contained another set of references to the popular understanding of what it meant to be a civilized person. The levels of elaboration in the arrangement of furnishings, and the fancy appearance of each individual item in the furnishing scheme, expressed what may be called the "aesthetic of refinement." Today "refinement" is usually conceived as a process where things are reduced to their essence. However, to the Victorians, "refinement" was associated with progress and proliferation, since civilized progress was believed to lead to greater material, social, and cultural complexity.[21] "Refinement" in etiquette was conceived as attention to social detail and the nuances of polite behavior. "Refinement" in science and technology was the process of perfecting and proliferating the activities that increased human comforts and embellished basic needs. Regarding "refinement" in the home, one author put it thus:

> Our American home is . . . the valued result of years of conquest in the realms of commerce and science. It is curious to observe how, in each advancing step, fresh wants are created which, in turn, encouraged and accelerated the efforts of science and art as applied to the convenience and embellishments of the home.[22]

In other words, "refinement" meant more, and more elaborate, possessions, reflecting as much accomplishment and artifice as their owners could buy or assemble. The refined eye delighted in a high degree of obvious technical skill in objects, in visual puns and play, and in what I have elsewhere called equivalent levels of visual detail.[23] In this kind of looking, the eye always had as much to take in as it could manage, whether looking at a shelf lambrequin twelve inches long, or an entire room (of which such a lambrequin was only a small part).

Why bother trying to contain a material summary of the outside world inside a house or, more incredibly, within a single room? The peculiar logic and necessities of domesticity must be credited with this phenomenon. While they believed deeply in the necessary separation of the world and the home, Victorian Americans were fascinated with what their culture had wrought and wanted to celebrate it. Working inside its dichotomy, domesticity suggested that the world be brought into the house and mediated, miniaturizing it and giving it its stamp of approval for family consumption. Thus the most worldly room in middle-class houses also contained the world in microcosm and, as we saw with Alice Neupert's family and with the parlor of Abbie and Samp, rendered it in a peculiar form of shorthand.

By the 1890s, the memory palace ideal of parlor furnishing seems to have reached its broadest popular acceptance. Scores of essays published in magazines like *The Decorator and Furnisher* illustrated and described ideal parlors, in accounts running as long as several thousand words.[24] Mail-order and furnishings and dry goods catalogs, along with photographs of individual parlors, indicate that there was no sudden rage for simplifying rooms at the turn of the century. Parlors that were deliberately simplified did begin to appear in this decade, but they still contained some objects intended to trigger associative thought—rocking chairs, displays of mementos on mantels or tabletops, and prints of famous paintings, for example.

By the decade beginning in 1910, however, most authors of furnishing advice, with the exception of those whose readership was well-to-do and able to continue having both a drawing room and a sitting room, promoted the idea of the "living room" in preference to a parlor. By 1920, the term *living room* had completely replaced *parlor* in the national periodical of the furniture trade, the *Grand Rapids Furniture Record*. Sets of model rooms displayed in furniture stores no longer included parlors, either.[25] The term *living room* had once referred to a multipurpose room in small, very modest households, a room one had on the way to economic success and future parlor making. Now it designated one principal room used for both family and guests. The modern living room was intended to be less overtly and enthusiastically artificial than the parlor, both in the social life taking place there and in its mirroring decor.

Did people follow this advice? Some did, but Victorian tastes and patterns of room use survived at least through the 1920s. The transformation of the parlor into the living room did occur, but it was gradual and uneven, reflecting the way Victorian culture itself slowly evolved into the modern era. A scholar trying to unravel the process of change from parlors to living rooms must sort out a range of factors, comparing changes in plans for newly constructed houses and actual patterns of living there, and looking for continuity and change in rooms found in older houses with Victorian floor plans. Suggestions for domestic social life described in advice literature must be compared with the activities that really took place at home, and furnishing advice with the actual material culture of living rooms. The advice literature is copious and readily available, but how are actual patterns of living to be reconstructed?

The Middletown Living Room

One study that still offers a useful diagram of the changes in material conditions, attitudes, and behavior that squeezed the memory palace out of existence is *Middletown* (1929), Robert S. Lynd and Helen Merrell Lynd's study of Muncie, Indiana, in the 1920s. The research that led to the publication of *Middletown*, a "venture in contemporary anthropology," compared life in the 1920s with the baseline of that same community in 1890.[26] While the Lynds documented significant change in every part of daily life as Middletown became "modern," they acknowledged that "it is not uncom-

Fig. 22. "An Inexpensive Living-Room in the Modern Style." Edward Stratton Holloway, *The Practical Book of Furnishing the Small House and Apartment* (Philadelphia: J.B. Lippincott, 1922), plate 2, facing p. 24.

mon to observe 1890 and 1924 habits jostling side by side," as in "a family with primitive back-yard water or sewage habits, yet using an automobile, electric washer, electric iron, and vacuum cleaner."[27]

The living room—a return to a multipurpose space—evolved partly from the fact that families had less room in newly built apartments, old houses that were split into two or more residences, and new single-family houses, particularly by the 1920s (figure 23). The typical Victorian house-plan, with its special-use rooms, was actually nothing more than a series of decorated boxes enclosing space. The walls rarely contained ducts, pipes, or wiring. Smaller new houses were one outcome when people opted for expensive, recently-perfected systems of heating and plumbing, cutting into the amount of money they once used for simply enclosing space from the elements in a decorative fashion. The Lynds noted that simply digging a basement for a furnace and water system added seven hundred dollars to house costs in 1920 Muncie, as much as the cost of an entire small house some years earlier.[28] Thus the disappearance of separate parlors was some-times a choice by families for systems over ceremony.

Further, some new house types, such as bungalows, had open plans where public rooms flowed together, making difficult the separation of

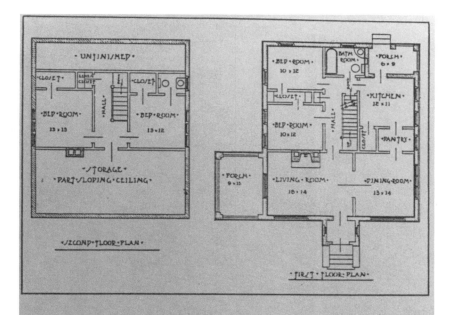

Fig. 23. Bungalow houseplan and elevations. This typical bungalow plan elimi-
nates the buffer zone of the entry hall. The living room and dining room are essentially one space, and the architectural hierarchy of front/back, public/private is
blurred by the location of the bedrooms on the first floor. Charlotte Wait Calkins, *A
Course in House Planning and Furnishing* (Chicago: Scott, Foresman, 1916), p.
23.

public and private functions so characteristic of Victorian houseplans and domestic routine. The new open plans were not embraced wholeheartedly, however. Architectural historian Alan Gowans has argued that some segments of the house-buying public resisted the open floor plan precisely because it neglected longstanding concerns for providing buffer zones such as entry halls and the "owners' continuing preference for individual privacy."[29]

In such a transitional moment in house history, the fate of the parlor was determined by many factors, including the social class and age of the occupants of a house. The Lynds noted that, at least in prosperous working-class homes, where the parlor had arrived last, it still survived. These families spent their evenings at home in the dining room. This was part of a general trend in which working-class living habits seemed to be one generation "behind" those of what the Lynds called the "business class."[30] Progressive-era social workers had noted a similar persistence of formal parlors among prosperous working-class families in Pittsburgh and New York City. Often these rooms were set apart from the uses of everyday living, at some sacrifice on the part of the owners, and employed much of the middle-class vocabulary of parlor furnishing from the 1880s and 1890s. While such parlors no longer contained the panoply of cultural references characteristic of middle-class parlors, they did reflect both domesticity and some references meaningful to their occupants, such as pianos or parlor organs and pictures of Catholic saints.[31]

The genteel rituals that formed middle-class parlor social life—calling, teas, musicales, and amateur theatrics—had declined dramatically by the years of the Lynds' research. They attributed this to Middletown's new, "more highly diversified and organized leisure." Modern leisure pursuits were facilitated by shorter working hours and by a wealth of new inventions, from motion pictures to the automobile. These new activities necessarily took place out of the house; still, sometimes it almost seems as though family members simply couldn't wait to get out of the house and away from one another.

Some of the city's residents were finely attuned to the effects wrought even by so small an invention as the telephone, which had begun to replace neighborly "calling." (The carryover of the term from face-to-face visit to telephone contact is itself significant.)[32] In the leisure time at home that did survive, the *Middletown* researchers noted a narrower range of activities, principally card playing and dancing to recorded music. It is unclear why the rich range of homemade entertainments disappeared when people did stay at home; perhaps this is further evidence of the erosion of the logic of domesticity, which insisted on bringing the world of culture into the home. Again, anecdotal evidence suggests that some families maintained traditions of Victorian types of parlor entertainment through the 1930s.[33] Paradoxically, the private Victorian home was *less* private than its modern successor, when seen in terms of the number and kinds of activities taking place there.

Although the Lynds did not treat this subject, the rites of passage that once took place in parlors gradually were being professionalized out of the home, just as leisure seemed to be. Funerals in commercial "funeral parlors" were part of the professionalization of death that, beginning in the 1880s, included licensed "funeral directors" and the national casket industry. Nonetheless, the typical funeral of 1920 still took place, when space permitted, in the family home.[34] As with space allocation itself, families made decisions about the suitability of their homes for such traditions based on a personal calculus that bears further research.

If the modern living room really was a different kind of space, one has to ask where and how the energies and values that created the memory palace parlor were redirected. Did families become less "domestic," in the Victorian sense of the word, less fretted by the need for formal social life? Did they no longer require a public facade that was, ironically, contained inside their houses? What was their relationship to the cultured world, if the living room was unlike the old memory palace?

Deliberately simplified living-room decor was indeed one harbinger of changing priorities among middle-class women in particular. They had less household help than their Victorian mothers, or none at all, and by the 1920s the lives of many such women had become more public due to new kinds of shopping and increased participation in new forms of leisure, from organized clubs to the movies. Advice literature reflected and encouraged this change. The authors of *The Modern Priscilla Home Furnishing Book* announced to readers, "We have discovered that the world is full of a number of things beside the routine of housekeeping."[35] The careful collections of possessions that were integral to the rhetoric of the memory palace were, in the words of interior decorator Edward Stratton Holloway, simply "small objects—attractive enough in themselves, perhaps, but entailing how much work in their dusting and handling day after day?"[36]

Changing attitudes on the part of homemakers was part of a larger shift in values away from Victorian culture's capacious interpretation of domesticity. Still, the domestic ideal of home-as-haven survived in an attenuated form. A common advertising pitch for new construction of single-family houses in the 1920s took the theme of the house as a psychological fortress against the pressures of the world of business.[37]

The genteel worldview that prized high culture and etiquette, and so recalled eighteenth-century gentility, also was in slow decline. Particularly after 1915, advice authors began to regard longstanding forms of parlor social life as "old-fashioned pomposity."[38] The decline of "formalism" has been well documented elsewhere; still, parlors (along with libraries, conservatories, and other single-purpose rooms with memory-palace functions) continued to survive among families whose members believed in the hierarchies of value and the priorities of genteel culture. For example, a formal parlor, complete with horsehair upholstery, survived in the Ruth family house in Lebanon, Pennsylvania, until the 1950s. This family, whose members were all college-educated, resisted the popular culture and new technologies of leisure that swept over America in the 1920s.[39]

Thus the smaller living spaces, changes in housekeeping routines and priorities, new and compelling outlets for spending discretionary income, and new forms of social life were accompanied by the decreasing power of the vision of the parlor as the world within a room, both an emblem of a public family identity and a memory palace of culture. In decorating advice books of the 1910s and 1920s, the living room was described as a room carefully stripped of many of the objects that Victorian Americans enjoyed displaying and contemplating. Hazel Adler, the author of *The New Interior: Modern Decoration for the Modern Home* (1916), instructed her readers that "objects of sentimental associations, of affected culture, together with certain heirlooms and souvenirs which the scheme of decoration refuses to assimilate, should find a happy end in a memory chest where the viewing of them at intervals provides a source of interest and amusement."[40] Another author insisted that each room was intended to be "simply the background of the people who live in it."[41] While such statements do not mean that possessions no longer served as indicators of their owner's cultural membership as well as their social aspirations, they do suggest that some commentators posited a different relationship between people and their possessions. Scholars of twentieth-century consumer culture have suggested that consumer goods were sometimes seen as one medium for articulating individual personality rather than formal cultural identity, as aids to consolidating fragmented identity (impression management), or even, by extension, interchangeable masks to be removed at will.[42] This model of consumption differs from the one that underlay the cultured facade of gentility, which was a collective identity shared by choice. It fits well with our understanding of the charms of new forms of commercialized leisure of the late nineteenth and early twentieth century such as the amusement park—a "gigantic stage set that engulfed visitors in new roles" and promised "not stability but transformation."[43] There is more work to be done on consumer mentality in the transitional decades of 1890 to 1920, but one can hypothesize that, by the 1920s, cultural memory was not believed to reside in household possessions; only much depleted, evanescent personal memory was contained there.[44] This change would explain why advice authors such as Hazel Adler were able to suggest to their readers that even personal mementos were somehow trivial.

Perhaps the most important new medium for statements of identity, such as they were, through possessions was the automobile. By the 1920s, when credit buying was extended to automobiles, middle- and working-class families now had access to what can be described as a portable facade. The Lynds noted that working people often planned to spend one week's wages per month on car payments and that the car was the single most important competitor for dollars once spent on houses.[45] (Along with furnaces and other systems, it should be noted in passing here that new homeowners also diverted some portion of house-building funds to construction of a garage, a house for their portable facade.) By the 1930s, as many as half of the thirty million households in the United States owned or had access to a car.[46]

Simultaneously, the aesthetic of refinement was under attack by design reformers, who were often Progressives with ties to the Arts and Crafts movement, manual arts training, and social work. Reformers offered criticism of the parlor and its contents based upon a narrow, proto-modernist definition of "function." When function was defined as "physical use," it ruled out the Victorian conception that furnishings could be used to make complex rhetorical statements of identity. Charlotte Wait Calkins' *A Course in House Planning and Furnishing* (1916), a booklet intended as a workbook for a home economic course, suggested that students ask themselves such questions as "Will [this article] serve this purpose in a simple, honest, straightforward manner?"[47]

Calkins was one of many home economists who attacked the old aesthetic of refinement, with its love of ornament, visual play, and visual complexity; she did this through a series of comparison exercises. A plate comparing "good" and "bad" sofa pillows was accompanied by the statement, "Pictures on sofa pillows and all other objects are out of place. No one should want to rest his head on anything that resembles real rose thorns, tennis rackets, pipes, flags, Indian heads and the like."[48] Another author railed against the "Early Pullman period of American home decoration; when the cozy corner held its sway and chenille curtains, crocheted tidies, beaded portieres, ubiquitous grill-work, plush upholstery and embroidered piano drapes formed dust catchers all over the house."[49] Her model room arrangements attacked the levels of complexity treasured by the refined eye, reasserting utility over rhetoric. One unexplored issue that seems to underlie this attack on the memory palace is the possibility that the argument being advanced was predominantly a feminine one, as self-consciously modern women attacked the subculture of Victorian women by finding no value in, and aggressively eliminating, just what the older generation treasured.

Finally, memoirs repeatedly indicate that some families used living rooms as they once had their parlors, reserving them for special occasions and confining everyday living to their dining rooms and kitchens. The Charlotte, New York, house in which Robert Vance Stewart grew up in the 1910s and 1920s is one case in point. The house had a "living room," simply furnished, that was used as if it were a parlor. It was used "Saturdays, Sundays, and holidays, when we had company. When Eleanor [his sister] was taking piano lessons," she spent dismal evening hours alone in the living room practicing while the rest of the family sat in the kitchen.[50] This is an urban pattern as well as a rural one, and, for the time being, its implications for our understanding of changing patterns of everyday life remain unclear. Further, average consumers may have simplified their living rooms somewhat, but many of the furnishing styles most popular through the 1920s—Jacobean revival and various other interpretations of colonial and European historical styles—embodied the design qualities much criticized in advice manuals.

Much work remains to be done on topics in house history along the lines of the "room history" examined in this essay. Writing such histories can do more than help historic preservationists and museum professionals prepare more accurate reconstructions of rooms. A house, its contents, and its occupants are a complex constellation. Change in the components of the house—change from a Victorian parlor to a modern living room—reflects more than a simple desire to stop dusting so frequently. A wide range of cultural, social, and material factors impinged on the Victorian memory palace, and some of the more intriguing factors must remain the objects of speculation for now.

Notes

1. For a fuller account of this development in house planning, see Katherine C. Grier, *Culture and Comfort: People, Parlors, and Upholstery, 1850–1930* (Rochester, N.Y.: Strong Museum, 1988), esp. ch. 2, "The Comfortable Theater: Parlor Making in the Middle-Class Household, 1850–1910," 19–58.

2. S.B. Reed, *Modern House-Plans for Everybody* (New York: Orange Judd Co., 1878, 1900), is a useful volume for understanding the thinking behind construction of modest houses in the latter part of the 19th century. The copy in my possession contains a label indicating that it was purchased from Sears, Roebuck and Co.

3. Clarence Cook, *The House Beautiful: Essays on Beds and Tables, Stools and Candlesticks* (1878; rptd. Croton-on-Hudson, N.Y.: North River Press, 1980), 47; and Ralph A. Cram, "The Reception Room," *Decorator and Furnisher* 1, no. 4 (Jan. 1883):119.

4. Harriet Beecher Stowe [Christopher Crowfield, pseud.], *House and Home Papers* (Boston: Fields, Osgood, and Co., 1869), 34.

5. One of the most frequently reproduced images of this kind of gala social life is the American artist Henry Sargent's painting *The Tea Party* (ca. 1821–25), in the collection of the Museum of Fine Arts, Boston. A vivid account of the social rounds of tea parties, balls, and receptions or "routs" in elite private households in the early 19th century may be found in Barbara G. Carson, *Ambitious Appetites: Dining, Behavior, and Patterns of Consumption in Federal Washington* (Washington, D.C.: American Institute of Architects Press, 1990).

6. Examples of these various parlor activities may be found in Grier, *Culture and Comfort.*

7. Progressive-era social workers were struck, and occasionally distressed, by elaborate parlors in small working-class houses and apartments. See, e.g., Louise Bolard More, *Wage Earners' Budgets: A Study of Standards and Costs of Living in New York City* (New York: Henry Holt, 1907, rptd. New York: Arno, 1971).

8. Catharine E. Beecher and Harriet Beecher Stowe, *The American Woman's Home* (New York: J.B. Ford and Co., 1870), 18–19, 20.

9. For a discussion of the symbolism of the center table, see Grier, *Culture and Comfort,* 86–89.

10. Lawrence Taylor, "Death in *Godey's*: Women and Death in Nineteenth-Century America." Paper presented at the Winterthur Museum, Winterthur, Del., Apr. 1982, p. 16.

11. Emily Thornwell, *The Ladies' Guide to Perfect Gentility* (New York: Derby and Jackson, 1856), 66.

12. *The Institutio Oratoria of Quintillian,* trans. H.A. Butler, 4 vols. (New York: G.P. Putnam's Sons, 1922), 4:223. The author was first introduced to the history of artificial memory systems in Jonathan Spence, *The Memory Palace of Matteo Ricci* (New York: Penguin). The definitive work on this subject is Frances A. Yates, *The Art of Memory* (New York: Penguin, 1969).

13. Kenneth Ames, "Murderous Propensities: Notes on the Dining Iconography of the Mid-Nineteenth Century," manuscript, Winterthur Museum, Winterthur, Del., 1975; and Kenneth Ames, "The Battle of the Sideboards," *Winterthur Portfolio* 9 (1974):1–27.

14. Penelope Eames, "Furniture in England, France and the Netherlands from the Twelfth to the Fifteenth Century," *Furniture History* 13 (1977):55–60.

15. Neil Harris, "Museums, Merchandising, and Popular Taste: The Struggle for Influence," in *Material Culture and the Study of American Life,* ed. Ian M.G. Quimby (New York: Norton, 1977), 145.

16. For a discussion of this type of popular history, see Rodris Roth, "The New England, or 'Olde Time,' Kitchen Exhibit at Nineteenth-Century Fairs," in *The Colonial Revival in America,* ed. Allen Axelrod (New York: Norton, 1985), 159–83.

17. See, e.g., Philip T. Sandhurst, *The Great Centennial Exhibition* (Philadelphia and Chicago: P.W. Zeigler and Co., 1876), one of a number of inexpensive illustrated accounts of the fair. One-volume cyclopedias proliferated in the 1880s and 1890s; they were sold door-to-door and through the mail, as well as in bookstores. See, e.g., Charles E. Beale and M.R. Gately, eds., *Gately's Universal Educator: An Educational Cyclopedia and Business Guide* (Boston: M.R. Gately, 1883). The copy in the collection of the Strong Museum notes on its title page, "Eleventh Edition Revised. Sixtieth Thousand," suggesting the popularity and longevity of such volumes.

18. Mary Gay Humphries, "The Parlor," *Decorator and Furnisher* 11, no. 5 (May 1888):52.

19. Several Pompeiian examples, of a couple holding tablets and a scroll and of a cultivated woman writer, are published in Philippe Aries and Georges Duby, gen. eds., *A History of Private Life,* vol. 1, *From Pagan Rome to Byzantium,* ed. Paul Veyne, (Cambridge, Mass.: Harvard Univ. Press, 1987), pl. 6, facing p. 274.

20. Alice Hughes Neupert, "In Those Days: Buffalo in the 1870's," *Niagara Frontier* 24, no. 4 (Winter 1977):77–78.

21. This definition of refinement is supported by the *Oxford English Dictionary.* By the 18th century, refinement implied progress: "an instance of improvement or advance toward something more refined or perfect," as in "to polish or improve (a language, composition, etc.); to make more elegant and cultivated."

22. "An Antiquarian" [pseud.], "Our Home: Its History and Progress, with Notices of the Introduction of Domestic Inventions," *Household Journal* 28 (Sept. 1861):407.

23. For a more complete explanation of the aesthetic of refinement, see Grier, *Culture and Comfort,* ch. 5, "The Quest for Refinement: Reconstructing the Aesthetics of Upholstery, 1850–1910," 129–62.

24. See, e.g., J.R. Pugh, "The Best Room: Its Arrangement and Decoration at Moderate Cost," *Decorator and Furnisher* 13, no. 1 (Oct. 1888):19.

25. See, e.g., manufacturers' advertisements for "living room" furniture, such as that of the Greilick Manufacturing Co. of Traverse City, Mich., in *Grand Rapids Furniture Record* 38, no. 1 (Jan. 1919):91; and the model rooms featured in E.P. Wakefield, "Margeson Bros., Home Furnishing Specialists," *Grand Rapids Furniture Record* 38, no. 3 (Mar. 1919):113–18.

26. Robert S. Lynd and Helen Merrell Lynd, *Middletown: A Study in Modern American Culture* (New York: Harcourt, Brace and World, 1929, 1956), 5.

27. Ibid., 97.

28. Ibid., 98–99.

29. Ellen Elizabeth Frances, "Progressivism and the American House: Architecture as an Agent of Social Reform" (M.A. thesis, Univ. of Oregon, 1982), 59; Alan Gowans, *The Comfortable House: North American Suburban Architecture, 1890–1930* (Cambridge, Mass.: MIT Press, 1986), 27.

30. Robert Lynd and Helen Lynd, *Middletown*, 98–99.

31. More, *Wage-Earners' Budgets*, 133–34, 146; Margaret Byington, *Homestead: The Households of a Mill town* (1910; rptd. Pittsburgh, Pa.: Univ. of Pittsburgh Press, 1974). Byington's book features several Lewis Hine photographs of working-class parlors.

32. Robert Lynd and Helen Lynd, *Middletown*, 275.

33. I knew of two families who did participate in regular parlor games. One was a group, actually, of professionals (doctors and lawyers) in the 1920s and 1930s (maybe earlier?) who spent weeks preparing for scenes—silhouettes also [tableaux vivant], I think—the productions were in my acquaintances' Victorian parlors. . . . Wood nymphs, fairies, boatmen, etc. . . . Another instance of parlor games involved a large extended Irish-heritage family that summered in Newfields [Mass.]. They would spend Satur*day* itself getting ready for an evening's entertainment, for themselves, of recitations, dances, songs, piano pieces, group songs. . . . All the family and guests were expected to perform. . . . This was a large teacher's family. (Mrs. John A. O'Brien to Florence Smith, museum educator, Strong Museum, Rochester, N.Y., 29 Nov. 1989)

34. James J. Farrell, *Inventing the American Way of Death, 1830–1920* (Philadelphia: Temple Univ. Press, 1980), 172–77.

35. *The Modern Priscilla Home-Furnishing Book: A Practical Book for the Woman Who Loves Her Home* (Boston: Priscilla Publishing Co., 1925), 162.

36. Edward Stratton Holloway, *The Practical Book of Furnishing the Small House and Apartment* (Philadelphia: J.B. Lippincott, 1922), 93.

37. Gowans, *Comfortable House*, 8, 13.

38. *Vogue's Book of Etiquette: Present-Day Customs of Social Intercourse with the Rules for Their Correct Observance* (New York: Conde-Nast, 1924), 173.

39. The family described here includes the grandparents, parents, and aunts of the author's father.

40. Hazel H. Adler, *The New Interior: Modern Decorations for the Modern Home* (New York: Century, 1916), 38.

41. *Modern Priscilla Home Furnishings Book*, 9.

42. See T.J. Jackson Lears, "From Salvation to Self Realization: Advertising and the Therapeutic Roots of the Consumer Culture, 1880–1930," in *The Culture of Consumption: Critical Essays in American History, 1880–1980,* ed. Richard Wrightman Fox and T.J. Jackson Lears (New York: Pantheon, 1983), 1–38. The implication of the modern vision of "selfhood"—"an empty vessel to be filled and refilled according to the expectations of others and the needs of the moment"—was that consumption of the proper goods eased and aided this necessary shifting. See also Roland Marchand's ingenious analysis of advertisements containing the "Parable of the First Impression," ads which capitalized on this new concern with mastering impression management, in Marchand, *Advertising the American Dream: Making Way for Modernity, 1920–1940* (Berkeley: Univ. of California Press, 1985), 206–17.

43. John Kasson, *Amusing the Million: Coney Island at the Turn of the Century* (New York: Hill and Wang, 1978), 65.

44. T.J. Jackson Lears, in "From Salvation to Self-Realization," 16, suggests that history and cultural memory were themselves devalued.

45. Robert Lynd and Helen Lynd, *Middletown*, 105.

46. Ruth Schwartz Cowan, *More Work for Mother: The Ironies of Household Technology from the Open Hearth to the Microwave* (New York: Basic Books, 1983), 83.

47. Charlotte Wait Calkins, *A Course in House Planning and Furnishing* (Chicago: Scott, Foresman, 1916), 55.

48. Ibid., 63.

49. *Modern Priscilla Book of Home Furnishing*, 2.

50. Robert Vance Stewart, "When Grandpa Was a Boy: Reminiscences of Robert Vance Stewart," 1982, p. 7. Typescript, Collections of the Genesee Charlotte Lighthouse Historical Society.

CHAPTER THREE

Children in the House, 1890 to 1930

Karin Calvert

Anyone who has visited a museum or historic house dating from the colonial era more than likely has seen a room devoted to the children of a colonial family—a room furnished with diminutive beds and dressers, little chairs and scaled-down rugs; a room filled with toys and decorated with child-related prints or paintings on the walls. Such rooms are very popular with museum visitors because they express what we who live in a very child-oriented and child-conscious society expect. Such rooms also fulfill the expectations of the museum curators who furnished them and took it as a given that there would have been separate children's rooms to house the children of an eighteenth-century family, and that the age and gender of the young occupants would have a major bearing on the furnishings plan of their quarters.

The reality was quite different, however, for children's rooms, children's furniture, and even distinctive children's dress and most toys, are, for the most part, all very recent innovations, not much older than the American Civil War, and not really common until the period under discussion—1890 to 1930.

The Colonial Child: Image and Implements

Adults in the colonial period viewed infants as rather inadequate creatures, terribly vulnerable to accident and disease, irrational and animalistic in their behavior, and a drain on the family's resources and energy. The best thing for the children and the family was to get infants through the dangerous first year of life and up on their feet, as soon as possible, as independent and functioning members of the family. Parents believed that children would not progress on their own but had to be forced to develop. What goods existed specifically for children were, therefore, designed to push them into the adult world as quickly as possible. The common artifacts of the period were swaddling—long linen bandages wrapped firmly around an infant's arms, legs, and body to encourage straight growth; standing stools or posts that secured an infant in an upright position to strengthen leg muscles and encourage early walking; and walking stools with wooden wheels (but without seats) to support the toddler's uncertain steps. Ambulatory children of both sexes wore cumbersome petticoats and long gowns over padded corsets which helped to ensure good posture and curb childish exuberance. Little boys in long gowns did not look feminine to contemporary eyes, anymore than little girls in blue jeans look masculine to us today. Long skirts characterized the dress of all dependent members of a family, regardless of sex, and visually distinguished them from the authority vested in older boys and men in knee breeches. Childhood essentially ended at about the age of seven, when boys discarded childish skirts for their first pair of knee breeches. This does not mean that either boys or girls of seven were regarded as adults, but that they were ready to begin taking their place in the world, through either school, work, or apprenticeship. By the age of seven, children had entered upon the age of responsibility.[1]

Colonial parents expected even their young children to accommodate themselves as best they could to an adult world. Children slept wherever there was space—with parents, siblings, servants, guests; in full-sized beds or on pallets on the floor in often crowded rooms. They ate sitting on an adult's lap or standing by the table in order to reach their plates. They played with amusements such as balls, whistles, cards, or whirligigs, which were made as much for adults as for children; or possessed few toys if their religious sect disapproved of play in general. Adults viewed childhood as a vulnerable, frustrating period of human inadequacy. They therefore believed that children should work, play, eat, and sleep in the company of adults in order to learn from them and grow up quickly.[2]

The Victorian Child: Child-Specific Dress and Artifacts

Beginning about 1770, Americans began to take more interest in their families. Increasingly marriages were based on affection rather than economics, and parents took delight in the peculiarly childish natures of their children. Middle-class mothers wrote letters to absent fathers detailing the baby-talk and antics of their infants, and both parents more often enjoyed playing with their little ones. As parents found pleasure in the childishness of their children, they abandoned the artifacts of previous generations, which had been designed expressly to push children beyond infancy as quickly as possible. They stopped swaddling their babies and gave up the use of standing and walking stools. They abandoned tight corsets and heavy gowns in favor of very light cotton frocks, three to four feet long for babies and ankle length for toddlers, and they permitted boys of four to seven the freedom of long trousers instead of long skirts. Parents continued, however, to room children with adults so that the child might learn from constant association with his elders. The wealthy Virginia planter Robert Carter, for example, assigned his son to sleep in a room with the children's tutor, and his young nephew shared a room with Carter's secretary. Likewise, George Washington's grandson shared a room at Mount Vernon with Washington's secretary.[3]

Only after 1830, with the advent of the Victorian era in England and America, do we begin to see widespread use of specialized goods and rooms for children. Both boys and girls after 1830 dressed in colorful knee-length frocks and white trousers (or pantaloons). The new costume looked very masculine to contemporary eyes. Little boys had always been dressed in frocks for their first few years, and had worn trousers for several generations, so the new costume was easily accepted on them. But because, in Western culture, only males had ever worn pants of any kind, many people were at first shocked to see such a masculine garment on little girls. Girls had always worn skirts, of course, but never pants, not even in the form of underwear. In letters to the editor and sermons, concerned citizens of the 1830s warned that such attire would coarsen American girls, diminish their maternal instincts, and endanger the future of the American family. Nonetheless, the new style gradually lost its strangeness and became quite acceptable by the 1840s.

By then, the new androgynous costume was complemented by a confusion of hairstyles. Some boys and girls sported very short hair, cut off above the ear in the then-popular Brutus or Titus cut. Other girls and boys wore their hair in long curls down on the shoulders. The androgynous affect was deliberate, reflecting a new perception of children. Beginning in the 1830s, the popular image of children came to be that they were entirely sweet and innocent (i.e., sexless) beings who descended directly from heaven to their earthly homes. Parents believed that their children were born pure and angelic, and any faults of character they might develop would be due to contamination by contact with the coarseness of this earthly world. It was

Fig. 24. A.R. and Kenneth Lawrence, Yonkers, N.Y., 1893. A.R.'s long baby gown
kept little ones warm and discouraged crawling on all fours, since Victorian parents
were still uncomfortable with such an animalistic form of locomotion, no matter
how temporary. Kenneth's velvet suit, consisting of jacket and skirt, was commonly
worn for best by boys who had outgrown the more feminine toddler's frocks but
were still too young for short pants. Collection of Karin Calvert.

therefore the task of parents to protect their children from just such contamination. The new costume was an appropriate visual reference to the then-popular theories regarding the innocent nature of children, since it emphasized the sexual innocence of children as well as their separateness from the adult community.[4]

In its need to sequester children from the evils of the world, the Victorian middle class adopted specialized rooms and furniture forms. The new furniture accomplished two important functions: it protected the children from the world, and protected the house from the children. The Victorian home was an elaborate environment, a veritable thicket of damageable goods. Tables, shelves, mantels, bookcases, and chests were covered with loose fabrics, the better to display delicate ceramic figurines, art glass, hair sculpture, and heavy brass objects. Such knicknacks were as dangerous to small children as children were to them. Victorian families therefore adopted the jumper, a seat or harness on a spring which could be fastened in any doorway, to tether their toddlers in one safe place. The child could jump and swing energetically while firmly restricted to that one spot. Significantly, advertisements for jumpers assured parents that the devices were big enough to hold children of six years of age, thereby restricting the movements of the older child as well as the baby. Similarly, parents abandoned cradles, trundle beds, and shared adult beds for a new form of children's furniture which developed around the turn of the nineteenth century, the crib. In theory at least, even a toddler could be confidently left within the confines of a metal crib. The new furniture for children protected them and the domestic environment by confining them to a safe spot, away from the bustle of adult activities.[5]

Dining in the Victorian home was an elaborate and formal affair. The middle-class table was set with white linen and delicate china and glass. Parents expected their children to absorb and demonstrate the manners, knowledge, and dexterity that were prerequisite to the art of dining. In addition, physicians and child-rearing authorities had warned that children should be kept to a bland diet, avoiding the rich meats, sauces, and desserts that their elders enjoyed, but which could, it was believed, overstimulate young bodies. The highchair with attached tray developed as a solution to a double problem. It kept young children from damaging the dining accoutrements, and it prohibited them from helping themselves to the many forbidden foods before them, enforcing, as one retailer promised, "a well-regulated demeanor at the table." Like the jumper in the parlor and the crib in the bedroom, the highchair protected children by restricting their access to the world around them.[6]

Fig. 25. Paul Merlyn Cornelius, age 2 years and 4 months, ca. 1895, Reading, Pennsylvania. Paul wears a short frock, a straw hat, and a white ribbon tied in a bow in his golden curls. The androgynous look pleased Victorian parents who wished their children to project an air of sweetness and innocence. Beginning in the 1850s, pantaloons became increasingly shorter until, by the 1880s, they disappeared from view altogether. The invisible became the unmentionable, and pantaloons became bloomers, the first real underwear. Collection of Karin Calvert.

Fig. 26. Child in rompers, ca. 1920–25. The introduction of rompers marked a major change in child-rearing practices in America, since, for the first time, babies had free use of their legs and could crawl and climb as they learned to walk. Collection of Karin Calvert.

Nurseries and Playrooms: Environs and Equipment

The best sanctuary for the protection of Victorian children, however, was not a single piece of furniture, but a separate space within the house where children could remain secure and sequestered from the dangers of the adult world. By the 1830s, then, a few parents began setting aside one room as a nursery for their young children. The nursery was usually located at the back of the house on the second or third floor—as far away from the normal activity of adults as possible. This arrangement protected the children from too much exposure to adult activities and adults from nursery noise. The new nurseries were usually sparsely furnished, containing only the beds, tables, and chairs necessary for the care of all the young children in the family. Rugs, curtains, and other fabrics were kept to a minimum to leave the space uncluttered, airy, and free of dust. Parents viewed the nursery as a functional space and felt no need to decorate it. Indeed, they usually furnished it with any available pieces too old and shabby for use anywhere else in the house. Virtually all of the furnishings of a typical Victorian nursery would have been secondhand adult-sized goods that the family had accumulated over time, with only the cribs and perhaps one or more child-sized chairs specifically purchased to accommodate their new little owners.[7]

Traditionally, the indoor play area for children had always been the garret—a fairly large storage space that allowed plenty of room for rough-and-tumble play during inclement weather, with little danger that the children would damage anything of value. Gradually, as houses became increasingly large in the late nineteenth century, parents sometimes reserved a second room for children, called either a day nursery (as opposed to the night nursery used for sleeping) or a playroom. Like the garret before it, the nineteenth-century playroom was usually a large, virtually empty space located near the top of the house, which provided children with space for active play. Nothing much was done about furnishing or decorating these early playrooms. Such attentions were reserved for areas visible to visitors, and children's rooms were among the most private spaces in the Victorian home.[8]

In many comfortable middle-class homes after the Civil War era, the nursery was a secluded, self-contained unit. All of the young children of the family slept, bathed, dressed, played, and sometimes ate there, under the supervision of their nurse. Wages were low enough during what was actually a period of deflation that even families of very modest means could hire a young girl to help with the house and look after the children. As the children reached "a certain age," which was determined differently by each family, they moved into whatever regular bedrooms were available—ideally, separate rooms for each child or at least separate rooms for brothers and sisters. The nursery, then, had a lifespan extending from the birth of the first child to the adolescence of the youngest, whereupon it was regulated to other uses.[9]

The Modern Child: Playful and Gender-Specific Surroundings

During the last decades of the nineteenth century, an alternative perception of the nature of children emerged. Some scholars, writers, child-rearing authorities, and parents began to doubt the absolute innocence of all children. Mischief, according to this view, was natural, normal, and healthy, especially in the development of young boys. Mark Twain, for example, expressed the new sentiments when he wrote the adventures of Tom Sawyer and Huckleberry Finn, who were basically good and likable boys even though they were almost always in trouble. Sigmund Freud later codified the new perception in his descriptions of infants as born with desires, instincts, and selfish impulses. Growing up, according to the new theories, was a process of channeling those natural impulses. Since no child was perfect, parents did not have to guard their children quite so assiduously. Any display of disobedience, stubbornness, or selfishness could be treated as natural and correctable, even harmless, rather than as the first sign of worldly corruption. In fact, when parents no longer regarded any act of disobedience as a fall from grace, infant naughtiness actually could seem comical and endearing, a viewpoint which would have shocked earlier generations. The sweet kitten, pet lamb, or chick of the antebellum era had become, by the end of the century, "King Baby," "the little emperor," or the "Little Tyrant," whose demands could sometimes be indulged without fear of permanently damaging the child's character. As parents came to want their children to be more independent and self-assertive, they sought environments that could stimulate and channel youthful energy.[10]

Parents who accepted the newer perception of children believed that it no longer was necessary to protect their little ones quite so diligently from contact with the world around them. In fact, they believed that the intellectual stimulation derived from physical activity, play, and exploration would help children adapt and mature. Parents felt they could relax a bit and give their children more freedom, since children could benefit even from their own mistakes. Changing parental perspectives led to changes in many of the popular artifacts of childhood. Clothes became shorter and looser, as long baby dresses gave way to rompers which bared the legs and permitted crawling and climbing. Loose, tough playclothes gradually gained acceptance. Children in the late nineteenth century had played in everyday clothes styled very much like their school or dress clothes. Children had played in dresses or knickers of sturdy fabrics, or in clothes too worn for best, or, in summer, had found relief by rolling up their sleeves, removing boots and stockings, or stripping down to play in just their underwear. By the early decades of the twentieth century, many parents preferred specially designed playclothes for their young children. Dungarees, shorts, overalls, sunsuits, and sandals became popular and accepted for both boys and girls. School or dress clothes also became lighter, looser, and shorter, leaving much of the leg bare between either shorts or short dress, and ankle socks. By the mid-twenties, young adults sported so-called resort wear of shorts, sandals, knit halter tops, and jersies, which were really no more than larger versions of the playclothes they had enjoyed as children. Play by then had become acceptable for all ages.[11]

The new focus on freedom of movement altered American preferences in children's furniture. The playpen replaced the baby jumper, providing a secure, contained environment, but one that allowed little children to sit, stand, crawl, or lie down as they wished. Articles in women's magazines encouraged mothers to make their homes safe for their babies, so that toddlers could be given free run of the house without fear of injury. Mothers were advised to rid their homes of the stacks of Victorian bric-a-brac by then considered old-fashioned and fussy anyway. Go-carts became popular for the first time since the colonial era, but the new versions contained seats that permitted toddlers some mobility without putting undue strain on immature legs. Advocates of the new Arts and Crafts movement further argued for replacing ornate parlors with simpler living rooms containing sturdy furniture, bare wood floors which could stand up to rough play, and cozy inglenooks beside the fireplace for quiet reading or reverie. Americans came to see children as mischievous, curious, adventurous, and impulsive beings who needed a stimulating environment that integrated them into the life of the family while offering them safety and protection.[12]

In 1899, the *Ladies' Home Journal* published a description of an ideal playroom for children. The room was located in the garret, and the roof had been replaced with skylights to let in plenty of sunshine. Among other marvels, the playroom contained a full-sized tent, a sandbox, a small pond

Fig. 27. Architect's rendering of a child's playroom, ca. 1925. In the early years of the twentieth century, architects, designers, and child-rearing authorities began advocating rooms furnished to stimulate a child's imagination and creativity. Collection of Karin Calvert.

of water in which to sail toy boats, a plot of earth for growing real flowers and vegetables, a croquet set, a four-sided swing, a marble course which circled the room and ended in the sandbox, an aquarium, large upholstered nooks in which a child could curl up to read, daydream or sleep, wall space for the children's art work, and a zoetrope with little painted figures that seemed to move when the drum was spun. Such a wonderful room probably never existed, what mother would allow large quantities of sand, dirt, and water on the third floor? but the proposal made its point. The playroom of the early twentieth century was not just a more or less empty indoor space in which to romp, but a carefully designed environment meant to stimulate children. Photographs of the period indicate that many children did enjoy rooms furnished with toys, blackboards, potted plants, aquariums of goldfish, and alcoves, nooks, and window seats as private sanctuaries.[13]

Above all, playrooms held toys. Since the 1770s, parents had provided children with educational toys to encourage their development. Some of the earliest toys had been fashion dolls (to teach girls grace, taste, and etiquette), alphabet blocks, and children's books. The Victorian nursery often was filled with toys, including scores of moral or educational board and card games, and miniature versions of adult artifacts, such as carpentry sets to develop manual skills in young sons and diminutive teasets to foster domestic instincts in little daughters. With the exception of sports equipment and humorous toys, most antebellum toys represented objects found in the real world, such as horses and farm animals, locomotives and steamboats, and elaborate wardrobes for fashionable dolls. The purpose of such toys was to prepare children for the roles they would one day play as adults. The urge for educational toys continued and expanded in the twentieth century, but what was really new in this century was the acceptance and encouragement of a fantasy world for children. Colonial and antebellum parents shunned make-believe as the propagation of falsehood. At best, make-believe confused children; at worst, it was lying. Only in the last quarter of the nineteenth century, with the acceptance of the mischievous child, did most middle-class parents accept make-believe as a harmless pleasure for the young. To the traditional children's stories of young protagonists faced with moral dilemmas now were added the stories of *Peter Pan, Alice in Wonderland, Winnie the Pooh,* and *The Wizard of Oz,* and the tales of Beatrice Potter. Soon after the introduction of stories of make-believe, the hard, elaborately dressed dolls of china and porcelain, the metal locomotives, and the wooden or metal toy animals which had been the playthings of Victorian children were joined in the nursery by soft, cuddly Brownies, Kewpies, and Golliwogs, and anthropomorphic rabbits, toads, and, of course, bears. The tactile pleasure of the new stuffed toys offered their little owners comfort and security, and the companionship of a little friend. Children live in a world where everyone else is bigger, stronger, and smarter than they. They therefore often find relief and delight in the company of someone smaller and weaker than themselves whom they can dominate or protect. Raggedy Ann and Winnie the Pooh were important to a child's immediate sense of well-being. Soft toys have remained popular throughout the twentieth century, and have become such a commonplace of childhood that we tend to forget how very modern and revolutionary they actually are.[14]

With the new emphasis on exploration and child-directed play, child-sized furniture became increasingly popular. While the Victorian highchair and jumper served the parents' needs to isolate the young and protect both child and house from each other, early-twentieth-century sets of play tables and little chairs were meant to accommodate the needs of the children themselves for comfortable and serviceable furniture. As a result, it became more common to furnish children's rooms with furniture bought especially for them, rather than with goods no longer deemed presentable downstairs.

Furniture manufacturers began producing child-sized tables and chairs for reading, coloring, or tea parties, toy chests, low bookshelves, and open storage shelves that children could reach easily (and that, in theory, would encourage children to put away their books and toys themselves). Similarly, low, child-sized beds and dressers offered children safer and more comfortable surroundings. Most of the furniture used in the daily care of children which has become standard in the twentieth century first developed in the nineteenth. The crib, carriage, highchair, bassinet, and jumper were all products of Victorian parents' concern for the care and safety of their children. What is new in this century is an interest in furniture for play, from blackboards and play tables to bookcases and playhouses, all in child-sized proportions.[15]

In the decades around the turn of the century, childrearing authorities, interior decorators, and parents, particularly mothers, came to believe that children's rooms should be visually identifiable as children's rooms, that they should carry a visual code of childishness which would set such rooms apart from rooms inhabited by adults. If adults saw children as intrinsically different from themselves, then, arguably, their rooms should be decorated differently as well, with children's tastes and interests in mind. In actuality, children's rooms of the early twentieth century (and the decades since, for that matter) exhibited an artificial code of childishness devised and implemented by adults. Adults, for example, assigned certain colors to young children. First pastels were in vogue for children's rooms, primarily blue for babies and pink for young children. By the mid-twenties, parents preferred white furniture with brightly colored decals. Certain motifs were given age-specific connotations including balloons, clowns, clouds, sailboats, ducks, all baby animals, and characters from nursery rhymes. Special wallpapers, friezes, rugs, curtains, and even furniture decorated with the new child-specific codes gained considerable popularity. By 1920, parents expected babies' rooms to look like babies' rooms; that is, to display the new code of color, design, and motif associated in the public mind with children. Parents wanted their children's rooms to be pleasant, stimulating, and personal, although the code probably carried more meaning for parents than for young children. A baby may see no difference between wallpapers decorated with red balloons or red peppers, but to parents, the distinction mattered. Images of red balloons and baby ducks served as visual references to the popular definition of the nature of childhood and reiterated parental commitment to that definition.[16]

If new theories of the psychological nature of children resulted in a growing acceptance of childish high spirits and a growing recognition of children's need for stimulation, it was also responsible for introducing the somewhat more disquieting idea of infant sexuality. Victorian parents had roomed their boys and girls together in the common nursery, confident of their children's absolute innocence and purity. Late-nineteenth- and early-twentieth-century parents were far more uncomfortable with the idea of mixing the sexes in a single bedroom. Instead, they began to think in terms of separate girls' rooms and boys' rooms. Once that distinction had been made, "nursery" became a name for the bedroom housing the latest baby. Older children moved into separate or single-sex bedrooms, and a visual code to distinguish the gender of the room's occupant(s) developed fairly quickly.

By 1910, boys' rooms and girls' rooms looked very different from each other. Boys' rooms tended to be very spartan, drawing on a visual vocabulary borrowed from the military. Usually the rooms were sparsely furnished with simple, unadorned furnishings. Wood and metal furniture in the new Arts and Crafts styles were popular. Floors were usually wood, perhaps with a small area rug in a nautical or native American pattern. Textiles were kept to a minimum—simple straight curtains or venetian blinds and a very plain, usually dark, bedspread. Very few pictures decorated the walls. By the 1920s, military themes were very explicit and popular. Boys' rooms contained campaign furniture, foot lockers, prints of maps and military scenes, model planes or sailboats, ship's lanterns, an anchor design on the bedspread, or a window shaped like a porthole. Bunk beds, with their naval history, were strictly for boys. The rooms also encouraged study (or so parents hoped) with large desks, bookshelves, maps, and globes.

Girls' rooms of 1910 were, for the most part, the antithesis of boys' rooms. Where the environment for boys was spartan and plain, with lots of natural wood and dark colors, girls' rooms remained highly Victorian, giving them a cluttered air of old-fashioned charm. Girls were more likely to have rooms furnished with antiques or reproductions, carpets and draperies, and artwork on the walls. For their daughters, parents favored ornate metal beds painted white, wicker chairs, cushioned window seats, pastel colors, and an abundance of textiles, with ruffles everywhere. Rugs, drap-

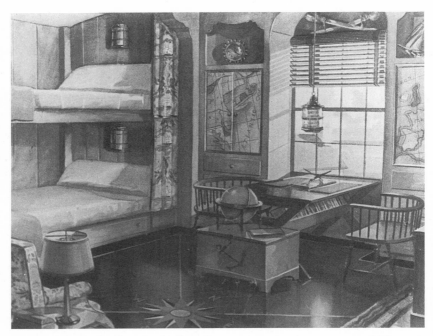

Fig. 28. A room for "a pair of jolly sailormen too young to put to sea." Women's magazines of the 1920s and 1930s encouraged women to decorate their sons' rooms in accepted masculine motifs. Military images were the most popular. This room incorporates maps, lanterns, swords, a toy ship, and images of a ship's wheel, anchor, and compass to create a suitably masculine atmosphere. Bunk beds, with their nautical associations, were considered particularly suitable for boys. *American Home,* June, 1930. Collection of Karin Calvert.

eries, dresser scarves, bedspreads, and pillow shams softened and rounded virtually every surface. Large mirrors and vanity tables were common in girls' rooms, while rooms decorated for boys rarely contained a mirror of any sort. As tastes changed during the 1920s, girls' rooms became somewhat less frilly, although the furniture was usually still painted white or a light pastel, and floral motifs continued to decorate furniture, wallpaper, and textiles. No theme emerged for girls as clearly as the military theme for boys, and desks and bookshelves were usually smaller or missing altogether, perhaps because a girl's future would not be defined by education and career as much as by a culturally-defined air of femininity. In families with both sons and daughters, parents found the new gender-specific codes more expensive to implement than the Victorian emphasis on unadorned utilitarian nursery furniture.[17]

The fundamentals of a playroom actually designed for a child are here in the small lightweight rugs, sturdy furniture and uncluttered spaces

Fig. 29. "The Child's Own Room for Work and Play." This is an accurate sketch of a room occupied by a little girl and her baby brother. Infants of either sex were commonly placed in a room with older sisters. Once past infancy, a little boy would move to a separate room or in with other brothers. Girls' rooms had less clearly defined themes, since girls were defined more by their gender and less by their career possibilities. Girls' rooms contained more color, frills, and ornament, with an emphasis on flowers. The tools in the corner of this room were a gift to the baby brother. *American Home,* March 1929. Collection of Karin Calvert.

By the 1920s, the Victorian nursery had ceased to exist in most middle-class American homes. Smaller families and a desire to separate the sexes made the single large children's room obsolete. Instead, parents frequently placed the infants directly into the room he or she would inhabit throughout childhood, and which visually reflected the baby's age and gender. The new model was a room and furnishings that could be altered to "grow with the child." Women's magazines and books on interior decorating showed mothers how precisely to match the room to their child. A baby boy, for example, could be housed in a room decorated with ducks and boats, and sporting a brightly colored toy chest. A few years later, as the boy grew older, the ducks could be removed, the boats could be retained (assuming, of course, that the particular image of boats did not look too childish, since the code by this time had become very sensitive to nuances of presentation), and the toy chest could become a foot-locker (freshly painted brown, green, or navy blue) providing useful storage for sports equipment. Similarly, a child-sized tea table eventually could be replaced with a full-sized vanity table for a growing girl, both items painted in whatever colors were at that time considered feminine. Over time, each room underscored the fluid process of maturation and the constancy of gender. By the early decades of the twentieth century, childhood had been divided into an elaborate scheme of subdivisions, each one requiring a different visual environment for the optimal growth and proper adjustment of the child.

This elaborate and very precise calibration of the correct material surroundings for a particular child developed during the 1920s and ended with the end of the decade. The concept that children outgrew wallpaper in the same way they outgrew their clothes seemed frivolous during the hard realities of the Great Depression. However, the idea of a room materially coded to the age and sex of the child returned with increased momentum in the 1950s and still remains so common at this, the end of the century, that we fail to recognize the novelty of the idea and assume that this is how things have always been.

Notes

1. For further information on childhood and family in the 17th and 18th centuries, see Philippe Aries, *Centuries of Childhood: A Social History of Family Life*, trans. Robert Baldick (New York: Random House, 1962); Philip Greven, *The Protestant Temperament: Patterns of Child-Rearing, Religious Experience, and the Self in Early America* (New York: Meridan Press, 1979); David Hunt, *Parents and Children in Early History: The Psychology of Family Life in Early Modern France* (New York: Basic Books, 1970); Ross W. Beales, Jr., "In Search of the Historical Child: Miniature Adulthood and Youth in Colonial New England," *American Quarterly* 27 (Oct. 1975);379-98; Catherine Scholten, *Childbearing in American Society, 1650-1850* (New York: New York Univ. Press, 1985); Peter C. Hoffer and N.E.H. Hull, *Murdering Mothers: Infanticide in England and New England* (New York: New York Univ. Press, 1981); Edmund S. Morgan, *The Puritan Family: Religion and Domestic Relations in the Seventeenth Century* (New York: Harper, 1966); Lloyd de Mause, ed., *The History of Childhood* (New York: Psychohistory Press, 1974); Karin Calvert, "Childhood in American Portraits: 1670 to 1810," *William and Mary Quarterly* 39 (Jan. 1982);33-63; and Joseph M. Hawes and N. Ray Hiner, *American Childhood: A Research Guide and Historical Handbook* (Westport, Conn.: Greenwood, 1985).

2. For further information on play in the colonial period, see Bernard Mergen, "The Discovery of Children's Play," *American Quarterly* 27 (Oct. 1974):339-423;

Bernard Mergen, "Toys and the American Culture: Objects as Hypotheses," *Journal of American Culture* 3 (Winter 1980):743–52.

3. Philip Vickers Fithian, *Journal and Letters of Philip Fithian: 1767–1774*, ed. John Roger Williams (Princeton, N.J.: University Library Press, 1900), 240; David A. Fletcher, *Privacy in Colonial New England* (Charlottesville: Univ. Press of Virginia, 1972). For further information on childhood and family in the era of the New Republic, see Daniel Blake Smith, *Inside the Great House: Planter Family Life in Eighteenth-Century Chesapeake Society* (New York: Harper, 1980); Joseph F. Kett, *Rites of Passage: Adolescence in America, 1790 to the Present* (New York: Basic Books, 1977); D.D. Hitchcock, *Memories of the Bloomsgrove Family* (Boston: Thomas & Andrews, 1790); William Buchan, *Advice to Mothers on the Subject of Their Own Health; and the Means of Promoting the Health, Strength, and Beauty of Their Offspring* (Philadelphia: Joseph Bumstead, 1809); and An American Matron [pseud.], *The Maternal Physician: A Treatise on the Nurture and Management of Infants from Birth until Two Years Old* (Philadelphia: Clark & Roser, 1818).

4. For additional information on Victorian attitudes towards children, see William Alcott, *The Young Mother or Management of Children in Regard to Health* (Boston: George Light, 1839); Lucy Larcom, *A New England Girlhood* (1889; rptd. Boston: Houghton Mifflin, 1924); Lydia Child, *The American Frugal Housewife* (Boston: Carter, Hendee, 1835); also see fashion, editorial, and fictional material from *Godey's Lady's Magazine*, incl. "Children," *Godey's* 64 (Jan. 1862):9; and "Childhood," *Godey's* 20 (Dec. 1840);280.

5. William P. Dewees, *A Treatise on the Physical and Medical Treatment of Children* (Philadelphia: Carey & Lea, 1832); and see jumpers, swings, and rocking swings in the *Montgomery Ward* and *Sears, Roebuck* catalogues of the 1880s and 1890s.

6. Quote from design used as a filler, *Furniture Gazette* 14 (Sept. 1870):43; Lydia Child, *The Mother's Book* (Boston: Carter, Hende, 1837). For additional information on Victorian child rearing, see *Hints for the Improvement of Early Education and Nursery Discipline* (Philadelphia: John M. Putnam, 1826), 83; Walter R. Houghton, *American Etiquette and Rules of Politeness* (New York: Standard Publishing House, 1883); Catharine Beecher, *A Treatise on Domestic Economy* (New York: Harper & Bros. 1848); Mrs. Charles Harcourt, *Good Form for Women* (Philadelphia: John Winston, 1907); and Karin Calvert, "Cradle to Crib: The Revolution in Nineteenth-Century Children's Furniture," in *A Century of Childhood, 1820–1920* (Rochester, N.Y.: Strong Museum, 1984), 33–63.

7. Dewees, *Treatise on Physical and Medical Treatment of Children*, 86; John W. Bright, *The Mother's Medical Guide: A Plain, Practical Treatise on Midwifery and the Diseases of Women and Children, in Seven Parts* (Louisville, Ky., 1844), 249. For further information, see Kate Douglas Wiggins, "The Training of Children," in *The House and Home* (New York: Scribner's, 1894), 317–39; J. West Roosevelt,

"Hygiene in the Home," in *The House and Home* (New York: Scribner's, 1894), 263–317; and Marion Harland, *Common Sense in the Nursery* (New York: Scribner's, 1885).

8. Journal of Eliza Ridgely, Hampton, Md., 1841–42, manuscript Phii3, Phoenix Belknap Memorial Library, Winterthur Museum, 9–10, 15–16, 18–19; and Ann Wentworth, "Playrooms and Nurseries," *House Beautiful* 21 (July 1911):57–58.

9. Louis Starr, *Hygiene of the Nursery,* 7th ed. (1871; rptd. Philadelphia: P. Blackston's Sons, 1902); and O.S. Fowler, *Creative and Sexual Science* (Philadelphia: National Publishing Co., 1870).

10. "Babies," *Appleton's* 1 (April 1869):12; J.E. Panton, *From Kitchen to Garret* (London: Ward & Downey, 1893), 130; *The Upholsterer* 6 (Fall 1890):116; "Good Night Papa," *Nursery* 25 (Mar. 1879):86–87.

11. See *Sears, Roebuck* and *Montgomery Ward* catalogues, 1900–1930. All carry an array of the newly fashionable practical children's playclothes.

12. For the Arts and Crafts philosophy regarding children, see Gustav Stickley, *Craftsman Homes* (New York: Craftsman Publishing Co., 1909); and Gustav Stickley, *What is Wrought in the Craftsman Workshops* (New York: Craftsman Publishing Co., 1903); and *The Craftsman* 2 (June 1903 and Aug. 1903) and 4 (Aug. 1905).

13. "A Modern Playroom," *Ladies' Home Journal* 16 (July 1899):39.

14. For further information on children's toys, see Katherine Morrison McClinton, *Antiques of American Childhood* (New York: Clarkson Potter, 1970); Constance Eileen King, *The Collectors' History of Dolls* (New York: Bonanza Books, 1977); Edith Webster, "Teaching Children to Play," *Ladies' Home Journal* 16 (April 1899):57; Inez McClintock and Marshall McClintock, *Toys in America* (Washington, D.C.: Public Affairs Press, 1961); and Brian Sutton-Smith, "Toys for Object Role and Mastery," in *Educational Toys in America: 1800 to the Present,* ed. Karen Hewitt and Lorine Roomet (Burlington, VT.: Robert Hull Fleming Museum). For in-depth studies of the development of children's literature, see Gillian Avery, *Nineteenth-Century Children's Heroes and Heroines in English Children's Stories, 1780–1900* (London: Hodder and Stoughton, 1965); Percy Muir, *English Children's Books, 1600 to 1900* (London: B.T. Batsford, 1954); F.J. Harvey Darton, *Children's Books in England* (Cambridge, England: Cambridge Univ. Press, 1960); Monica May Kiefer, *American Children Through Their Books, 1700–1835* (Philadelphia: Univ. of Pennsylvania Press, 1948); and Anne Scott MacLeod, *A Moral Tale: Children's Fiction and American Culture, 1820–1880* (Hamden, Conn.: Archon Books, 1976).

15. Alice M. Kellogg, *Home Furnishing—Practical and Artistic* (New York: Frederick A. Stokes, 1904), 99.

16. For descriptions of children's rooms of the period, see Edith Wharton and Ogdon Codman, Jr., *The Decoration of Houses* (New York: Scribner's, 1919);

Hazel H. Adler, *The New Interior* (New York: Century, 1916); Ross Crane, *The Ross Crane Book of Home Furnishings and Decoration* (Chicago: Frederick J. Drake, 1925); Lucy Abbott Throop, *Furnishing the Home of Good Taste* (New York: Robert M. McBride, 1920); Amy L. Rolfe, *Interior Decoration for the Small Home* (New York: Macmillan, 1926); Mrs. T.W. Dewing, *Beauty in the Household* (New York: Harper & Bros., 1882); Henry W. Frohne, Beatrice Holloway, and Edward Stratton Holloway, *The Practical Book of Furnishing the Small House and Apartment* (Philadelphia: J.B. Lippincott, 1922).

17. For further information on age and gender-specific decoration of children's rooms, see Alice Jackson, *Color Schemes for the Home and Model Interiors* (Philadelphia: J.B. Lippencott, 1919), 87–102; "For a Pair of Jolly Sailormen Too Young to Put to Sea," *Ladies' Home Journal* 47 (July 1930):86; "For a Pair of Jolly Sailormen Too Young to Put to Sea," *American Home* 15 (June 1930):455; and Christine Frederick, "Grown-Up Accessories for Small People," *American Home* 13 (Dec. 1928):94.

CHAPTER FOUR

Home Libraries: Special Spaces, Reading Places

Linda M. Kruger

A heightened interest in the library in the American home has occurred in recent years. Book readership and book ownership are on the rise,[1] while many urban-dwelling Americans find themselves desperate for shelf storage space for books at home (apartments, townhouses, or small single-family houses being the characteristic urban domestic architectural format). Popular periodicals of the 1980s include articles on how to create space for books in the home, while other articles reveal how to decorate such space once the commitment is made to create it.[2]

The historical precedent for this phenomenon resides in our recent past, relatively speaking, for one need recede no farther than 1890 to document the architectural roots of this trend. We may postulate that, to the extent that significant numbers of suburban American book-buying/book-reading individuals reside in "older" homes, i.e., structures built between 1910 and 1940, in cities such as Boston, New York, Philadelphia, and Chicago, a separate room originally intended as a library or den is likely today to be used for reading purposes.

Furthermore, the mail-order house plan purveyors (Home Planners, Inc., of Farmington Hills, Michigan, is preeminent among such vendors) offer—and have for at least a decade—a wealth of plans that provide space for books.[3]

To understand the historical continuum surrounding the placement of books in the American home, this inquiry seeks to identify in what part of the American home reading occurred between 1890 to 1930. Prior to 1900, book placement was confined most typically to a specific room, which mail-order houseplan catalogs and domestic economy manuals of the period called a library, study, or den. The "library" in the American home gradually ceased to occupy consolidated space in a specifically named room and became a collection of books housed throughout the house. Thus, in the context of this study, the American home library is both a collection of books and a physical space.

Robert Darnton, the Princeton historian, cites scholars who "share a conception of literature . . . [as] something that happens every time a reader reads a book. It's an activity—in fact, the act of reading."[4] A burgeoning body of knowledge continues to document the nature of readers and reading, prompting Darnton to comment on the "where" of reading. American impressionist paintings depict men and women reclining on chaise lounges, in hammocks, or on garden benches. As we move away from the intimacy of the boudoir and into the more readily identifiable space in the home known as the library, the den, or the study, Darnton advises: "The general understanding of reading would be advanced if we thought harder about its iconography and accoutrements, including furniture and dress."[5]

To such queries we may add: What did the rooms or spaces look like? What types of furniture accompanied the act of reading? Why is this forty-year period regarded retrospectively as the halcyon days of book buying, of book collecting, and of the development of the home library? Darnton emphasizes the importance of library catalogs as source materials for such analysis: "To go over the list of books in Jefferson's library is to inspect the furniture of his mind, and the study of private libraries has the advantage of linking the 'what' with the 'who' of reading."[6] Benjamin Franklin and Thomas Jefferson both owned, even by today's standards, impressive private libraries, Jefferson's being in excess of six thousand volumes.

The Commerce of Books: An American Tradition

By 1890, the American home library symbolized a continually evolving Anglo-American tradition. The American home library tradition had its genesis at least by 1675, with books on travel, exploration and discovery, law, medicine, Bibles, and almanacs found in the earliest colonial homes.[7] By the 1720s, imported and indigenous books and periodicals were commonplace. By the mid-1730s, in New York City, Philadelphia, and Boston—given the absence of public libraries—impressive private libraries existed among the citizenry's learned and affluent.[8] Studies of intellectual circles that were based on commonality of interests suggest members' willingness and ability to loan and buy books. Learned societies emerged to respond to specific interests and goals: scientific, artistic, trade, etc.[9]

The growth and importance of this emerging print culture is well documented, especially for the post-Revolutionary decades. Our nation's unprecedented population growth and westward expansion was paralleled by the advancing technology of the printing press. Along with these developments came sophisticated book distribution networks, aided by a vast railroad transportation system and special postal rates for printed materials. Thus urban and rural populations were able to buy books cheaply and quickly.[10]

During this time, readers throughout the land were serviced by circulating libraries,[11] and throughout the nineteenth century rural reading clubs proliferated.[12] A recent study demonstrates the vitality and dynamism "in a new mass culture of reading and writing," one in which "reading becomes a necessity of life."[13] Although Gilmore's study deals with an earlier period and circumscribed place, his findings would have been broadly applicable throughout America during an entire century (1835–1935).

Nineteenth-century Americans were fascinated by the lives, contributions, and beliefs of America's founding fathers. Franklin and Jefferson personified the American love for travel.[14] This love, driven by an emerging bibliophilia and thirst for knowledge, led many educated and affluent citizens to visit the great English and Continental libraries.[15] British country house visits were commonplace for Americans "doing" the requisite Grand Tour.[16]

As American curiosity and interests widened, beginning in 1830, publishers such as Harper Brothers began to publish books in series, each series being termed a "library." By 1879, Harper was responding to some midwestern competition; its Franklin Square Library of 1878 was designed to counter competition by the Chicago Donnelly firm's Lakeside Library and the New York Munro's Seaside Library. By 1879, one popular Harper author, Jacob Abbot, had seven series totaling seventy-two volumes.[17]

A relevant subgenre of this series format so common in the third quarter of the nineteenth century is the phenomenon of railroad literature: cheap reprints designed for railroad travel reading. Houses such as A.K. Loring of Boston (Railway Companions Series); Peterson of Philadelphia; Putnam and Appleton of New York; and the notorious and colorful New Yorker, Frank Leslie, published huge editions. Leslie produced four series of railroad literature, often reprinted from his journal contributions. In 1877, after a well-publicized transcontinental rail journey, during which he observed a lacuna in travel literature—light in weight, subject matter, and cost—he created his Home Library of Standard Works by the Most Celebrated Authors. The Home Library, despite its name, was targeted for railroad travelers. Distributed through the American News Company network and priced at ten and twenty cents per copy, this fiction was displayed at newsstands and kiosks and hawked through the trains by train boys. Leslie's book production tripled in 1876–77, at the height of the "Silver Seventies" of rail expansion.[18] The majority of the 27.5 million people who attended the 1893 World's Columbian Exposition undoubtedly arrived there by train and were, at least to some extent, a captive audience for the culture of print.

Also contributing to this heightened interest in the commerce of printed materials was the Chautauqua program, a forerunner in the organization of reading circles, particularly throughout America's rural areas. The Chautauqua Literary and Scientific Circle (CLSC), founded in 1878, was a four-year program of directed home reading. By 1891, 180,000 were enrolled, and by 1918 membership in CLSC reached 300,000. In its first twenty years, 10,000 local circles were formed, 25 percent of which were in villages of less than 500 population and 50 percent in communities of 500 to 3,500 in size. Even train crews on western railroads organized circles! The monthly *Chautauquan* was one CLSC journal, begun in 1880, that summarized the content of the reading lists of the Home Reading Series. Other Chautauqua-sponsored series were the Chautauqua Library of English History and Literature, the Garnet Series, the Chautauqua Text-Books, and the Home College Series. Indeed, the CLSC was the first book-a-month club in America.[19]

"And Everywhere, Books": The 1893 Columbian Exposition

The Columbian Exposition had a major impact on the growth in book-buying, the marketing of books, and the way in which Americans furnished their home libraries. Therefore we shall explore in considerable detail the impact on those Americans in attendance, particularly in comparison with subsequent American worlds' fairs. We can theorize that this exposition's books and the interior architecture selected for their display, including furnishings and other accoutrements, impressed Frank Lloyd Wright, who, in the next thirty-five years, invariably included a provision for book placement in his residential designs. He, in turn, vastly influenced (and continues to influence) several generations of residential architects, from his peers among the house plan catalog architects of the turn of the century (fellow members of the Chicago Arts and Crafts Society) to the Taliesin apprentices of 1930–60 and their students practicing today.

American serial publishing was duly noted at the dedication ceremonies of the Chicago World's Fair on October 21, 1892, when the Honorable Chauncey M. Depew of New York State described Americans as a nation of newspaper readers.[20] Depew attributed the existence and growth of a serial/series press to indigenous enthusiasm as well as material prosperity.

No subsequent American world's fair of our period appears to have contained as many books and related displays as the 1893 Chicago Exposition. The 1915 Panama-Pacific International Exposition, held in San Francisco, contained many of the same interior architectural features surrounding displays of books and other accoutrements of literacy as the 1893 exposition. The well-known rare book dealer John Howell held court in an Elizabethan bookshop near Funk and Wagnalls' entranceway, which consisted of quartered oak flanked by Corinthian columns and a Palladian pilaster. Above the interior bookshelves of the latter, lithographs hung on silver-gray burlap walls. A revolving stand in the middle contained lithographic plates. A writing table and "all needful stationery" were provided for the comfort of the visitor.

In 1933, when the Century of Progress International Exposition opened in Chicago, fair attendance reached 48.8 million visitors. Kroch's 128-page catalog of a model library of four thousand books, printed by Donnelly in an edition of one hundred thousand copies, included selections from a consortium of publishers. At this model library, visitors were ushered into "luxurious" red leather chairs. Travel books were prominent among the genres, which included fiction, children's books, and foreign books. Another "comfortably furnished" room was occupied by five religious publishers.[21]

Two architectural styles predominated at the 1893 Columbian Exposition: the neoclassical Beaux Arts revivalist styles and the lesser known but more broadly applicable Arts and Crafts aesthetic that was to be widely publicized via the mail-order catalog. The presence of book exhibits at this fair did not escape the attention of twenty-six-year-old Frank Lloyd Wright, whose firm, Adler & Sullivan, had been invited by Daniel Burnham to design the Transportation Building.[22] Awash in a sea of Beaux Arts eclecticism, the Transportation Building's central portal, the "Golden Gate," which Wright worked on, evinced certain characteristics of Wright's famous horizontal line, a line that emerged later in his concept of home library design and in his placement of books throughout the common areas of a home. In Wright's mind, images of childhood building blocks became linked to images of his family's books and their placement in his mother's home. Thus his childhood exposure to books became as architectonically intriguing as it was intellectually stimulating.

Books were displayed throughout the Columbian Exposition grounds. The American Library Association displayed a model collection of five thousand volumes. Publishers, including Harper, George A. Plympton, Funk and Wagnalls, and the medical publisher William Wood put on an impressive display. "Tiffany & Co. displayed illuminations on parchment, and copper and steel engravings. The J. Ottman Lithographing Company demonstrated the entire process of making lithographic plates and printing lithographs."[23]

Because women supported circulating libraries and literary clubs, the Lady Managers of the Woman's Building insisted on a library, a large west room on the second floor, its location recommended and interior decor executed by Candace Wheeler, a Tiffany associate, author, and author-editor of two popular "how-to" books; *Principles of Home Decoration* and *Household Art*.[24] This library contained dark oak bookcases, wash leather green upholstery, Italian Renaissance furniture placed against blue-green walls, busts of notable women, a huge leaded-glass window, and heavy blue drapes.[25] Wheeler felt that "a library was 'not only to hold books' but to make people feel 'at home in a library atmosphere'."[26]

A plaster and gilt frieze occupied space between bookcase tops and ceiling, with a ceiling painting executed by Wheeler's daughter. The decor of the room was well received. One critic stated that the colors created "a general tone that invited rest and quiet and suggested elegant, literary ease." *The Art Amateur* described the room as "reposeful, quiet and cheerful . . . It must be reckoned among the very best bits of interior decoration in the Fair."[27]

The Woman's Building Library also displayed fine bindings. Of particular note among decorated publisher's cloth covers produced for a mass market was the G.P. Putnam display with bindings by Alice C. Morse. *Publishers' Weekly* of July 1, 1893, described the booth of a New England binder and book-cover designer, Sarah Whitman, as:

> built on the order of a Greek temple, finished on the inside in olive green and old English Oak. Windows of amber-stained glass give a soft, restful light to the interior. A large, cheerful tiled fireplace occupies the far end,

and is flanked by comfortable, old-fashioned straightback settees. The room was designed as an ideal American library by Mrs. Henry Whitman, of Boston, who has designed many of the original book-covers of this house. Over these cases are placed the busts of some of their authors—Holmes, Longfellow, Emerson, Hawthorne, Lowell, Whittier, and Harriet Beecher Stowe.[28]

In the Manufacturers Department, suites of furniture thought appropriate for the home library were displayed. Exhibitors included Dean & Company, Chicago; Berkey & Gay Furniture Company of Grand Rapids, Michigan; the Indianapolis Furniture Exchange; S. Karpen & Brothers, Chicago; and the Rockford, Illinois, Furniture Exchange. Desk supplies included stationery, bookbinding materials, printing papers, inkstands, writing implements, bookbinding leathers and vellum, and embossed leather for furniture, wall decoration, etc.[29] By 1900, library furniture was readily available in New York City retail furniture stores. R.J. Horner & Company devoted an entire floor to library furniture and display of a model library.[30]

At the same time that Frank Lloyd Wright indulged his love of books at the fair, he perceived the eastern architectural establishment's preference for Beaux Arts architecture.[31] Coincidentally, in the year of the fair (1893), New York City witnessed the founding of the Beaux Arts Institute of Design by American architects who had attended the Paris École des Beaux Arts. The institute's curriculum, modeled after that of the École, influenced several generations of American architects. The first American École student was Richard Morris Hunt, architect of many home libraries, the most famous being the George Vanderbilt library of twenty thousand volumes at Biltmore, a Beaux Arts chateau at Asheville, N.C.[32] It may not be accidental that between 1890 and 1930 provision for a library in American homes was executed by a cadre of architectural practitioners who emerged from the Beaux Arts schools to relocate throughout America. This Academic Revival movement—replete with frequent literary and neoclassical allusions—had a measurable effect, as a dominant design thrust, on home libraries of this period.

One American Beaux Arts architect whom Wright encountered at the 1893 fair, who incorporated a separate library room in many New York City town house designs, was the Chicagoan Emery Roth, a draftsman on the fair's design staff. Roth's unpublished autobiography reveals the international flavor experienced by Wright: "There were men of all nationalities among the hundred or more draughtsmen: Frenchmen from the École des

Beaux Arts, Norwegian Moderns, Germans from the famous Wagner School, and above all the pick of America."[33]

Wright later continued that enrichment when he rejected a grant-funded period of study at the Paris École for a self-designed two-year European stint that included a residential year in Italy.[34] Many of Wright's built-in bookcases and their placement bear a resemblance to drawings published in folios of architectural interiors of the time[35] or in Arts and Crafts interiors depicted in emerging periodicals such as *House Beautiful* (1896), *The Craftsman* (1901), *House and Garden* (1901), and *American Homes and Gardens* (1905).[36]

Around 1880, Frank Lloyd Wright's mother, Anna Lloyd-Jones Wright, of Welsh ancestry, lived in a home in Madison, Wisconsin, described by a Wright biographer as "an oasis of simple good taste." Wright described this Gorham Street cottage as containing "new-laid, white, waxed maple floors, the cream-colored net curtains hanging straight beside the windows. The centers of the room floors covered with India rugs—cream-colored ground with bright-colored patterns and border. Maple and rattan furniture. And everywhere, books."[37] What led Wright's mother to disperse her books throughout the house?

Books in "Close Companionship": Their Placement in the Home

In 1878, Clarence Cook published *The House Beautiful,* a taste manual at once acerbic, opinionated, and popular. It appeared after the 1876 Philadelphia Centennial Exhibition, at which, as at the 1893 exposition, the public demonstrated a renewed interest in books and home libraries. (Wright's parents had attended the Centennial Exhibition.)[38]

Cook declares that "these chapters are not written for rich people's reading." Since very few are privileged to have single-purpose rooms such as a library, then the living room (formerly the parlor) must "admit the ornament of life—casts, pictures, engravings, bronzes, books, chief nourishers in life's feast." To provide for the accommodation of books, Cook recommends a rectangular living room table with two shelves below for folios and large books of prints and atlases.

Cook discusses the importance of a stand for print portfolios, describing it generically as "the most troublesome member of the living room ornaments, and yet the one we can least do without." He further shows a "little movable": book shelves *cum* letter pad *cum* cupboard, the latter "for

Fig. 30. R.J. Horner & Co., New York City, *Library Furniture,* ca. 1900. Courtesy of Avery Architectural and Fine Arts Library, Columbia University, New York, N.Y.

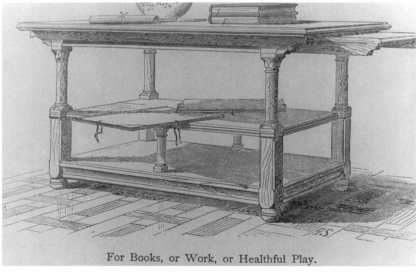

For Books, or Work, or Healthful Play.

Fig. 31. Living room book table. Clarence Cook, *The House Beautiful,* 1878. Courtesy of American Life Foundation.

books that are too valuable to be handled by everybody." Another example is a "writing-table with book-shelf above and drawers at the side."

Cook reserves his most cutting aside for the bookcase: "Hardly any piece of furniture is more troublesome to bring into harmony with the conditions of our modern room than the bookcase . . . We want to have our books in our living room . . . We want our books . . . in close companionship, and where we can get at them easily." Cook elaborates: "For lovers of books, however, a house without books is no house at all; and in a family where books make a great part of the pleasure of living, they must be where they can share in the life around them and receive some touches of the humanity they supply and feed."

Cook argues against solid or glass doors on bookcases because "they are inhospitable and hinder close acquaintance." To protect against dust he recommends a curtain of thin silk affixed with metal rings to a metal rod running along the entire bookcase front and designed to hold four hundred to five hundred books, depending on size.[39]

A decade earlier, the British Charles Eastlake's *Hints on Household Taste* had favored the library as a separate room, furnished with oak, and consigning "silly knick-knacks" to the drawing room. Eastlake, too, recommended leaving the oak light (as Wright did with his famous white and "honeyed oak"). The Eastlake look was medieval in feeling—heavier, thicker, fussier. Eastlake preferred scalloped and gilded leather valances as "dust ruffles" for the shelf edges. He favored black-stained mahogany with white metal finishes and admonished the reader to avoid "bright and violent hues" in paint colors.[40]

Each decade from 1890 to 1930 had its *dernier cri* among domestic economy manuals.[41] Ogden Codman and Edith Wharton's *The Decoration of Houses* (1897), which contained a chapter "The Library, Smoking-Room, and 'Den'," was written to counter the influence of Eastlake and Cook. Richard Guy Wilson states that "the book, which sold very well and was reprinted in England and later in America, helped change taste in decoration on both sides of the Atlantic."[42]

Edith Wharton's two personal libraries, first at Land's End in Newport, Rhode Island, between 1892 and 1897, and later at The Mount in Lenox, Massachusetts, in 1900–1901, represent the continuing refinement in home library design espoused in *The Decoration of Houses*. Ogden Codman supervised the remodeling of Land's End. Its library contained "delicate Louis XVI paneling, medallion scroll work, and leafage but was set off with the overstuffed furniture and dark bookcases that would be attacked in *The Decoration of Houses.*" Wharton differed with Codman over his selection of library wall color at Newport, preferring "a uniform pink" to his "dark red."[43] She remained the final arbiter of color choice for the library at Land's End.

The Mount's renovation was consigned to a Beaux Arts architect from Providence and New York, Francis L.V. Hoppin, whose library there "received perhaps the most attention" of any room in that house:

> Louis XVI style dark oak cases filled with leather-bound sets of books reach to the ceiling on three sides, while a tapestry dominates the other. The carving in the overdoor panels and bookcases is more elaborate than suggested in *The Decoration of Houses.* A portrait of Edith's great-grandfather Stevens hung over the mantel. The furniture, such as a lit de repos or Louis XVI chairs brought from Newport and two Regency-style writing tables, were background—as stated in *The Decoration of Houses*—to the books and the conversation that would take place.[44]

Codman's 1916–17 library at Hautbois, in Jericho, Long Island, in the home of Walter and Eunice Maynard, remains his exemplar of

> timeless elegance and taste. It was paneled in black and gold Directoire boiserie . . . and the recessed shelves filled with leather-bound books provided an important element of color and texture . . . As stated in *The Decoration of Houses,* "a room should depend for its adornment on a general harmony of parts, and on the artistic quality of such necessities as lamps, screens, bindings, and furniture."[45]

Library Aesthetics: Beaux Arts and Arts and Crafts

Let us examine two home libraries designed on a smaller, more intimate, more manageable scale than the libraries of Codman and Wharton. These two libraries, exemplars of (1) the Neo-Georgian/Beaux Arts tradition and (2) the Arts and Crafts aesthetic tradition of home library interiors, represent the prevailing trends from the turn of the century to 1930. Although the following examples may be thought elitist in being designed by architects, similar examples appeared simultaneously in the house plan and mail-order catalogs of the period and in articles in the periodical press.[46]

In 1903, Robert Todd Lincoln, son of the late President Abraham Lincoln and president of the Pullman Company (an exhibitor at the 1893 fair),

Fig. 32. Living room bookcase. Clarence Cook, *The House Beautiful,* 1878. Courtesy of American Life Foundation.

Fig. 33. Library, Hildene, home of Robert Todd Lincoln, Manchester, Vt., 1907. Courtesy of the Archives of Hildene.

commissioned the Boston and Chicago architectural firm of Shepley, Rutan and Coolidge to build a twenty-four-room Georgian Revival house in Manchester, Vermont. This was his home for six months of every year from 1907, when the house was completed, until his death at eighty-two in 1926. The plans included a library and an office. On the architects' blueprints, the library is termed "the den" and is 24'9"×17'; the office is 11'×17'.[47] The south wing library has French doors facing east (commanding a spectacular view of the Green Mountains), adjacent to a loggia with awnings and Ionic columns, furnished with wicker, and overlooking formal gardens. Opposite the loggia wall is a windowed west wall; a south wall interior door leads into Lincoln's "home office," a southwest 1908 addition.

The library and office wallpaper is a "raspberry sherbet" grasscloth (an original sample survives on an inside wall of an office cabinet). The original lined drapes are a velvet russet pinstripe of 1905. The floors are quarter sawed white oak. The four-shelf-high bookcases follow the Cook specifications in length and height, leaving room at the top for Oriental vases, figurines, busts, and globes. Much of the furniture was inherited from Mrs. Lincoln's family (her father was U.S. Senator James Harland of Mount Pleasant, Iowa, who was also president of Iowa Wesleyan University and died in 1899). It was heavy and dark, with a tinge of linearity suggestive of an Arts and Crafts influence, as in the modified wing chairs. The appointments dating from around 1900 include an eighteenth-century-style tripod tilt-top table with decanter and glasses; a mahogany book table on cabriole legs; a humidor; a bronze and marble inkwell; a William-and-Mary style settee; an Oriental rug; a tufted horsehair sofa; and a brass electric lamp with silk shade.

Books appear throughout the house. Bookcases reside in almost every bedroom, and a regal neoclassical glass-door bookcase dominates a parlor wall. The second-floor stair landing terminates in a sun-filled 18'×20'6" sitting room (designated a bedroom on the blueprints), painted white and housing two glass-door bookcases, a secretary-bookcase, comfortable upholstered settees and chairs, and magazines such as *International Studio* (1927), *Needlecraft* (1924), and *Town and Country* (1923).

The concept of a second-floor sitting room at the head of the stairs or centrally placed on the second floor persisted throughout the 1920s, a vestige of the English "living hall." A splendid example is the 1928 second-floor sitting room of Carter's Grove, an eighteenth-century Williamsburg, Virginia, plantation house. The owners, a socially prominent diplomat and his wife, undertook the transformation of this space as both her office and a center for family life.

Concurrent with this Beaux Arts eclecticism, which included a den, library, or study, the lesser-known English Arts and Crafts movement[48] emerged and rapidly gained proponents in Boston, New York, and Chicago,[49] particularly among the anonymous architect-draftsmen of the vernacular mail-order house plan catalog.[50] So numerous were these catalogs that rural and suburban American homeowners soon were as *au courant* concerning home library design as were those who engaged an architect. As Stevenson and Jandl relate, "Little is known about the architects of most Sears houses, but this much is certain: Sears houses followed rather than set architectural styles."[51]

As stated earlier, Frank Lloyd Wright, working at this time in the Arts and Crafts tradition, appears to have incorporated his Columbian Exposition experiences into a home library aesthetic and thus immeasurably influenced succeeding generations of architectural purveyors of home library design. Some members of the Chicago Architectural Club at the turn of the century had houseplans published in the architectural press and new homemaker magazines.[52] Frank Lloyd Wright was not only a member of this club but also a founding member of the Chicago Arts and Crafts Society in 1897.[53] Wright's employment, first with J.L. Silsbee on a shingle-style house and then with the firm of Adler & Sullivan, further exposed him to domestic architecture in the Richardsonian style, reinforcing his beliefs about the placement of books in the home.[54] By the opening of the Columbian Exposition, Wright was partially practicing independently, having undertaken ten private home commissions, most of which had libraries. (These were his "bootlegged houses," as he termed them, for they were planned and/or executed while he was still in the employ of Adler & Sullivan.)

In Wright's Blossom House—his only Palladian-Colonial one—the library was positioned left of the front hall and was hardly wider than the hall itself. His 1894 Dutch Colonial Bagley House in Hinsdale, Illinois, contained a separate octagonal library connected to the main house by a covered passage. Manson elaborates: "It has an octagonal roof of low pitch; it is lighted by means of a continuous clerestory, permitting uninterrupted shelf-space below. Although somewhat incongruous in its Dutch Colonial context, it makes a very functional library."[55] Three other Wright houses of this period position the library centrally among the three rooms spanning the front of the houses. The floor plans suggest that the main entrance is through the library doors.[56] These square, centrally-placed libraries all include huge, sweeping five-sided bays, indications of Wright's desire to merge indoors and outdoors.

The "back to nature" movement in domestic architecture was chronicled by a Wright competitor, Hermann Valentin von Holst, in his 1913 book, *Modern American Homes*. A majority of the floor plans shown in this book reflect the Prairie School's dedication to an organic approach, as shown in the fluidity and use of interior space with respect to the placement of books.[57] Designed to be built at moderate cost by city dwellers moving to the suburbs or building second homes, these houses featured wide portals, lack of interior doors, and sufficient built-in seating and storage space (so designated on the plans) to allow homeowners maximum autonomy in the selection of interior reading sites. Among Wright's notable Prairie houses revealing dispersement of books throughout the premises are the following.

Glenlloyd, Kankakee, Illinois (1900). For B. Harley Bradley. The living room has a built-in bookcase adjacent to the bay window wall, and a desk is placed in front of the banquette under the bay.[58] This placement anticipates features of the Francis Little house, executed twelve years later, a house which, so far as books are concerned, makes Wright's ultimate design statement.[59]

Darwin D. Martin House, Buffalo, New York (1904). One end of the living room is a library area: a banquette sofa with high sides is flanked by a book-topped table on one side and, on the other, a tall four-shelf bookcase for folio-size volumes.[60]

Ray Evans House, Chicago, and the *Avery Coonley House, Riverside, Illinois (both 1908).* In both, library furniture is a dominant presence in the living rooms. The Evans golden oak library table, now in the Chicago Art Institute, matches the interior woodwork of the living room.[61] The Coonley library table is of mammoth proportions (almost 39″ deep, 65-1/4″ long, and 28 1/4″ high). Like his other Prairie School living rooms, the Coonley living room, as pictured in Wright's portfolio of architectural drawings,[62] in design concept resembles the library-hall, living room–library, and den interiors depicted in the *120 Intérieurs en Couleurs.*[63]

Meyer May House, Grand Rapids, Michigan (1909). This house features a living-room bookcase situated perpendicular to the fireplace, creating an angular anchor not seen before in Wright living rooms.[64] The placement heralds the architectonic placement of folio volumes on the lower shelf of

Fig. 34. Frank Lloyd Wright (1867–1959), living room, *Meyer May House,* Grand Rapids, Mich., 1909. Courtesy of Steelcase, Inc.

the living-room desk of the Francis Little House (1912), now in the Metropolitan Museum of Art.

Francis Little House (1912). Wright's *pièce de resistance* among library rooms, however, remains that of the Francis Little House, now installed in the Allentown Art Museum, Allentown, Pennsylvania. Located to the left of the entrance of the original house, the library commanded a vista through "leaded" glass windows to a wide expanse of lawn to the south. Four leaded-glass windows, executed by the Temple Art Glass Company of Chicago, comprised the east wall and overlooked a terrace. The west wall contained recessed white oak shelving 4′8″ high.

The Littles used the room as a reception room and furnished it with an oak desk and chair, wicker chairs, two floor lamps, a dark red Oriental rug, and a Hiroshige woodcut on the wall. The 1912 wall lights are silk shades over bare bulbs. The clients appear to have rejected much of Wright's furniture design for this room. Thus what we see is a recreation by a Wright apprentice, a Taliesin Fellow for twelve years, Edgar Tafel, whose long as-

Fig. 35. Frank Lloyd Wright (1867–1959), library, Francis Little House, 1912–14.
Allentown Art Museum, Allentown, Pa., gift of Mr. and Mrs. Bernard Berman,
1972. Photo courtesy of Allentown Art Museum.

sociation with Wright has enabled him to capture Wright's bibliophilic essence so successfully that, when schoolchildren visit, they later describe
feelings of peace, calm, and a "churchlike" atmosphere in this room.

The room bespeaks a dignity, restraint, intimacy, simplicity of line, and
small scale that are Oriental in character. Because the room originally was
used by the family as a reception area, the museum has wisely selected
handsomely bound sets in gilt for display here. Although not indigenous to
the family or the room, the titles have been selected from among those in a
contemporaneous library.[65]

Contrary to popular belief, Wright did not eschew the mundane practitioners of the American Arts and Crafts movement. He used Mission furniture in some of his "secondary" rooms (e.g., bedrooms), when, as Hanks
reveals, "his own furniture could not be afforded." Wright's famous oak
settee with leather seat cushion (circa 1912) resembles a Gustav Stickley
design depicted in the October 1901 issue of *The Craftsman.*[66]

Precisely who influenced whom or who borrowed from whom may never be known, for there were many Arts and Crafts practitioners who placed books throughout the home: Will Bradley, first in Boston, then in New York; Gustav Stickley, first in western New York and later in his Craftsman commune in Morris Plains, New Jersey; the Roycrofters in East Aurora, New York, near Buffalo. What is known is that architects, artists, bookbinders, and printers enjoyed collaborative efforts, social and professional, in such Arts and Crafts Society chapters as Boston, where the Beaux Arts architects Bertram Grosvenor Goodhue and Ralph Adams Cram consorted with socialite binder Sara Whitman, printer Daniel Berkeley Updike, and authors Oliver Wendell Holmes, James Russell Lowell, and Charles Eliot Norton. In fact, Wright reveals in his *Autobiography* that he grew "to love the smell of printer's ink." Indeed, in 1896–97 he printed a book entitled *The House Beautiful,*[67] which reflects the influence on him of William Morris and Louis Sullivan. This endeavor was a logical expression of Wright's naturalism, as he mirrored a *modus operandi* initiated by confreres in New England.

The Midwest became the largest center for the dissemination of the Arts and Crafts aesthetic for home library decor, primarily through the preeminence of Sears, Roebuck, Montgomery Ward, and numerous other creators of mail-order house plan catalogs.[68] Moreover, as the hub of the rail transportation network, this was a likely region for millwork vendors and other specialty manufacturers, e.g., sash and door and furniture makers, as they were well positioned geographically to obtain raw materials. The president of the Muscatine, Iowa, Sash and Door Company (founded in 1889) had, by 1901, built himself a grand home library. Another Muscatinian had to settle for something less grand: a modest hall library corner.[69]

E.L. Roberts & Company published a 1903 millwork catalog featuring an Arts and Crafts library interior in "unselected" birch, with a wood-bedecked stairwell. The customer was asked to specify whether "with or without bookcase."[70] The Charles P. Limbert Company, cabinetmakers of Grand Rapids and Holland, Michigan, in its Book No. 119 (circa 1906) offered several versions of an Arts and Crafts home library[71] characterized by Mission style bookcases, settees, and rocking chairs, like Wright's. Desks of this type began to exhibit open bookshelves on their sides and bottoms, and the classic geometric rectilinearity in the treatment of chandeliers, wall sconces, windows, and doors.

A previous study discusses the millwork and houseplan catalog vendors' depiction of home libraries in greater depth.[72] Suffice it to say that people in every geographical area of the country were able to be serviced by mail-order vendors throughout the 1920s. One such catalog, recently discovered, incorporates the Hispanic tradition: The Palm Beach architectural firm of Seelig & Finkelstein owned a 1927 catalog reflecting the placement of books in living room areas. Issued by Economy Planning Service, obviously for a geographically specialized market, its "Toledo," "Barcelona," "Milano," and "Carcassonne" house models, all designed for southern city lots forty to fifty feet wide and containing no more than six rooms, each made provision for books against a living room wall, on shelves, or in cases to either side of the fireplace—"right where one wants books—by the fireside."

Each model's prose description, below a charming sketch, made mention of the provision for housing books. "An attractive feature likewise is the fireplace with its accompanying nook, seats and bookcases," read one. And for the "Carcassonne": "The fireplace is the heart of most of the French homes . . . as in this plan, the fireplace is usually recessed in a nook . . . this feature is the principal one in the living room . . . with the attendant effect of 'hominess'."[73]

Conclusion

"Comfort" and "hominess," standard descriptors for home library decor, are as applicable today as they were at the turn of the century.[74] Residential interiors do not change as quickly as clothing fashions. And it is fair to postulate that home *library* decor changes even less rapidly, as anyone who has ever moved a home library can guess.

The two predominant modes of home library decor remained the ones prevalent throughout the 1920s. The neoclassic, eclectic Beaux Arts style for the library in the home was seen in architectonic, pillared, pilastered, floor-to-ceiling linear bookcases executed in dark, elegant, and sometimes exotic woods, derived from Greco-Roman models and embellished by Renaissance and rococo furniture styles replete with thick upholstery and floral-patterned fabric, accented with the obligatory Oriental carpet, and accessorized with the artifacts of travel.[75]

The Arts and Crafts home library aesthetic was based on simplicity of line, elimination of detail, and a heightened respect for materials. Objects were preferably handmade but, in America, could be machine-made. These qualities tended to enhance, not diminish, the presence of books. The forty-year period under consideration was a golden era, literally and figuratively, of the decorated book cover and its contents. Open shelves, uncarved cases, and golden oak and paler wall colors enabled these often resplendent expressions of American home culture to display their properties instead of being upstaged by an architectural presence (as pediments and colonnades are wont to do).

Indeed, a most remarkable book entitled *American Home Culture* appeared in Chicago in 1902. Created as an etiquette manual, its pictorial content almost exclusively refers to home libraries. Thirty-five examples from Washington, D.C., to Chicago are interspersed throughout chapters on how to visit, how to travel, how to serve tea, how to give and attend a ball or reception. The book aims, as its lengthy subtitle states, to be "a complete guide to correct social forms and artistic living—to represent the very best in the home life of intellectual America." The authors quote Sidney Lanier: " 'Three things are essential to a real home—music, fire, and love.' By this he no doubt meant that the ideal home is founded on culture, comfort, and courtesy . . . All wise statesmen are agreed in declaring that the perpetuity of a government depends on the home life of its people."[76]

H. Allen Brooks, a preeminent historian of the Prairie School, in describing why its design precepts long outlasted its creators, relates: "The greater sense of restfulness, relaxation and repose, and the new richness to be experienced in living, were benefits which the average client assuredly did not foresee and probably never wholly attributed to the architect. He got more than he asked for, but hardly realized it. He 'loved' his house, but didn't know exactly why."[77] This inquiry into the nature of the American home library between 1890 and 1930—why it came into existence, what it looked like, and where books were placed in the home—may help to explain why we love our houses and the books within them.

Notes

1. Deborah Selsky, "Library Market Outlook: American Reading Habits (and Education) on the Rise," *Library Journal* 114, no. 9 (1989):22.

2. Ken Collier, "Building a Home Library," *Family Handyman* 39 (July-Aug. 1989):32–39.

3. The Library of Congress has at least 40 catalogs of this firm, published between 1980 and 1989. A recent representative example is: Home Planners, Inc., *266 Affordable Home Plans* (Farmington Hills, Mich.: Home Planners, Inc., 1989).

4. Robert Darnton, "Scholarship and Readership: New Directions in the History of the Book," in *Books and Prints, Past and Future* (New York: Grolier Club, 1984), 34. I am grateful to Susan Otis Thompson, associate professor, Columbia Univ., New York, for bringing this article to my attention.

5. Ibid., 43–44.

6. Ibid., 36, 39. See also E. Millicent Sowerby, *Catalogue of the Library of Thomas Jefferson* (Washington, D.C.: Library of Congress, 1955; rptd. Charlottesville, Va.: Thomas Jefferson Memorial Foundation and the Univ. of Virginia, 1983).

7. Daniel J. Boorstin, "Culture Without a Capital," in *The Americans: The Colonial Experience* (New York: Vintage, 1958), 293–316, *passim.* See also his bibliographical notes that accompany this section, 412–15.

8. Linda M. Kruger, "The New York City Book Trade, 1725–1750" (D.L.S. diss., Columbia Univ., 1979), *passim;* app. A and G, leaves 308–12, pp. 348–50. See also Edwin Wolf 2nd, *The Library of James Logan of Philadelphia, 1674–1751* (Philadelphia: Library Company of Philadelphia, 1974); Edwin Wolf's numerous periodical writings on the Philadelphia book trade; Cadwallader Colden, *The Letters and Papers of Cadwallader Colden* vol. 3, 1743–47 (New York: New York Historical Society, 1920), *passim;* Louis B. Wright, "Books, Libraries and Learning," in Louis B. Wright, *The Cultural Life of the American Colonies, 1607–1763* (New York: Harper, 1957), *passim.*

9. Brooke Hindle, "The Natural History Circle," in Brooke Hindle, *The Pursuit of Science in Revolutionary America, 1735–1789* (Chapel Hill: Univ. of North Carolina Press, for the Institute of Early American History and Culture, Williamsburg, Va., 1956), 15, 127–45. Among the correspondence of members of this circle can be found references to book borrowing, e.g., *Colden Papers,* 3:160, 3:206, 3:226–27, 3:276.

10. Madeleine B. Stern, "Dissemination of Popular Books in the Midwest and Far West During the Nineteenth Century," in *Getting the Books Out: Papers of the Chicago Conference on the Book in 19th-Century America,* ed. Michael Hackenberg (Washington, D.C.: Center for the Book, Library of Congress, 1987), 76–97, *passim.*

11. David Kaser, *A Book for a Sixpence: The Circulating Library in America* (Pittsburgh, Pa.: Beta Phi Mu, 1980).

12. An example discovered recently is the "Elmira [New York] Farmers' Club Library," rules and regulations for use, inserted in George Woodward and F.W. Woodward, *Woodward's Graperies and Horticultural Buildings* (New York: George E. Woodward, 1865), Chemung County Historical Society, Elmira, N.Y.

13. William J. Gilmore, *Reading Becomes a Necessity of Life: Material and Cultural Life in Rural New England, 1780–1835* (Knoxville: Univ. of Tennessee Press, 1989), 255–56.

14. Edward Everitt Hale, *Franklin in France* (Boston: Roberts Bros., 1888), 2 vols.; Edward Dumbauld, *Thomas Jefferson, American Tourist* (Norman: Univ. of Oklahoma Press, 1976); Darwin Stapleton, *Accounts of European Science, Technology and Medicine Written by American Travelers Abroad, 1735–1860* (Philadelphia: American Philosophical Society, 1985).

15. Foster Rhea Dulles, *Americans Abroad: Two Centuries of European Travel* (Ann Arbor: Univ. of Michigan Press, 1964); Allison Lockwood, *Passionate Pilgrims: The American Traveler in Great Britain, 1800–1914* (Rutherford, N.J.: Fairleigh Dickinson Univ. Press, 1981).

16. Paul Fussell, "The Eighteenth Century and the Grand Tour" and "The Heyday," in *The Norton Book of Travel,* ed. Paul Fussell (New York: Norton, 1987), 127-32, [271].

17. Eugene Exman, *The House of Harper: One Hundred and Fifty Years of Publishing* (New York: Harper & Row, 1967), 50, 137.

18. Stern, "Dissemination of Popular Books," 82–83; Madeleine B. Stern, "The Frank Leslie Publishing House," in *Publishers for Mass Entertainment in Nineteenth Century America,* ed. Madeleine B. Stern (Boston: G.K. Hall, 1980), 185–86.

19. Joseph E. Gould, *The Chautauqua Movement: An Episode in the Continuing American Revolution* (New York: State Univ. of New York, 1961), 8–9; Arthur Eugene Bestor, *Chautauqua Publications: An Historical and Bibliographical Guide* (Chautauqua, N.Y.: New York: Chautauqua Press, 1934), *passim;* Pauline Fancher, *Chautauqua: Its Architecture and Its People* (Miami, Fla.: Banyan Books, 1978), 28–29, 98.

20. Chauncey M. Depew, *The Columbian Oration Delivered at the Dedication Ceremonies of the World's Fair at Chicago, October 21, 1892, by the Hon. Chauncey M. Depew* (New York: Edwin C. Lockwood, ca. 1892–93), 18–19.

21. *Publishers' Weekly* 87, no. 2 (9 Jan. 1915):105; 87, no. 10 (16 Mar. 1915):671; 87, no. 22 (29 May 1915):1654–55; 124, no. 1 (1 July 1933):22; 124, no. 13 (23 Sept. 1933):1061.

22. Grant Carpenter Manson, *Frank Lloyd Wright to 1910: The First Golden Age* (New York: Van Nostrand Reinhold, 1958), 32–33.

23. Jeanne Madeline Weimann, *The Fair Women* (Chicago: Academy Chicago, 1981), 354.

24. Candace Wheeler, *Principles of Home Decoration* (New York: Doubleday, Page & Co., 1903); Candace Wheeler, ed., *Household Art* (New York: Harper and Bros., 1893).

25. Weimann, *Fair Women,* 371.

26. Candace Wheeler, as quoted in Weimann, *Fair Women,* 357.

27. *From Art Amateur,* as quoted in Weimann, *Fair Women,* 375.

28. "The Publishers' Exhibits at the World's Columbian Exposition: The United States," *Publishers' Weekly* 44, no. 1118 (1 July 1893):12.

29. Moses P. Handy, ed., *The Official Directory of the World's Columbian Exposition, May 1st to October 30th, 1893: A Reference Book* (Chicago: W.B. Gonkey, 1893), 241–42, 231.

30. R.J. Horner & Co., *Our American Homes and How to Furnish Them* (New York: N.P. [ca. 1900]), pp. [20–21, 24].

31. The Beaux Arts style espoused principles of symmetry, solidity, and monumentality as manifested in the aesthetic of Greco-Roman classicism, but the approach allowed for creative interpretation. The architect could draw upon diverse architectural traditions: Italian Renaissance, French Baroque, French and Belgian Art Nouveau, and German and Austrian Secessionism. The Library of Congress subject heading for this unbridled amalgam of disparate forms is "Eclecticism in architecture." Among the American architectural schools embracing this philosophy were Columbia, Cornell, MIT, Harvard, Yale, Princeton, Notre Dame, Ohio State, and the state universities of Pennsylvania, Texas, Virginia, Illinois, and Southern California.

32. Elisa Urbanelli, *Beaux-Arts Institute of Design,* Landmarks Preservation Commission LP-1667 (New York, 1988), pp. 1–2. See also Stapleton D. Gooch, *Library at Biltmore* (Charlottesville: Univ. Press of Virginia, 1967).

33. Emery Roth, *Autobiographical Notes,* typescript, 242, as quoted in Nancy Goeschel, *Hotel Belleclaire,* Landmarks Preservation Commission LP-1507 (New York, 1987), p. 3.

34. An early patron, Edward Waller, seeing the completion of Wright's 1894 Winslow house in River Forest, Ill., with a large frontally placed library that could be entered through the main entrance and the porte-cochère, "offered to finance a six-year course of study for Wright abroad—four years at the École des Beaux Arts and two in Rome" (Manson, *FLW to 1910,* 48).

35. *120 Intérieurs en Couleurs: Suite de la Couleur dans l'Habitation* (Paris: Librairie d'Architecture R. Ducher, [1913?]).

36. H. Allen Brooks, *Frank Lloyd Wright and the Prairie School* (New York: George Braziller, in association with the Cooper-Hewitt Museum, 1984), 11–12.

37. Manson, *FLW to 1910,* 11: "Young Wright . . . developed an insatiable appetite for reading, and, in a household which was bookish, there was a good deal of material to satisfy it, albeit haphazardly." Wright's sister adds another bookish aside in describing Wright's bedroom in their mother's house. Termed "the Sanctum Sanctorum" (after Thomas Jefferson, whose study was so named), this room contained "an odor of printer's ink . . . there was a printing press" (Maginel Wright Barney, *The Valley of the God-Almighty Joneses* [New York: Appleton-Century, 1965], 74–75).

38. Clarence Cook, *The House Beautiful: Essays on Beds and Tables, Stools and Candlesticks* (1878; rptd. Croton-on-Hudson, N.Y.: North River Press, 1980); Barney, *Valley of Joneses,* 64; Manson, *FLW to 1910,* 5.

39. Cook, *House Beautiful,* 45, 48, 81, 83, 89, 109, 166, 170–71, 166–67.

40. Charles L. Eastlake, *Hints on Household Taste in Furniture, Upholstery and Other Details* (1868; abridged reprint, *Late Victorian Decor from Eastlake's Gothic to Cook's House Beautiful,* ed. Hugh Guthrie [Watkins Glen, N.Y.: American Life Foundation, 1968]), 56, 59–60.

41. For a more extensive treatment of this point, see Linda M. Kruger, "The Library in the American Home, 1865–1920: Based on the Trade Catalog Collection, Avery Architectural and Fine Arts Library, Columbia University" (paper given at the symposium on *Books and Reading in America, 1840–1940,* Strong Museum, Rochester, N.Y., Nov. 1986 [New York: Greenwood, Beta Phi Mu monograph, in press]).

42. Richard Guy Wilson, "Edith and Ogden: Writing, Decoration, and Architecture," in *Ogden Codman and the Decoration of Houses,* ed. Pauline C. Metcalf (Boston: Boston Athenaeum/David R. Godine, 1988), 158.

43. Ibid., 140, 146.

44. Ibid., 169.

45. Pauline C. Metcalf, "Design and Decoration," in *Ogden Codman and the Decoration of Houses,* ed. Pauline C. Metcalf (Boston: Boston Athenaeum/David R. Godine, 1988), 97.

46. Kruger, "Library in the American Home"; Harold M. Otness, "A Room Full of Books: The Life and Slow Death of the American Residential Library," *Libraries and Culture* 23, no. 2 (Spring 1988): [111]–134.

47. Blueprints of Shepley, Rutan and Coolidge, 1903, Hildene, Manchester, Vt.

48. Alan Crawford, "The Arts and Crafts Movement in Context," in *The Decorative Arts in the Victorian Period,* ed. Susan M. Wright (London: Society of Antiquaries of London, dist. by Thames and Hudson, 1989), 89–96.

49. Robert Judson Clark, ed., *The Arts and Crafts Movement in America, 1876–1916* (Princeton, N.J.: Princeton Univ. Press, 1972), *passim.*

50. James L. Garvin, "Mail-Order House Plans and American Victorian Architecture," *Winterthur Portfolio* 16, no. 4 (Winter 1981): [309]–334; Kruger, "Library in the American Home."

51. Katherine Cole Stevenson and H. Ward Jandl, *Houses by Mail: A Guide to Houses from Sears, Roebuck and Company* (Washington, D.C.: Preservation Press, 1986), 32.

52. H. Allen Brooks, *The Prairie School* (New York: Norton, 1976), 23–24.

53. Ibid., 17.

54. In addition to his notable institutional library buildings, H.H. Richardson's home designs usually included a library.

55. Manson, *FLW to 1910,* 51.

56. Ibid., 53.

57. In Oct. 1910, Wright wrote to Darwin Martin (for whose 1904 house in Buffalo, N.Y., Wright had designed some resplendent library furniture) to request that Martin intercede on Wright's behalf with a potential client, C.R. Wills, of Detroit,

Mich., to woo Wills away from von Holst: "I have seen the plans and it is a crime to waste an opportunity like his [Wills] on stuff so weak . . . von Holst will do all he can to hold him, of course, but the client is to decide whether he goes on with the thing as it is or whether he wants an original." Frank Lloyd Wright, *Letters to Clients,* ed. Bruce Brooks Pfeiffer (Fresno, Calif.: The Press at California State Univ., 1986), 17–18. Herman Valentin von Holst, *Country and Suburban Homes of the Prairie School Period* (New York: Dover, 1982), plates 22, 25, 29, 31, 32, 34, 36, 41, 51, 55, 60, 63, 67, 68, 72, 82, 84, 87, 89, 91–93, 97. The characteristics of Wright's "natural organic unit" included:

> a house that was completely suited to its setting: low, horizontal lines; broad overhanging eaves, bands of leaded glass windows, an open plan with a central fireplace and rooms opening up to each other, corners dissolved in glass, the latest mechanical equipment, natural materials left unadorned, furniture in harmony with the architecture, a house designed for its occupants and its setting (Deborah S. Haight and Peter F. Blume, *Frank Lloyd Wright: The Library from the Francis W. Little House* [Allentown, Pa.: Allentown Art Museum, 1978], 8).

58. David A. Hanks, *Frank Lloyd Wright: Preserving an Architectural Heritage: Decorative Designs from the Domino's Pizza Collection* (New York: Dutton, 1989), 32, 35.

59. Edgar Kaufmann, Jr., *Frank Lloyd Wright at the Metropolitan Museum of Art* (New York: Metropolitan Museum of Art, 1985), 12.

60. Hanks, *FLW: Preserving,* 61.

61. Ibid., 64.

62. Ibid., 66; Frank Lloyd Wright, *Ausgeführte Bauten und Entwurfe* (Berlin: Wasmuth, 1910).

63. *120 Intérieurs en Couleurs.*

64. Steelcase, Inc., "Meyer May House Restoration," *Historic Preservation* 42, no. 1 (1990):[3] of cover.

65. The library of a Little family contemporary, Kate Fowler Merle-Smith of Beekman Place, New York City, and Oyster Bay, Long Island, was acquired by the Allentown Art Museum for display in the Little library. Some examples include: the Scribner's edition of Robert L. Stevenson, 28 vols.; Thackeray, a London edition of 22 vols., and another 9-vol. edition; *British essayists,* 30 vols.; *Museum of Painting and Sculpture,* 17 vols.; George Eliot, a 20-vol. set and a 5-vol. set.

66. Hanks, *FLW: Preserving,* 82.

67. William C. Gannett, *The House Beautiful* (River Forest, Ill.: Auvergne Press, 1896–97), page decorations by Frank Lloyd Wright, *passim.*

68. Stevenson and Jandl, *Houses by Mail,* 19.

69. *Picturesque Muscatine: A Booklet Descriptive of the "Pearl City" of Iowa* (Muscatine, Iowa: H.W. Lewis, 1901), [83].

70. E.L. Roberts & Co., *Roberts' Illustrated Millwork Catalog: A Sourcebook of Turn-of-the-Century Architectural Woodwork* (1903; rptd., New York: Dover, 1988), 155, 204.

71. Charles P. Limbert Co., Cabinet Makers, *Book No. 119* (ca. 1906; rptd., New York: Turn of the Century Editions, 1981), [3], [5], [7], 42.

72. Kruger, "Library in the American Home."

73. Economy Planning Service, *Spanish and Italian Homes of Real Character and Distinction* (West Palm Beach, Fla.: Economy Planning Service, ca. 1927), 22, 34, 40.

74. A recent term embracing the concept of leisure hours spent at home in pursuit of library-type activities is "couch potato." See David Blum, "Couch Potatoes: The New Nightlife," *New York* 20, no. 28 (20 July 1987): 26. An April 1986 Gallup Poll revealed that one-third of all Americans chose to stay home. Most watched TV, but some read.

75. Charles Eugene Banks and Marshall Everett, *American Home Culture and Correct Customs of Polite Society: . . . with Views of Rooms, Corners, Libraries, Dens . . . a Complete Guide to Correct Social Forms and Artistic Living . . .* (Chicago: Henry Neil, ca. 1902), 245, 254.

76. Ibid., [1–2] of preface.

77. Brooks, *Prairie School,* 25.

CHAPTER FIVE

A History of American
Beds and Bedrooms, 1890–1930

Elizabeth Collins Cromley

Life in the nineteenth- and twentieth-century American home could hardly have proceeded without the bedroom. This room not only satisfied everyone's need for a setting in which to sleep, but it also provided what to the middle class in this period was an essential property of a home: a private place in which to do it. Indeed, the bedroom appears to offer the very definition of privacy. But the bedroom of this time was also the site for many activities and cultural expressions beyond those specifically connected to sleeping. This study will provide a glimpse of the many other things that a bedroom is, besides an obviously private site. It should complicate our understanding of how this particular household space functioned, and provide a fresh perspective on the nature of privacy in the home.[1]

The Organization of Household Space and the Implications for a Place Called "Bedroom"

The structure of household space supports the sleeping aspect of household life, and as that structure changes, the location of sleeping and the relationships between sleeping and other activities change, too.[2] The pattern of this change can be traced through house plans. In rural houses of the mid-nineteenth century, there were often one or more bedrooms on the ground floor of the house, linked to the reception rooms. A detached cottage design with a main-floor bedroom was published by pattern-book author Gervase Wheeler in 1855. Intended for a suburban or country location, it had a square body, with a one- or two-story wing at the rear. A ground-floor center hall plan placed a parlor at the front (5); a sitting room across from it (2); a dining room at the rear, communicating with the kitchen in the wing; and, in the corner of the ground floor, a bedroom. This bedroom was linked to the dining room through an entry fitted with built-in drawers and a "wardrobe," and to the parlor by another door.[3]

A volume published by the Cooperative Building Plan Association of New York in 1886 provided builders with plans for low-cost houses. One of the plans called for a ground-floor bedroom, plus several more bedrooms on the second or chamber floor. The bedroom on the main floor opened into both the kitchen and the entrance hall. Another plan showed a double (or two-family) house, in which the lower unit had a room called "bedroom or sitting room" opening into both dining room and parlor. The upper unit had two bedrooms—one opening into both the dining room and the hall, and a second bedroom opening into both the parlor and the hall.[4]

All of these designs, significantly, include a chamber on the main floor attached to the most important reception rooms in the house. While a ground-floor chamber was sometimes appropriated as a sickroom to save invalids and their caretakers from climbing stairs, more often this ground-floor chamber belonged to the heads of the household. The room provided privacy to its occupants, allowing them to close the door upon other household activities, but, because it was located next to a parlor, entrance hall, or kitchen, the bedroom was also positioned for sociability and for connection to ongoing household tasks.

The link between prominent social rooms on the ground floor and a sleeping room is reminiscent of seventeenth- and eighteenth-century practices at all class levels. Then the parents slept in a ground-floor parlor or chamber, and children and servants shared attic and outbuilding sleeping spaces. However, by 1850 this relation marks a difference in class. At the high-cost end of published house designs, the preferred location of all chambers was on a separate "chamber floor" clearly segregated from the social zone of the house; the urban middle-class and well-to-do households in both country and city had grown away from the ground-floor sleeping room.

In many early-twentieth-century examples of middle-class houses, the chamber floor absorbed *all* the sleeping spaces, continuing a nineteenth-century trend begun by the wealthy. The *Delineator* magazine, a home and fashion monthly, held a competition for a three-thousand-dollar house for a middle-class family in 1909. Frank Choteau Brown designed the first-prize winner. Its ground floor had kitchen, dining room, and living room. The chamber floor had four sleeping rooms: one servant's room, two chambers, and a nursery.[5]

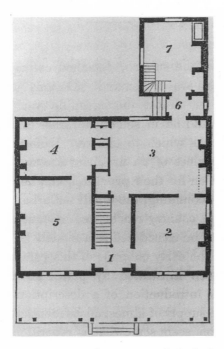

Fig. 36. Plan of a cottage with the bedroom linked to the parlor and the dining room. Gervase Wheeler, *Homes for the People in Suburb and Country* (New York: Scribner's, 1855), p. 322.

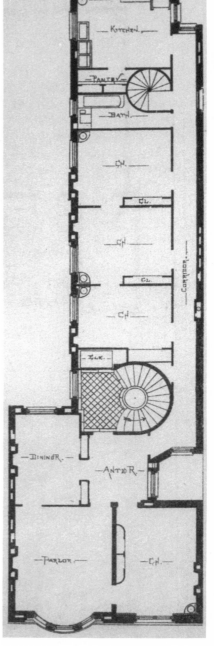

Fig. 37. An apartment unit plan with the chamber and parlor linked, 21 East 21st Street, New York, N.Y. *American Architect and Building News,* 4 May 1878, plate 123.

Two kinds of changes in the *Delineator* house suggest increasingly functionalist thinking about the house plan. The typical bedroom had a single entrance from a discrete corridor—not the multiple entrance points of the earlier first-floor bedrooms described above—better guaranteeing privacy. This plan clarified room location by function rather than by status of occupant, placing all household members' sleeping rooms together on the second floor (although the servant's room was separated from the others by three steps). The plan asserts that the privacy of sleeping is more important than the segregation of family members by rank, which had been characteristic of seventeenth- or eighteenth-century houses.

There is an historical movement in location of bedrooms from the first floor, linked to a parlor or dining room and having several means of access, to bedrooms segregated on upper floors, with access limited to a door into a passage and perhaps a door into an adjoining bedroom. This movement seems linked to the family's desire to present itself as middle class or as rising on the social ladder by making a show of privacy. Bedrooms also shift from status-determined locations, where a principal bedroom was linked to the most valued social zones in the house and servants were separated from other family members, to function-determined placement, defining all chambers as sleeping rooms and creating a sleeping zone with owners and servants on one floor. That is, by the early twentieth century, the category "sleeping zone" prevails over competing categories, such as "servants' zone" and "family zone."[6]

The designers of single-floor homes in the later nineteenth and early twentieth centuries confronted additional problems in locating their bedrooms. A one-floor plan forces one to ask what functions could go next to a sleeping room and which ones had to stay apart. Early apartment unit plans for single-floor household space often mixed sleeping rooms for family with the family's other more social rooms, as seen in Bruce Price's 21 East 21st Street apartment house of 1878. In his plan, a chamber and a parlor are linked; their windows overlook the street—always the privilege of the "best" rooms. Price's remaining bedrooms march toward the rear of the apartment along a corridor which leads finally to the kitchen. Servants, family members, and guests all pass by the "private" bedrooms on the way to the parlor, dining room, or kitchen.

By the first decade of the twentieth century, apartment designers preferred grouping all family bedrooms together in a sleeping zone instead of linking a bedroom with reception spaces. An apartment designed by William Boring for 520 Fifth Avenue in 1910 clustered all the family bedrooms together and allowed a separate zone for the servants' and service rooms. Both are cleanly separated from social rooms where guests would be received, preserving strong boundaries between the private and the more public zones through planning devices.

Bungalows, two- and three-family flats, and modern houses of the ranch style also have all rooms laid out on one floor and have to manage the relation of bedrooms to social spaces. Two Aladdin Redi-Cut one-story bungalows of 1918–19 handle this relation in radically different ways.[7] One deploys its bedrooms all around the social spaces, with every bedroom's door opening into the living and dining rooms; the other groups all its bedrooms off a little hallway which completely buffers the bedrooms from the social spaces. One plan enhances privacy, while the other house preserves opportunities for intrafamilial surveillance of bedroom activity from the living room or kitchen.

Although this history of the spatial location of bedrooms at first seemed to argue for a clarification of rooms' uses, toward a room that was pure "bedroom" and toward an isolation of all bedrooms in a pure zone of privacy, the bungalow examples return us to the complexity of the question. Bedroom locations and their relationship in space to other rooms of the house remain problematical, determined sometimes by their sleeping function and sometimes by other family demands or class preferences.

Who Gets a Bed or a Room of One's Own?

Sharing a bedroom would have been unavoidable for members of low-income families. In middle-class houses, however, there often were many bedrooms to be assigned to the several members of a household. The question of who had the right to her, his, or their own bed or room was answered differently in different decades.

The late-nineteenth-century owners of a house, the parents of the family, normally occupied the principal bedroom together. In a humorous 1872 article, journalist Matthew Browne suggested that it was so taken to be a rule that married couples must sleep together, that if anyone wanted to try sleeping alone, it would become the talk of the neighborhood (although he maintained that sleeping alone is good for everyone, at least once in a while).[8]

But there were times when the married couple was advised to sleep apart. Dr. Alcott's 1859 medical handbook advised that, when pregnant, women should sleep in a bed separate from their husbands or even in a separate room. This allowed them to get good air and helped prevent their having intercourse (which it was thought might damage the health of the fetus). The husband might sleep in the same room in his own bed, or in an adjoining room with the door open between them.[9] According to some sex reformers, women, even when not pregnant, should sleep separately from their husbands, in order to preserve themselves from a man's insatiable, bestial lust. Separate bedrooms could keep the frequency of marital sexual intercourse down to a reasonable once-a-month pattern.[10]

Some nineteenth-century medical advisors asserted that a double bed was always unhealthy and that each member of a married couple should have a separate bed. No two people can comfortably and naturally sleep on the same mattress and under the same bedclothes, wrote a doctor in *Appleton's* magazine of 1880: they disturb each other by wiggling or dragging at the bedclothes, and shock their partners with bad breath![11]

The Crystal House at the 1934 Chicago "Century of Progress" Exposition was a modern design in which "his" and "hers" suites of rooms revealed an erosion of the belief that married couples should always share a room. Her and his suites filled the third floor of the house; they served basically the same purposes but were furnished differently. "Her" room had its own bathroom with a bathtub and no shower, suggesting her greater leisure, while "his" bathroom had a shower and no tub, as befits a man's greater businesslike efficiency. "His" room had his bed, a single size; "her" room and "their" bed, a double. "Her" room was the site of marital congress; "his," perhaps, of solitary pleasures.[12] The 1920s and 1930s saw the rising popularity of twin beds for married couples who did not have the budget or the taste for completely separate suites of rooms.

Before the mid-nineteenth century, infants and small children often shared the beds of their elders, who did not believe there was any need for them to have their own beds or bedrooms. Reformers concerned with health, however, felt that even the youngest infant should have its own bedstead, so it would not have to share air with its mother, an impure practice. In its own bed, it would also be protected from mothers, who sometimes were recorded as rolling over on infants, crushing their limbs. When children were put to sleep with their grandparents, another common nineteenth-century practice, the aged bodies were said to rob the children of "vital warmth" and enfeeble them, according to health reformers; so sleeping in single beds was recommended, to assure a child's healthy growth. An American doctor advised young mothers in 1838 not to let the child sleep with dogs, cats, or younger persons, either.[13]

When they grew up a little, children did deserve their own rooms, but since children, in the nineteenth and early twentieth centuries, were the members of the household who did not yet have a gender, they comfortably shared space and perhaps shared beds. As Sally McMurry has shown, nurseries as shared rooms for all the infants and children of a family, regardless of sex, were already by the 1830s being promoted to aid in the discipline and education of the young.[14]

But when the children had grown to preadolescence, had become boys and girls, then many home decorating books advised parents on the role of separate rooms for each. One of the high points of a girl's life, wrote journalist Martha Cutler in 1906, is acquiring a room of her own. Such a room is for a person "who has reached that longed-for period in life when her needs are worthy of consideration, when a quiet, retired spot is deemed a necessity for [her] study and work . . . Her sense of individual possession is coupled with a delightful sense of importance and newfound dignity, which renders her association with 'the children' unworthy to her seriousness."[15] This description of the needs of early adolescence omits any mention of emergent sexuality, but this, too, may have motivated parents to find separate rooms for their growing boys and girls.

Another important inhabitant of the nineteenth- and early-twentieth-century middle-class household was the servant, who also needed a bed, if not a room, of her own. Every family who keeps more than one servant should provide each with her own single bed, advised the Beecher sisters in 1869, so she "might not be obliged to sleep with all the changing domestics, who come and go so often." If the servants' room were too narrow, they advised the use of a "truckle bed" pulled out at night to sleep the second servant.[16] Mr. and Mrs. Stockton's 1872 book, *Furnishing the House,* advised that one of the best ways to retain a good servant was to give her her own comfortable room. Even if a servant were a poor one, giving her a good room might help make her better at her work.[17]

As the numbers of servants declined radically in the first two decades of the twentieth century, so did advice on the maid's room. Instead, the guest bedroom or spare room gained the attention of advice-book writers in the second half of the nineteenth century, and continued to concern them well into the twentieth. Guest rooms were often "decorated" with family castoffs and then never visited by family members, so their lack of comforts might go unnoticed. An 1888 etiquette book, *The Social Mirror,* reminded housekeepers that a spare room should always have a hairbrush and comb, a pincushion, a shoe buttoner, a box of matches, a train schedule, writing paper, and envelopes. The bed linen should be changed for each newcomer, even if the previous guest used the bed for only one night, while the hairbrush should be cleaned once a week![18] By the 1910s, guest rooms had become more lavishly outfitted in prosperous households. *House and Garden*'s writer believed that the guest room should have its own bathroom, telephone, twin beds, and, "if the house has electricity," a reading lamp.[19] Smaller houses of the 1930s and 1940s which did not provide any "spare" rooms constrained middle-class hospitality and gave rise to multipurpose rooms which could serve family members as a den or game room, as well as convert to a guest room when needed.[20]

Finally, invalids were family members who needed bedrooms of their own in the days before hospitals and nursing homes replaced home care. Those who might spend a day feeling a little under the weather, weeks at a time being cured of an illness, or whole lifetimes with more permanent complaints needed a bedroom. For the type of room suitable for a chronic invalid, create something that is half bedroom, half boudoir, recommended Mr. and Mrs. Stockton.[21] Supply the invalid with an easy chair, a carpet in a single sober tone with a bright border, curtains in lace, light-colored wood furniture, and a cool-toned picture on the wall. For invalids of the moment, "A little gem of a tete-a-tete service on a small corner table in the sleeping-room is pleasantly suggestive of a day or so of invalidism, when one is just sufficiently out of sorts to be waited on and 'made of'," wrote *Appleton's* home decoration columnist Ella Church in 1877.[22] The mid-nineteenth-century ground-floor bedrooms common in inexpensive pattern-book houses served well for invalids who could not use the stairs.

Answers to the question of which persons get their own bedrooms, then, depend on the social and economic relations within the household and the health ideas of the moment. Putting the baby to sleep with its grandparents was common in the nineteenth century, when one or more grandparents shared homes with younger generations; in the late twentieth century, many children do not grow up in the same house with even two parents, much less two grandparents. Here changed social relations obviate health warnings to keep the baby out of grandma's bed. Giving an infant its own bed, instead of putting it to sleep in the parents' bed, has been a middle-class preference, supported over the past century by doctors although sometimes challenged today by breastfeeding advocates. Working-class families shared beds and bedrooms more often than middle-class households, in part because extra space was too costly to be within their grasp. Separating the children by gender has been common since the nineteenth century for any family that could afford separate bedroom space, but gender is assigned more insistently and earlier now than it was a century ago.

Bedrooms as the Site for Individual Expression

At the turn of the century, many writers gave the bedroom power to express the self. "Every opportunity should be given for the development of individuality in a room which is preeminently the corner of the home which is truly home to the occupant, where the taste of no one, either guest or relative, need be considered."[23] The other rooms must reflect the life of the whole family and their various occupations, but the bedroom "is the place for one's personal belongings, those numberless little things which are such sure indications of individual character and fancy . . . the one room where purely personal preference may be freely exercised."[24]

The individuality of bedrooms, wrote Ella Church in her 1877 home-decorating advice for *Appleton's Journal,* allows one to tell at a glance the mother's room from the brother's room. In the mother's room one finds an extra-large and comfortable bed, an easy chair, and a table—things used for "accommodating numerous inmates." The bachelor's room (for the uncle or brother) is full of newspapers, pipes, cigar boxes, and photographs of actresses. The young lady's room has muslin flounces on everything—usually either pink or blue; the grandmother's room has an old-fashioned four-poster bedstead, a three-story bureau, and a favorite easy chair. Only in the children's room, with its "snowy-draped" bed for the six-year-old Alice and a swinging crib for Floy, the two-year-old, are sexes combined and individual identity statements blurred.[25]

In E.C. Gardner's entertaining 1880s book, *The House that Jill Built After Jack's Had Proved a Failure,* an uncle of the family espouses the "individuality" position in regard to separate husband's and wife's bedrooms: "The personality of human beings should be respected. The chief object of home is to give each individual a chance for unfettered development. Every soul is a genius at times and feels the necessity of isolation. Especially do we need to be alone in sleep, and to this end every person in a house is entitled to a separate apartment."[26]

Bedrooms were also individualized for children: home-decorating books advised parents on the proper decorations for the boys and girls of the family. One advised making furniture of railroad ties for a boy's room. The boy's creativity should be encouraged by having him build his own drawing table or gun rack. A camping or an Indian theme were recommended for boys' rooms, as were pictures of ships, cowboys, and medieval knights.[27] Every girl, practicing for her future role as hostess, liked to entertain friends, so her room needed a little tea-table. Selecting her favorite wallpaper pattern and chintz curtains gave her "an opportunity to express her real self." Girls' rooms had junior dressing-tables as well as space for artistic and intellectual development.[28]

Bedrooms tested the understanding of the "mother or house-ruler," insofar as she allowed each occupant some space for self-expression, asserted Candace Wheeler in her 1903 book, *Principles of Home Decoration:* "Characteristics of the inmate will write themselves unmistakably in the room." If one put a college boy in "the white and gold bedroom," soon sporting elements and an outdoor-life atmosphere would creep in. "Banners and balls and bats, and emblems of the 'wild thyme' order will color its whiteness." Wheeler continued, "In the same way, girls would change the bare asceticism of a monk's cell into a bower of lilies and roses."[29]

What was represented by the authors of these quotes as the expression of individuality was often not so individual, but rather an expression constructed out of widely accepted markers of gender roles. This was made clear by the keeper of a boarding house who wrote advice on decorating young men's rooms. What might have been seen as "individualizing" in a private setting is revealed to be generic and gender-related in the boarding house.[30]

This boarding house keeper advised on the pictures in the boys' bedroom and sitting room. In a sitting room, the pictures should be "strong, bordering on frisky," with appropriate images including bulldogs, baseball players, college scenes, and horses. The pictures in the young man's sitting room should represent his "workaday life—that of a man among men." But in his bedroom he should have works "prophetic of his home life . . . His pictures there should be soft and inspiring like the caress of a good woman . . . The young man has no mother, sister, wife or child to keep his life sweet and clean, his ideals high and true; the influence of his landlady" is all he has. She should give him an American flag to cultivate his patriotism; hang a madonna in his room, and also a picture of "the Master." "One or two photographs of the mother or best girl should be neatly framed and kept nice—moreover they should be looked at every day."[31]

The urging of advice books to allow each bedroom's occupant plenty of latitude in self-expression through the choice of objects and furniture must be questioned. All this advice assigns predictable gendered signs to those presumed individuals. All girls should have ruffled dressing tables; all boys decorate their rooms with baseball bats or make their furniture of railroad ties. Young men all need to declare their individuality through "frisky" pictures of bulldogs; all mothers' rooms must express nurturance. In this literature, the bedroom's decor shapes its occupant into the correct gender roles, rather than encouraging the occupant to express individual taste in shaping the bedroom.

Bedrooms and the Question of Function

Throughout the centuries, bedrooms have served as more than sleeping spaces. Seventeenth-century New England parents slept in a room called "parlor," alongside tea-tables, chairs, pieces of tapestry, and silver—all the household's best items. Eighteenth-century parents' bedrooms, while more focused on the bed and the sleeping function of the room, still included sets of upholstered chairs, couches, and tables for receiving a visit or for supporting the formal rituals attached to birth and death, as such rituals were set in the bedroom. Nineteenth-century bedrooms were often furnished with manufactured suites of furniture that included washing and dressing equipment, clothes storage pieces and daybeds—all for functions in addition to sleeping in bed. Was there ever a time when the bedroom was just for sleeping?

A turn-of-the-century columnist for *Canadian Magazine,* Ms. Helliwell, described mythical "old days" (by which she meant the mid-nineteenth century), when each room in a house had an unambiguous function; she quoted Webster's dictionary to define "bedroom" as "'a room or apartment intended for a bed,' or 'a lodging room,' and that's that."[32] Her grandmother never would have received friends in her bedroom, said Helliwell; the easy chair was more likely to be found in the library, because bedrooms were for beds, a place to be only at night.

This imaginary purified bedroom, where only sleeping went on, provided contrast for Helliwell's description of the "modern girl" who lived by herself in one room and no longer had a bedroom proper. Her bed became by day a "cozy corner." Gay cushion covers hid night-time pillowcases. Toilet articles were hidden behind the mirror in a bag, while the jug and basin were concealed by a screen. Curtains hid "my lady's wardrobe." The furnishings in the modern girl's room, besides the normal bedroom furniture and cozy corner, included her desk, bookshelves, cabinets to hold curios, easy chairs, and upholstered boxes that provided storage and seating at the same time. Even the girl who still lived in her parents' home "regards her room less as a sleeping place than as a sort of combination boudoir, library, reception and sitting-room. Here she sews, reads, studies, writes her letters and club essays, receives her feminine friends, and frequently brews herself a private pot of tea."[33]

How to make a bedroom serve the additional "living" needs of the modern woman was the subject of architect D.N.B. Sturgis's 1904 article for *Architectural Record*. Twin beds had been in fashion for the past dozen years for bedrooms intended to serve also as sitting rooms, Sturgis noted, because they could more easily be disguised as something besides a bed during the day. Such a room needed a fireplace and some attractive *objets d'art*, a toilet table and full length mirror, a little stand with drawers that can easily be moved around, and a writing table for sending hasty notes "without going to the library below." Arranged thus, the bedroom becomes "a pleasant place in which to sit and, indeed, to live."[34]

These turn-of-the-century writers portrayed bedrooms as multifunctional places which served complex purposes. The seventeenth-century parlor, with its merged social and sleeping projects, is not so different after all from Helliwell's 1902 modern girl's bedroom, with its merged uses. In fact, a bedroom with a single use turns out to be a historical rarity.

Technological Inventiveness in the Bedroom

A special kind of furniture was marketed from the mid-nineteenth century on, to enable a single room to do duty both as a parlor or sitting room and as a bedroom. Mid-nineteenth-century patent furniture took various forms but generally was marked by its disguised identity: it looked like a piano, a desk, a bureau, a fireplace or a wardrobe, but it converted into a bed. In an illustration in an 1891 *Decorator and Furnisher,* the principal piece of furniture is a "parlor bed" in mahogany with a full-length mirror, carving, and two drawers at the base. This is shown being unfolded into a bed by the mistress of the house who moves it with no effort, thus turning the parlor of a too-small apartment into a bedroom.[35]

In their catalog of 1884, Boyington's recommended their folding beds because they could change most quickly from a cabinet to a bed and back to a cabinet: "A distinguishing feature of these Beds is the fact that, when closed, they are an exact representation of some piece of furniture other than a bed, such as Bureaus, Dressing Cases, Cabinets, Writing Desks, Side-Boards, Secretaries, etc., and there is nothing about their exterior suggestive of a bed, as there is in all other Folding Beds made."[36]

Scientific American magazine in 1896 reported a patent to Thomas Langdon of Los Angeles for a piece of furniture that combined in one item a single bed, a double bed, a sofa, and a detachable crib. The seat and back of the sofa were upholstered and hinged. With the hinged back upright, it was a sofa. With the hinged back down and resting on hinged folding legs, it became a double bed. The single bed and the crib were made by detaching various parts of the frame.[37]

Another *Scientific American* issue of 1898 described a bedstead made of metal that could be adjusted in both length and width by sliding rails. "Among the many advantages claimed for this bed are its structural firmness and its ready adjustability to conform with the accommodations afforded by various rooms."[38] This suggests that the size of rooms and not the sizes of mattresses, sheets, blankets, or people's bodies controlled the dimensions of beds, at least for this inventor.

Folding beds of this kind were a market success, according to the *Decorator and Furnisher* in 1885, because they did away with the need for extra rooms in apartment houses. "A family that wants to economize, can do so by hiring small tenements and using Boyington Folding Beds in their living rooms."[39] They owed their acceptance to the "attractive cabinet work, by which they not only simulate but serve as cabinets, secretaries, etc., in striking contrast with the clumsy and awkward concerns that at one time loomed up and disfigured the entire apartment."[40]

In the early twentieth century, wall beds such as the "Murphy bed" folded up against the wall or into a cupboard, aided by strong springs. A variant, the portal bed, dropped from a closet or dressing room into the living room. Advertisers claimed that such beds made extra bedrooms unnecessary and "practically eliminated the servant problem." They were recommended for any setting in which "convenience receives serious consideration," including apartments and apartment hotels, mansions, and bungalows—that is, commercial as well as private locations.[41]

But technological inventions have cultural reverberations, as a journalist observed in 1908: "A woman likes a folding-bed, she likes a washstand that shuts up into an imitation sewing table; she likes to keep the chinaware out of sight. A man cannot see that; he argues that every one knows that he has a bed and uses a washstand, and why should he be ashamed of them?"[42]

These mechanical, adjustable, fold-up, or hideaway beds provided a welcome solution for those living in constrained spaces. The extraordinary disguising of beds as pianos, fireplaces, or secretaries was no longer

Fig. 38. A fold-up parlor bed. *Decorator and Furnisher* (Oct. 1885):31.

Fig. 39. A screened sleeping porch built off an existing bedroom. C.M. D'Enville, "Sleeping Outdoors for Health," *Country Life in America* 16 (May 1909):45.

deemed necessary by the turn of the century, but most small apartments and many houses today still include a bed concealed inside the living-room couch.[43]

The Bedroom as a Focus of Health

Sleeping is, of course, essential to health, but bedrooms reflected many other health concerns as well. Cleanliness in the bedroom became a cause for mid-nineteenth-century reformers such as Catharine Beecher, who, in her 1841 *Treatise on Domestic Economy,* wrote on keeping the bedroom dust-free. The subsequent decades saw a continuation of similar concerns.

Fresh air in bedrooms was another cause of the period. An 1850 article in *Harper's Monthly* gave mock-serious instructions on how to make an unhealthy bedroom: Cover the fireplace up, so foul air cannot escape during the night; likewise shut the window. Don't use perforated zinc paneling: if you do, foul air will escape. Pull closed the curtains around your bed, an especially effective means of containing the "poison vapor bath" if the curtains are of a thick material. Cover yourself with a featherbed so the skin can't transpire, and wear a tight nightcap.[44]

By the turn of the century, the prevention of tuberculosis had become the most pressing health worry. Experts believed the disease could be combatted by means of fresh air. In order to avoid the "Great White Plague" (tuberculosis), some people even gave up kissing their kin, reported *Scientific American* in 1909. "Fresh air and plenty of it is the best preventive for consumption, the grip, bronchitis, common colds, and pneumonia."[45] The magazine also advised using tissue-paper handkerchiefs.

For the germ-conscious early-twentieth-century sleeper, fresh air for sleeping was critical. It was quite common for people to construct screened sleeping porches just outside their indoor bedrooms, either as a feature of a new house, or as an easily-made improvement to an older one. Patent sleeping bags were marketed to use on the sleeping porch; these left exposed only the head, which was then covered with a hood.

Even with protective clothing, one might get cold going from the warm changing room to the cold outdoor bed. Two tent-like solutions to this problem of both keeping the body warm and sleeping in the outdoor air directed fresh air over just the sleeper's head. One invention, called a window bed, extended the head of the bed out over the window sill at night, with the sleeper pulling an awning over his head to protect himself from rain. When used above the first floor, a *Scientific American* writer complained, this method makes the sleeper feel the possibility of falling and, worse yet, the "bed shows from the outside of the dwelling."[46]

Another method was a fresh-air tent, which was less conspicuous. It fitted around the open window and extended inward over the head of the bed and the head of the sleeper. Some tents had a window on the bedroom side so the sleeper could converse with others in the room, and it could be used in a double bed where only one person wanted the air. This type of tent protected the rest of the body from drafts and colds. If the weather were too cold, one could use a hood with a shoulder cape that left only eyes, nose and mouth exposed to the air.

Although much specialization had gone on inside normal house designs, so that each of the many family members could express her or his individuality in a separate room, in sleeping porches the family came together again. A contributor to *Country Life in America* in 1909 cited an example of a sleeping porch twelve feet square used by two adults in a double bed and three strong, healthy children on three cots, all enjoying a bedroom together. Another 1909 contributor to *Country Life in America* observed that outdoor sleeping and oxygenation for everyone had become immensely popular in the past year. Formerly known only as part of the treatment of tuberculosis, now these practices were viewed as good for everything from colds to insomnia and nervousness. In this magazine, a doctor from Philadelphia speculated that future generations would sleep in the open air and that the architecture of houses would change to make night outdoor life possible.[47]

A model house at moderate cost, designed by Ohio architect C.K. Shilling in 1909, recognized the new taste for outdoor sleeping and living. The dining room and living room each had an outdoor counterpart attached. On the second floor, four chambers had three attached sleeping porches. These had screens in the summer and canvas shields in winter, with floors of reinforced concrete. The outdoor spaces were incorporated under the main house roof, so they did not appear to be porches but rather integral parts of the body of the house.[48]

A Mr. Hoag in the same year described a little wooden house for sleeping out, created as an adjunct to his and his wife's permanent summer cottage. They called it their "sleeping machine" because it produced a lot of sleep. At eight by five feet, it cost twenty dollars. The house had a shed roof and flaps that opened up on its south and west sides, which were lined with "mosquito wire." The sleeper's head faced southwest to catch the prevailing breezes. Here the bedroom had broken entirely free of the house and lived a life of its own in the backyard.[49]

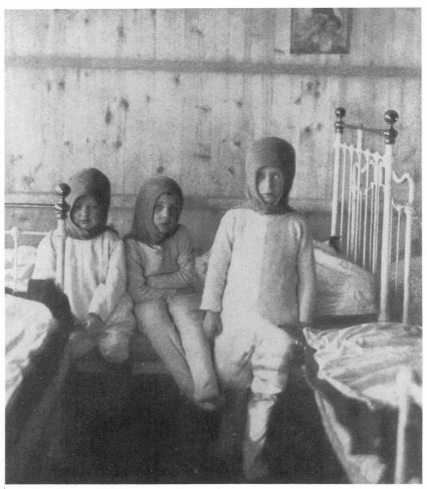

Fig. 40. Three youngsters on the family's shared sleeping porch. From C.M. D'Enville, "Sleeping Outdoors for Health," *Country Life in America* 16 (May 1909):45.

Fig. 41. Mr. Hoag's "Sleeping Machine," a free-standing bedroom in the back yard. C.G. Hoag, "A Sleeping Machine," *Country Life in America* 16 (May 1909):102.

Dreams

Bedrooms may literally break free of houses, but more usually they are places where freedom is situated in dreams and fantasies. A journalist in 1902 recollected how mysterious it was to go to bed in her grandmother's huge, canopied, mahogany bedstead; to a child it was so high, and its interior was cavernous and darkened by curtains. She remembers imagining fairies, gnomes, brownies, and angels as inhabiting the space enclosed by the room-like bed.[50] Hers is a fantasy of pure interiority, where enclosure is so complete that the inhabitant of the bed advances into a world of imagination.

A young man recalled his hall bedroom at the top of a city boarding house as the site for imaginary travel. Although his room was the size of a closet, it had a window which broke through the roof to the sky and looked upon the stars.[51] Dangling ropes controlled a skylight in the young man's hall bedroom. When he opened his skylight and turned out the gaslight, the moon and stars seemed as near as if he were in a meadow in the country. His room was so small and compact that he likened it to a ship's cabin and the muffled city sounds to those of the sea. Covered in snow, the skylight gave a greenish light, and he imagined he was in a cave rather than on a ship, "primitive man in the early wilderness." The temptations of the Hotel St. Regis were nothing to him; he preferred his imaginary voyages in the boarding house's hall bedroom.[52]

In the cavernous four-poster, the little girl was visited by goblins and angels; in the hall bedroom, the young man sailed out toward adventure. Both had their imaginations liberated by their bedrooms.

A journalist speculated in 1902: "Perhaps another generation will see the total disappearance of the bedroom proper, and weary individuals, when night falls, will merely sink to rest on the hygienically-covered floor of their library or sitting-room."[53] This has not happened for most of us yet. But while we still have bedrooms, let us not assume that we know them.

The nature of privacy in a bedroom is less simple than it first appears. While the bedroom often provides a personal haven for an individual occupant, that occupant's essentially public role in family and culture is structured into the bedroom's function, spatial location, and decoration. Any decade's theories about health, cleanliness, sex, and gender are imprinted on that decade's ostensibly private spaces. An exploration of bed and bedroom shows a remarkable wealth of meanings hovering over the innocuous word "bedroom" on the architectural plan.

Notes

1. The bedrooms studied here belong to a middle-class or upper-middle-class, heterosexual, family-oriented society. The research for this article is derived almost entirely from published sources, and its conclusions should be taken as provisional, pending further research. This study of the bedroom is part of a book in progress, which will cover a wider timespan and look at regional, class, and other differences. Variations on this topic by the author can be found in *Perspectives in Vernacular Architecture* 4 (1991) and *Journal of Design History* 3 (1990). I would like to thank Tom Schlereth and Tom Carter for comments on earlier versions of this work; Don O'Leary and Pat Best, my graduate assistants, for research; and the Winterthur Museum, Winterthur, Del., for a Forman Fellowship in 1988–89.

2. The words "bedroom," "chamber," and "sleeping room" will be used interchangeably in my text. In the 17th century, "chamber" indicated a withdrawing room where privacy could be found by the master and mistress of a crowded household; in the second half of the 19th century, "chamber" was the word used to de-

note an important or high status bedroom. "Sleeping room" merely points to one of the bedroom's common functions and does not hint at status.

3. The second floor is called "chamber floor" and has four large sleeping rooms and two small ones. Gervase Wheeler, *Homes for the People in Suburb and Country* (New York: Charles Scribner, 1855; rptd. New York: Arno, 1972), 321–27. A sleeping room for servants is in the wing.

4. Co-operative Building Plan Association, *The Builders' Portfolio* (New York: R.W. Shoppell): house plans with a ground-floor bedroom plus a chamber floor, vol. 1 (1886), pl. 16; house plans for a double house with bedroom-sitting room link, vol. 3 (1887), pls. 202 and 208. For ground-floor bedroom locations, see other houses in Gervase Wheeler, *Homes for the People in Suburb and Country,* 4.

5. *Delineator's Prize $3000 House* (New York: B.W. Dodge and Co., 1909) 12–13.

6. I have developed the concept of "zoning" residential space in Elizabeth Collins Cromley, *Alone Together: A History of New York's Early Apartments* (Ithaca, N.Y.: Cornell Univ. Press, 1990). The late-19th-century clarification of groups of rooms according to function may be a forerunner of urban zoning, which, in the first and second decades of the 20th century, enacted into law the separation of activity zones in American cities.

7. *Aladdin Homes,* Bay City, Mich., catalog for 1918–19 (rptd. Watkins Glen, N.Y.: American Life Foundation, 1985), "The Merrill," 53; "The Kentucky," 39.

8. Matthew Browne, "On Going to Bed," *Every Saturday* 13 (Aug. 1872):250–51.

9. William Alcott, *Physiology of Marriage* (Boston: John P. Jewett, 1859), 176.

10. William Leach, *True Love and Perfect Union* (Middletown, Conn.: Wesleyan Univ. Press, 1989), 81–98, traces several sex-reform arguments.

11. B.W. Richardson, "Health at Home," pt. 2, *Appleton's Journal,* n.s. 8 (1880):521–26, 524.

12. Dorothy Raley, ed., *A Century of Progress Homes and Furnishings* (Chicago: M.A. Ring, 1934).

13. B.W. Richardson, "Health at Home," 525. The nursery is a variant of the children's room, also not gendered in its decoration or its inhabitants. According to Richardson, the nursery should be the sunniest room in the house, since babies need sunshine to grow; every other room should go without sunshine in favor of this one. William A. Alcott, *The Young Mother* (Boston: George W. Light, 1838), 268, 273.

14. Sally McMurry, *Farmhouses and Families* (New York: Oxford Univ. Press, 1987), 178–85.

15. Martha Cutler, "Girls' Rooms," *Harper's Bazar* 40 (Oct. 1906):935–40.

16. See the section on servants' rooms in Catharine Beecher and Harriet Beecher Stowe, *The American Woman's Home* (New York: J.B. Ford and Co., 1869), 370ff. Servants often inherited cast-off furniture from the rest of the house, but Beecher

and others recommended buying a new metal bed for the servant because it was easiest to keep clean and free of bedbugs. A "truckle" or "trundle" bed is on wheels and rolls under a higher bed in the same room.

17. Frank R. Stockton and Marian Stockton, "The Home: Where it Should Be and What to Put in It," in C.D. Warner et al., *The American Home Book with Directions and Suggestions for Cooking, Dress, . . . House Furnishing, . . . Etc.* (New York: Putnam's Sons, 1872), 84–85. See also Candace Wheeler, *Principles of Home Decoration* (New York: Doubleday, Page and Co., 1903), 45: "Good surroundings are potent civilizers, and a house-servant whose room is well and carefully furnished feels an added value in herself, which makes her treat herself respectfully in the care of her room."

18. *The Social Mirror,* with an introduction by Rose Cleveland (St. Louis, Mo., 1888), 341–43.

19. Abbot McClure and Harold Eberlein, "The Hospitable Guest Room" *House and Garden* 23 (Mar. 1913):185–87. See also Mary Taylor-Ross, "Care of the Guest Chamber," *House Beautiful* 26 (Sept. 1909): 95; she advises a saucer of lime, rather than the burning of incense, to keep the air of a guest room fresh.

20. "Friendly Study-Guest Room," *Good Housekeeping* 131 (Nov. 1950):88, illustrated a pine-paneled room that would be comfortable "whether a foursome sits down to a game of Canasta or a guest arrives for the weekend."

21. Frank R. Stockton and Marian Stockton, "The Home," 52–53.

22. Ella R. Church, "How to Furnish a House," *Appleton's Journal* n.s. 2 (Feb. 1877):157–62, 161–62.

23. Martha A. Cutler, "Hygienic Bedrooms," *Harper's Bazar* 41 (Jan. 1907):78–82, 80–81.

24. "The Bedroom and Its Individuality," *The Craftsman* 9 (Feb. 1906):694–704, 595–96.

25. Church, "How to Furnish a House," 160.

26. Eugene Gardner, *The House that Jill Built* (New York: Fords, Howard and Hulbert, 1882):246–47.

27. C.B. Walker, "Railroad Tie Furniture to Furnish a Boy's Den," *Women's Home Companion* 32 (Oct. 1905):48; Amelia Leavitt Hill, "The Boy's Room," *Country Life in America* 49 (Feb. 1926):72–76; Marlin Butts, "Our Boy's Room," *American Home* 9 (Mar. 1933):189; Louise Shrimpton, "Furnishing the Boy's Own Room," *Woman's Home Companion* 39 (May 1912): 32; Verna Cook Salomonsky, "The Boy's Own Room," *House Beautiful* 55 (May 1924):531.

28. Nina Tachau, "The Girl's Room," *House Beautiful* 38 (June 1915):10–12; Agnes Rowe Fairman, "The Young Girl's Room," *Good Housekeeping* 65 (Dec. 1917):50–51; Louise Shrimpton, "Furnishing the Girl's Own Room," *Woman's Home Companion* 39 (May 1912):33.

29. Candace Wheeler, *Principles of Home Decoration,* 61–62.

30. Tekla Grenfell, "Renting Rooms to Young Men: How I Have Successfully Done it for Years," *Ladies' Home Journal* 25 (Sept. 1908):24.

31. Grenfell, "Renting Rooms to Young Men," 24.

32. M. MacLean Helliwell, ed., "Woman's Sphere," *Canadian Magazine* 20 (1902–1903):281–83, 281.

33. Helliwell, "Woman's Sphere," 282–83.

34. D.N.B. Sturgis, "American Residences of Today," pt. 4, "The Bedroom," *Architectural Record* 16 (Oct. 1904): 372–83, 382; see also Nancy Walburn, "For the Girl Who Lives in One Room," *House Beautiful* 41 (Jan. 1917):98, 104–05.

35. *Decorator and Furnisher* (New York) 18 (Apr. 1891): 19. The 18th century provided precedents for the hidden bed in the form of fold-up beds and truckle or trundle beds.

36. L.C. Boyington, *Folding Beds,* 1884 (trade catalog in collection of Winterthur Museum) 2, 3, 7.

37. "A Combined Bed and Sofa," *Scientific American* 74 (20 June 1896):390.

38. "A New Extension Bed," *Scientific American* (5 Oct. 1898).

39. L.C. Boyington, *Automatic "Chiffonier" Folding Beds,* 1885 (trade catalog in collection of Winterthur Museum), 10–11, 15.

40. *Decorator and Furnisher* 6, no. 3 (June 1885):81.

41. *VanDame Portal Wall Bed,* 1918, pamphlet in the collection of the New York Public Library, 2; "How Many Rooms Has This House?", advertisement of the Murphy Door Bed Co., *House Beautiful* 53 (Apr. 1923):418.

42. Grenfell, "Renting Rooms to Young Men," 24.

43. For an earlier version of the living-room bed, see "A Pullman for the Well Appointed Living Room," advertisement of the Pullman Couch Co., Chicago, in *House Beautiful* 55 (April 1924):449.

44. Harriet Martineau, "How to Make Home Unhealthy," *Harper's New Monthly Magazine* 1 (June–Nov. 1850):618–19.

45. Katherine Louise Smith, "Indoor Bed Tents," *Scientific American,* n.s. 101 (Dec. 1909): 423.

46. Ibid., 416.

47. C.M. D'Enville, "Sleeping Outdoors for Health: Outdoor Sleeping for the Well Man," *Country Life in America* 16 (May 1909): 43–46.

48. C.K. Shilling, "A Country Home with Outdoor Sleeping, Living, and Dining Rooms," *Country Life in America* 16 (May 1909): 71–72.

49. C.G. Hoag, "Sleeping Outdoors for Health," pt. 4, "A Sleeping Machine," *Country Life in America* 16 (May 1909):102.

50. Helliwell, "Woman's Sphere," 281.

51. "The Contributors' Club: Cave-Dwellers, or the Hall Bedroom," *Atlantic Monthly* 96 (July–Dec. 1905):574–75, 574.

52. Ibid., 575.

53. Helliwell, "Woman's Sphere," 283.

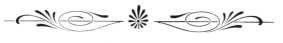

PART II

HOME LIFE

CHAPTER SIX

"The Family That Plays Together Stays Together": Family Pastimes and Indoor Amusements, 1890–1930

Donna R. Braden

In 1880, James A. Garfield, soon to be president of the United States, commented in an address to a Chautauqua assembly, "We may divide the whole struggle of the human race into two chapters: first the fight to get leisure; and then the second fight of civilization—what shall we do with our leisure when we get it."[1] For centuries, leisure had been identified primarily with a "leisured" class, a group free of any obligation to work. However, as urbanization and industrialization altered the fabric of society during the nineteenth century, a growing number of Americans were able to enjoy a certain amount of leisure in their daily lives.

By the 1890s, the loss of job satisfaction being experienced by employees of the new large corporations and bureaucracies was eroding the old work ethic, as the nation's economy shifted from one that was organized around scarcity and production to one that was based on surplus and consumption. Progressive-era social reformers passionately expounded the need for play, while government, church, and school programs were being reoriented toward a new acceptance of leisure as an antidote to the "violent, all-consuming busyness" of Americans.[2] Even conservative members of the middle class, who had long objected to the idleness and frivolity they connected with the term leisure, were beginning to support the notion that relaxation was important; increasingly they looked for personal expression and fulfillment in leisure activities rather than in work.[3]

Leisure and entertainment choices multiplied during the late nineteenth and early twentieth centuries, especially for those living in urban areas.[4] Increased discretionary time, rising income levels, and the growing popularity of the automobile all helped to increase the number of leisure activities and encouraged their support by the American public.[5] By the early twentieth century, public censure of many existing forms of entertainment, such as spectator sports and the theatre, had relaxed. At the same time, new diversions—for example, listening to ragtime music; engaging in faster, more intimate forms of dancing; going to amusement parks and to the movies; and participating in more active sports such as bicycling and tennis—attracted an ever-larger core of middle-class approval.

The home, of course, also became an important focus for the pursuit of leisure activities.[6] During the late nineteenth century, technological developments and mass production tremendously expanded the number and widened the scope of home amusements. Commercialized industries sprang up in connection with a broad range of home leisure pursuits, including such items as toys, games, musical instruments, sheet music, books, and magazines. The success of these industries ultimately led to a greater awareness and acceptance of their products, as well as to their standardization on a national basis.

Between 1890 and 1930, both the increased acceptance of leisure activities and their growing connection with America's consumer culture led to a proliferation of home amusements and family-oriented pastimes. Commenting on this, Frank De Puy wrote in his *New Century Home Book* of 1900:

In the best and happiest homes games and pastimes have their place. There can be no doubt that men and women are helped to happier and better lives by home amusements. The children who are permitted and encouraged to enjoy healthful and innocent games at home cling closer to their homes. They are not tempted to go elsewhere for the amusement for which Nature has given them the desire.[7]

The changing role of the home and the changing relationships between family members also had an impact on the nature of home amusements at this time. In the preindustrial home, work and amusements often had been interrelated. But, while the home had frequently served as the focus for extended social visits and for holiday and family celebrations, children were the primary participants in home pastimes. Parents and teachers alike pressed upon children the importance of engaging in amusements that were morally uplifting or instructional rather than simply entertaining.

As home and workplace became separated in America's increasingly urban industrial society, the daily lives and activities of individual family

Fig. 42. Boys playing "Cowboys and Indians" in an urban yard, ca. 1900. Courtesy of Henry Ford Museum & Greenfield Village, Dearborn, Mich.

members became more segmented. The strict conventions of Victorian so-ciety dictated appropriate home leisure pursuits for men, women, and chil-dren. These activities tended to be quite structured, especially those which, like calling, were engaged in exclusively by women. These also were often geared toward social advancement and continued overwhelmingly to em-phasize educational or spiritual values over simple enjoyment.

During the early twentieth century, even as home leisure pursuits became less formal and more often emphasized fun rather than edification, individ-ual family members still tended to go their separate ways. During this period, a distinct youth subculture emerged, and adolescents preferred spending more time in the company of their peers rather than at home with members of their families.[8] Increased mobility, one of the major forces in expanding leisure choices, ironically also contributed to the weakening of family ties by taking family members away from the home.

As a result of these factors, throughout the years between 1890 and 1930, home amusements and family pastimes were looked upon as potential means of reuniting the segmented family. For example, De Puy wrote in 1900:

> Parents . . . are better for joining in their children's games and pastimes. It lightens their cares; it helps to keep their brains clear for the larger duties of life; it aids in warding off physical and mental ills; it tends to keep them young in their old age. Above all, participation in your children's sports keeps you in that close and intimate touch with their lives, their thoughts, and their aspirations in which the truest family relations are found.[9]

And, in a similar statement three decades later, Mabel Travis Wood, in her book *Family Fun* (1931), advised adults that in play hours they "have a matchless chance to meet youth on common ground—not as dictators and disciplinarians, but as comrades and team-mates."[10] Whether the idea of family unity through home amusements was an attainable goal or an idealistic pipe dream, writers and advertisers of the period continually reinforced the notion that "the family that plays together stays together."[11] A closer look at specific games and family pastimes can reveal much about their role in the home during this period.

Parlor Games

Through the nineteenth century, family members and friends had often played parlor games at parties and family gatherings. Children, young people, and occasionally older adults participated in various memory games, games of charades, catching games such as blind man's buff and fox and geese, and games dictating that the loser pay a "forfeit" or penalty.

As parties became more formal and ritualistic during the latter decades of the nineteenth century, their organizers increasingly looked to the playing of games as a way of providing a purpose, a distinction, a play to what might otherwise turn into a dull evening. *Hill's Manual of Social and Business Forms* (1880) describes a typical nightmarish scenario that probably haunted the imaginations of many a nervous party planner at the time:

> The topics of conversation have been exhausted at the party; you have no musicians in the company, possibly, or if you have music, it no longer entertains. Under the circumstances, you bethink yourself of some light, pleasant indoor game that nearly all can play.[12]

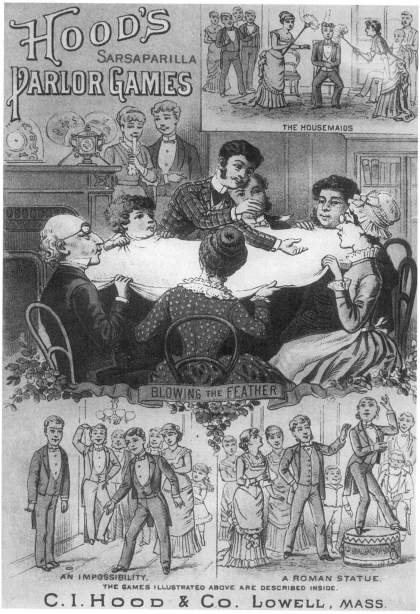

Fig. 43. Illustration of four parlor games. Back cover of a trade booklet for Hood's Sarsaparilla, ca. 1880. Courtesy of Henry Ford Museum & Greenfield Village, Dearborn, Mich.

Fig. 44. Illustration depicting the staging of a *tableau vivant* entitled "The Parlor Tableau of Blue Beard." *Frank Leslie's Illustrated Almanac,* 1875, p. 60. Courtesy of Henry Ford Museum & Greenfield Village, Dearborn, Mich.

During the last quarter of the nineteenth century, fortune telling, conjuring (doing magic tricks), and staging theatricals and *tableaux vivants* (in which a number of people grouped themselves to imitate a famous statue, painting, or story, while onlookers guessed what they were depicting) became particularly popular parlor entertainments. Many of these *tableaux* had moralistic themes, making them not only entertaining but supposedly edifying as well.[13]

A few more unusual party games, including soap-bubble blowing and "donkey party" (now called "pin-the-tail-on-the-donkey") became especially fashionable for adults during the 1890s. These soon would become obsolete or be relegated to children's parties.

During the second and third decades of the twentieth century, home entertaining became less formal than in previous decades, and playing games was considered more crucial than ever in keeping these occasions interesting and fun. Gloria Goddard wrote in *Party Games for Grown-Ups* (1927), "It does not matter whether the group be a dinner party, a dance or merely a general get-together sort of evening, a game or two will be the salvation of the affair."[14] Often, these games were now played in family living rooms, which were rapidly supplanting the earlier, more formal parlors as social centers of the home.

Board and Table Games

During the late nineteenth century, improvements in printing and paper manufacture, along with the growing interest in home amusements, resulted in a tremendous increase in the number of board, card, and other table games. Mary Elizabeth Wilson Sherwood wrote in her book *Home Amusements* (1881):

> That is a poorly-furnished parlor, think some people, which has not a chess-table in one corner, a whist-table in the middle, and a little solitaire-table at the other end near the fire, for grandma. People who are fond of games stock their table drawers with cribbage boards and backgammon, cards of every variety, bezique counters and packs, and the red and white champions of the hard-fought battlefield of chess.[15]

While some board games, such as chess, checkers, and backgammon, had been around for decades, the board-game industry really took off during the 1890s, when hundreds of thousands of games were manufactured and nationally distributed every year. Game manufacturers, including three major competitors (Milton Bradley, established in 1860; Selchow & Righter, in 1867; and Parker Brothers, in 1883), competed fiercely by continually introducing new games. Games that emphasized moral instruction were superceded by ones centered around such subjects as industry (for example, the Game of Banking, introduced in 1883), transportation, sports, and current events. The winners of these new games were no longer the most pious players who had accumulated the greatest joy in the next world, but they were more often the shrewdest players who had accumulated the most money.

During the 1920s, the popularity of certain table games, particularly bridge and mahjongg, reached fad proportions and conveniently lent themselves to themes around which entire parties could be organized.

Jigsaw puzzles, which had their origin during the nineteenth century, became especially popular during the Depression of the 1930s, as an inexpensive evening pastime for adults and children. Also during this decade (1935, to be exact), Monopoly, the largest-selling board game in history, was invented.

Sporting Pastimes

Many sporting pastimes which had been popularized by American socialites at exclusive clubs and resorts during the post–Civil War years became fashionable for both men and women of the middle class to play in their backyards. Capitalizing on the popularity of pastimes such as archery, croquet, and lawn tennis, manufacturers introduced a variety of rather sedate indoor games, such as parlor archery and table croquet, that adapted the action of their outdoor counterparts.

By the 1890s, the new interest in strenuous outdoor sports and the organization of physical education programs in schools brought a stronger emphasis on healthfulness and the value of exercise to home amusements. Earlier games were seen in a new light, as the comments of Frank De Puy, in his *New Century Home Book* (1900), attest;

> [O]utdoor games are preferable to indoor sports for their wider exercise in fresher air, but these are . . . not to be thought of in the long evenings of winter. . . . The familiar games of blind man's buff, bean bags, battledoor and shuttlecock, parlor ring toss, grace hoops, and parlor tenpins are excellent for children and grown folk who have had little exercise. They give mind and body mild but stimulating and healthful activity.[16]

Newer games, such as ping-pong, adapted for indoor play from lawn tennis, also represented a trend toward more active home amusements. The first official home version of this game (to be played on the dining-room table) was produced in 1902 by Parker Brothers, but versions of it had been played since its introduction to the public at the 1893 Chicago Columbian Exposition. The continuing popularity of Ping-Pong as a family pastime

THE GAME OF THE SEASON!
Horsman's Parlor Archery.

Fig. 45. Advertisement for an indoor adaptation of an outdoor sport, Horsman's Parlor Archery. *American Agriculturist,* 1878, p. 436. Courtesy of Henry Ford Museum & Greenfield Village, Dearborn, Mich.

and party game through the twentieth century points to Americans' interest in playing faster, more exciting, and more competitive home games.

Visual Entertainment

During the last few decades of the nineteenth century, various mechanical devices provided visual entertainment for home amusement. The zoetrope or Wheel of Life, patented in 1867 and manufactured by Milton Bradley, drew on earlier devices that created a semblance of motion when they were revolved. The magic lantern was another popular device for home use during this time. Adapted from its original function as a lecture aid, this contrivance beamed a picture onto a screen from transparent slides.

The hand-held stereoscope displayed two photographs taken at slightly different angles; viewing these simultaneously produced a three-dimensional effect. By the first decade of the twentieth century, millions of "stereo cards," or stereographs, were being produced inexpensively and sold for home entertainment.[17] Usually sold in sets, many of these cards depicted distant and exotic places, allowing families to take vicarious trips within the safe confines of their homes.

The development of cameras for still and moving pictures greatly enhanced the possibilities of visual entertainment in the home. While a number of hand-held cameras had been introduced to the American public by the 1880s, most had proved too cumbersome and complicated for the average user. The comparative ease of handling Kodak cameras, first introduced in 1888, helped considerably to increase the ranks of amateur photographers. Subsequent cameras introduced by Kodak and other companies during the 1890s and early in the twentieth century secured the popularity of snapshot photography among hobbyists and occasional users, while creating and looking at snapshot albums became fashionable family pastimes. During the 1920s and 1930s, home moving-picture projectors were adapted from commercial use, and taking and watching movies became the newly favored form of visual entertainment in the home.

Home Music

Music had long been an important and popular home amusement, whether it involved singing, playing an instrument, listening to phonograph records, or tuning in to a radio concert. Mary Elizabeth Wilson Sher-

Fig. 46. Humorous illustration of girl practicing piano. *Our Boys & Girls,* Oct. 1871, between pp. 692 and 693. Courtesy of Henry Ford Museum & Greenfield Village, Dearborn, Mich.

wood addressed the "transcendent powers" of home music in her *Home Amusements* (1881): "The family circle which has learned three or four instruments, the brothers who can sing, are to be envied. They can never suffer from a dull evening."[18] However, she added, "The only deep shadow to the musical picture is the necessity of practicing, which is *not* a Home Amusement; it is a home torture. If only a person could learn to play or sing without those dreadful first noises and those hideous shrieks!"[19]

By the 1890s, mass production had brought pianos within the reach of large numbers of middle-class families. Even before this time, less expensive upright pianos were replacing the bulkier square pianos of an earlier era. As a mounting tide of printed music, including dozens of simple, easy-to-follow "parlor songs," became available to the public, singing to piano accompaniment became a favored form of home entertainment.

Mass-production methods also were applied to the manufacture of smaller, less expensive instruments such as dulcimers, autoharps, and other instruments previously associated with specific types of ethnic and regional music.

Mechanical music devices presented an easy way for unskilled people to enjoy music at home. Cylinder-operated music boxes imported during the second half of the nineteenth century were among the earliest mechanical instruments to provide home entertainment. But the less expensive and operationally simpler disc music boxes, mass-produced in the United States from the 1890s until around the 1920s, enjoyed an even wider popularity.

Player pianos, activated by foot pedals or electricity and using perforated paper music rolls, also experienced enormous success during these decades. As Cleveland, Ohio, manufacturer J.T. Wamelink proclaimed in an advertisement, the performer on one of these pianos could achieve "Perfection without Practice." Because they reduced playing to a mechanical process, these instruments contributed greatly to the demise of piano-playing as a symbol of accomplishment, particularly for females, in the home.

The phonograph not only replaced most other forms of home music, but also made more music accessible to a larger group of people than ever before. During the 1890s, home phonographs using wax cylinders were making local and national performers known to a large home audience. By about 1910, however, easy-to-operate disc phonographs had become the standard for home entertainment. Disc records, which had the technical capability to record more complex dance music than the cylinders had, began to determine the course of popular music. Tunes were adapted to fit the three-minute playing time of the new records, and newly released disc recordings could rapidly make a song successful or condemn it to failure. Intricate dance music, ragtime, and Latin rhythms that were difficult to play on the piano could now be recorded by the finest musicians and enjoyed on home phonographs.

During the second decade of the twentieth century, phonograph and record sales mushroomed, as family members enjoyed being able to hear their favorite music when they wanted and as often as they wanted, right in their own homes. In 1919, some two hundred phonograph companies were producing about two million phonographs a year. Throughout the 1920s, the recording industry continued to expand in scope to meet specialized interests, while also helping to nationalize regional music. At the same time, phonographs became more substantial, often becoming requisite pieces of furniture in the family living room.

Record and phonograph sales finally plummeted in the early 1930s, when the comparatively free entertainment provided by radio took over. Sales did pick up again in the mid-1930s, however, as higher-quality records and combination radio-phonographs were introduced on the market.

Fig. 47. Advertisement for the Victor Talking Machine, a disc phonograph player. *Saturday Evening Post,* 24 Sept. 1904, back cover. Courtesy of Henry Ford Museum & Greenfield Village, Dearborn, Mich.

The Radio

Experiments with the wireless transmission of sound in the late nineteenth and early twentieth centuries had led to a growing realization of radio's vast potential to provide public entertainment. By 1920, experimental stations broadcasting news, music, and market reports encouraged hobbyists by the thousands to construct or purchase receiving sets. In an article published in the *American Review of Reviews* in January 1923 and entitled " 'Listening In,' Our New National Pastime," one observer noted that "the rapidity with which the thing has spread has possibly not been equalled in all the centuries of human progress."[20]

By 1924, families in about five million American homes owned radio receivers, the primary purpose being entertainment. Through the 1920s and into the 1930s, radio presented a varied offering of music, drama, and comedy. Programs generally were geared toward special audiences at different times of the day. For example, women's shows, especially "soap operas," and children's programs were scheduled during the daytime, while programs for general family listening dominated the evening hours.

During the Depression, "listening in" became a favorite inexpensive home amusement. By providing entertainment to be enjoyed in the comfort of the family living room, radios encouraged family togetherness at a time when Americans were becoming highly mobile. Commentators of the period, however, admitted that the reality of "listening in" often entailed more tension than harmony in families, as family members were likely to disagree on what program to listen to and when to listen to it. Reflecting this, the authors of "The Family and Its Leisure," an article in *Parents' Magazine* in April 1932, advised readers that "frequent compromise is necessary if all the members of the family are to find pleasure in the radio."[21]

Perhaps writers by the 1930s were becoming more perceptive about the difficulties and realities of family togetherness through home amusements. In describing her plan for a family playroom—a precursor to the present-day recreation room—Helen Sprackling wrote in *Parents' Magazine* in October 1932:[22]

[T]he ideal home must be all things to all members of its family. In this complex world of ours where ideals are difficult to achieve and maintain, and space so often costly, the success of the average home lies in the balanced adjustment of space and schedule to the various family needs.[23]

Fig. 48. Box cover for the Radio Game, ca. 1925. Courtesy of Henry Ford Museum & Greenfield Village, Dearborn, Mich.

Still she expressed the usual hope for family unity:

> Life is, after all, as many of us are learning these days, what we make it. Suppose we *are* a little worried. That is no excuse for not playing. Matching wits against the younger generation in a good stiff game of checkers or putting one over on them in ping-pong helps to clear the mind for tomorrow's struggles and aids digestion. It brings its greatest reward in a finer, closer understanding between children and parents. It's a serious matter, this play business; it deserves, whenever possible, a room dedicated to the sole purpose of family fun.[24]

Although these words were geared toward a Depression-weary audience, their message represents a synthesis of thought that had evolved along with home amusements themselves since the 1890s. These ideas, and the activities connected with them, laid the foundation for the family pastimes we engage in today, as well as for the way our culture perceives them. Indeed, the "play" business mentioned by Sprackling has continued to be pondered with the utmost seriousness, while editorials, magazine advertisements, and television commercials remind us daily that the dream of family unity is still a very lively topic for debate.

Notes

1. Jesse Lyman Hurlbut, *The Story of Chautauqua* (New York, G.P. Putnam's Sons, 1921), 184.

2. Daniel T. Rodgers, *The Work Ethic in Industrial America, 1850–1920* (Chicago: Univ. of Chicago Press, 1929), 102.

3. The classic work by Foster Rhea Dulles, *A History of Recreation: America Learns to Play,* 2d ed. (New York: Appleton-Century-Crofts, 1965), presents a concise historical overview of leisure developments in America. Donna R. Braden, *Leisure and Entertainment in America* (Dearborn, Mich.: Henry Ford Museum & Greenfield Village, 1988), presents a museum perspective on the subject. The important study by Robert S. Lynd and Helen Merrell Lynd, *Middletown: A Study in American Culture* (New York: Harcourt, Brace, 1929), provides insightful period documentation on leisure activities within one community during the late 19th and early 20th centuries. For some useful books on the growth of America's consumer society during these decades, see Stuart Ewen, *Channels of Desire: Mass Images and the Shaping of American Consciousness* (New York: McGraw-Hill, 1982); Neil Harris, "The Drama of Consumer Desire," in *Yankee Enterprise: The Rise of the American System of Manufactures,* ed. Otto Mayr and Robert C. Post (Washington, D.C.: Smithsonian Institution Press, 1981); and Daniel Horowitz, *The Morality of Spending: Attitudes Toward the Consumer Society in America, 1875–1940* (Baltimore: Johns Hopkins Univ. Press, 1985).

4. Dale A. Somers, "The Leisure Revolution: Recreation in the American City, 1820–1920," *Journal of Popular Culture* 5, no. 1 (1971):125–47, provides further insight on this subject.

5. Between 1890 and 1930, the average annual earnings for workers in the manufacturing sector increased from $439 to $1,488, while the average hours in their work week decreased from 60 to about 44.

6. For more detailed analysis on the subject of home amusements for women and children, see Harvey Green, *The Light of the Home: An Intimate View of the Lives of Women in Victorian America* (New York: Pantheon, 1983); Bernard Mergen, *Play and Playthings: A Reference Guide* (Westport, Conn.: Greenwood, 1982); and Mary Lynn Stevens Heininger, "Children, Childhood, and Change in America, 1820–1920," in *A Century of Childhood, 1820–1920* (Rochester, N.Y.: Strong Museum, 1984).

7. Frank A. De Puy, *The New Century Home Book* (New York: Eaton & Mains, 1900), 222.

8. For more information on this subject, see ch. 6, "The Rise of the Companionate Family, 1900–1930," in Steven Mintz and Susan Kellogg, *Domestic Revolutions: A Social History of American Family Life* (New York: Free Press, 1988). This trend is also discussed in the Lynds' study, *Middletown*.

9. De Puy, *New Century Home Book* 223.

10. *Family Fun: Games and Good Times for Children and Parents*, introduction by Mabel Travis Wood (New York: Parents' Magazine Press, 1931), xii.

11. For example, Wood advised readers that "families who have adopted regular home play evenings will assure you that 'the family that plays together, stays together.'" Ibid., 49.

12. Thomas E. Hill, *Hill's Manual of Social and Business Forms: A Guide to Correct Writing* (Chicago: Moses Warren, 1880), 150.

13. For example, the book *Entertainments for Home, Church, and School* (New York: Christian Herald, 1910) suggested the following tableaux: "dignity and impudence" "faith," "hope," and "charity."

14. Gloria Goddard, *Party Games for Grown-Ups*, Little Blue Book No. 1239 (Girard, Kansas: Haldeman-Julius Publications, 1927), 4.

15. Mary Elizabeth Wilson Sherwood, *Home Amusements* (New York: D. Appleton, 1881), 135.

16. De Puy, *New Century Home Book*, 224–25.

17. In 1901, leading stereograph manufacturers Underwood & Underwood were producing close to 25,000 stereo cards per day, totaling more than 7 million cards produced that year.

18. Sherwood, *Home Amusements*, 136.

19. Ibid., 137.

20. "'Listening In,' Our New National Pastime," *American Review of Reviews* 69 (Jan. 1923):52.

21. Benjamin C. Gruenberg and Sidonie Matsner Gruenberg, "The Family and Its Leisure," *Parents' Magazine* 7 (April 1932):24.

22. During the early 20th century, the playroom was generally associated with children and specific children's activities in the home. As the term "recreation" became more connected with adult and family leisure activities, esp. during the Depression, the term "recreation room" came to denote an informal multipurpose room in which all members of the family could entertain and partake of leisure activities. Recreation rooms in basements became esp. popular after World War II.

23. Helen Sprackling, "A Family Playroom," *Parents' Magazine* 7 (Oct. 1932):22.

24. Ibid., 51.

CHAPTER SEVEN

Parlor Piety: The Home as Sacred Space in Protestant America

Colleen McDannell

In 1869 Catharine Beecher and her sister Harriet Beecher Stowe published their drawings of a "Christian Home." As the famous author of *Uncle Tom's Cabin,* Harriet Beecher Stowe commanded the attention of many nineteenth-century Americans. The practical Beecher sisters, noted for their promotion of the efficient use of domestic space, showed no reluctance in discussing the designs of a house which would combine the functions of a church, a school, and a home. They explained in *The American Woman's Home: Or, the Principles of Domestic Science* that "a small church, a school-house, and a comfortable family dwelling may be all united in one building."[1] The main room of the house could be transformed into the nave of a church by a movable screen, the pulpit could be stored in the kitchen, and the chimney finished off outside as a steeple. After giving the architectural details of designing such a structure, Beecher and Stowe concluded that "the cost of such a building where lumber is $50 a hundred and labor $3 a day, would not much exceed $1200." All Americans should be able to build a Christian home.

The church house designed by the famous Beecher sisters serves as a quintessential example of how the creators of Victorian American culture—ministers, reformers, novelists, and architects—saw the home as a vehicle for the promotion of values. Like the church, the home as a physical space and a kinship structure was sacred. During the second half of the nineteenth century, mainstream Protestant Americans sought to make their domestic space holy by elaborating an ideology which placed the home, and not the church, at the center of the creation of religious and patriotic values. By adapting Gothic Revival architecture for house construction, they emphasized the connection between the design of homes and the design of churches. Constructing and displaying religious artifacts created a proper Christian environment in the household. Finally, the clerical promotion of family worship asserted the ability of the members of the family to aid each other in the mission of salvation. While it is impossible to know just how many families *really* participated in this domestic Protestantism, we have ample evidence in the existing material culture and advice literature that parlor piety made up a critical element of nineteenth-century American religious life.

By the beginning of the twentieth century, however, social and cultural changes in America weakened the common assumption of the sacred character of the home. Both secular and religious forces attacked the Victorian attitude that private morality created public virtue. Newly created professional social workers and sociologists discussed the declining birth rate, the rising number of divorces, and the disgusting conditions of urban slums. Theologians and social reformers urged Americans to look beyond their homes and view the whole world as needy of care and concern. At the same time, architects and interior designers stripped the home of what they saw as decorative clutter. Wax crosses, needlepoint biblical scenes, and elaborate family Bibles were no longer in fashion. By the 1930s domestic religion no longer functioned as a unifying force which transcended Protestant denominational differences. Home Bible reading, placing pious sayings in the living room, and believing in the saving forces of domesticity marked one as a conservative Protestant who was critical of modern perspectives on Christianity.

The Victorian Home as Church

Although Americans of the seventeenth and eighteenth centuries upheld the importance of the family as an educational, economic, and religious center, it was not until the mid-nineteenth century and the evolution of a strong middle-class evangelical Protestantism that the home achieved its sacred character. During the nineteenth century, both ministerial and secular writers increasingly argued that all good Christians could achieve heavenly happiness. Since salvation could be accomplished by leading a good life, the creation of God-fearing Christians became more and more important. Theologian Horace Bushnell, in his classic work on Christian nurture, stated that salvation need not be signaled by a radical, emotional conversion experience but could be achieved slowly, over the individual's lifetime. "The house, having a domestic Spirit," Bushnell noted in 1847, "should become the church of childhood, the table and hearth a holy rite, and life an element of saving power."[2] More than ever before, the home became the focal point of salvation.

During the nineteenth century, good family life was seen as the means by which the nation and its religion were maintained. Americans believed the home to be the nursery of both patriotism and piety. Home life taught the mutual dependence and reciprocal responsibility of each citizen. By connecting the individual to the community at large, the family instilled notions of morality, order, stability, education, purity, refinement, and discipline. Although the church also played an important role in creating good Christians, the Victorian preoccupation with the family saw home life as the more crucial purveyor of ethics and piety.

It was not merely life in a family which made good Christians—a notion as old as Martin Luther—but Victorian writers emphasized that the *house itself* shaped the character of its inhabitants. Beginning with British art critic John Ruskin, Victorians came to believe that right mental states and moral feelings could be produced by good architecture. Architecture was not morally neutral, it actively created either a productive or a destructive society. Americans eagerly embraced the ideas that good architecture produced good people and that good people produced good architecture. "There is so intimate a connection between taste and morals, aesthetics and Christianity," architect William Ranlett wrote, "that they, in each instance, mutually modify each other."[3] Physical space, as well as positive kinship relations, shaped the moral outlook of Americans. Housing design, rather than being merely a matter of taste, provided the means by which good family life could be accomplished.

By the mid-nineteenth century, housing builders began to see themselves as members of a profession whose goal it was to raise the level of refinement and morality of American society. William Ranlett, in his work *The Architect* (1847), perceived his position as one of a public benefactor "who corrects a vicious or improper development of public taste."[4] Many of these housing reformers divided American society into the virtuous, who possessed proper taste and sensibilities, and those who lacked aesthetic and moral character. Phrenologist Orson Fowler, who designed a remarkable octagonal house, argued that only the lowest types of people built primitive homes. "The slack, low-minded and 'shiftless' aspire only to some hut or hovel, dug out of a bank just to ward off the major part of the storm and cold," he wrote in 1853.[5] Those with lofty and high-toned minds showed their moral quality through the homes they built. Builders Cleaveland and Backus echoed this view: "Certainly, no race, or community, or family or individual, while dwelling contentedly in filth and discomfort, can be called respectable, or deemed happy."[6] Not only did good architecture raise the character of the people, but bad architecture encouraged sinfulness. The city, the site of much of that which the housing reformers condemned, became a symbol of what was wrong with America.

While housing reformers promoted many different styles of architectural design, one style especially summarized the close relationship between space and religious sentiment. From 1840 to 1870, Gothic Revival designs enlivened American ecclesiastical, commercial, and domestic architecture. From Richard Upjohn's Trinity Church in New York to the mortuary chapels at Laurel Hill Cemetery in Philadelphia and the cottages of Colorado mining towns, Gothic Revival captured the imagination of the American people. Drawing its impetus from European Romanticism, Gothic Revival emphasized the vertical over the horizontal, exploited medieval designs, and created a playful and dramatic interior space. Even after the preference for this style of domestic architecture subsided, colleges adopted it for library buildings and cities for governmental offices. Gothic Revival buildings and decorative arts evoked both tradition and spiritual uplift in a rapidly changing nineteenth-century society.

In 1846, Henry Bowen, cofounder and later owner of the influential Congregational journal *The Independent,* had a Gothic-style home built in Woodstock, Connecticut. Called "Roseland," the house had windows with wooden tracery, board-and-batten woodwork, and steeply pointed gable roofs, all of which gave the house a medieval air. A cloverleaf-cross motif on the bargeboards imitated those found on Gothic cathedrals, where they represented the Trinity. Thomas Brooks designed the Gothic-style furniture, which looked like it belonged in an Anglican church. Stained-glass windows helped convey a pious atmosphere. Even if the family showed little interest in organized religion, such a sacred environment helped promote Christian values. The physical character of the house would uplift the spirituality of the family—even if unconsciously. "Our minds and morals are subject to constant influence and modification," explained architect Oliver Smith, "gradual yet lasting, by the inanimate walls with which we are surrounded." Victorian sensibilities combined aesthetics with morality, causing an emotional and aesthetic response, which simultaneously evoked a moral and domestic response.[7]

Christian Home Decorating

For those who had neither the money nor the inclination to construct a house that looked like a Gothic cathedral, the production and display of

Fig. 49. Hand-carved picture frame, ca. 1860. Museum of Religious Americana, Archdiocese of Philadelphia Archives and Historical Collections, Overbrook, Pa.

explicitly religious art also created a sacred environment in the home. Under the influence of Romanticism and the Victorian predilection for conspicuous consumption, Protestants departed from the Calvinist distrust of religious art. A mother's (and through her, the family's) domestic sentiments, artistic accomplishments, and spiritual devotion came to be measured by her ability to decorate her home. Nonsectarian in character, religious home decorations reflected popular taste. Handmade objects included perforated cardboard fancywork which required time, skill, and patience to produce the intended religious message. One series of advice books included instructions for making home crosses.[8] These crosses were made of wood decorated to look like marble. The style of the cross could be adjusted seasonally. Christmas crosses had imitation icicles, summer crosses had vines entwining through them, and Easter crosses had lilies. Unfortunately, craft books gave no indication as to how these crosses were used. They probably were not used in family worship but served to evoke a general religious sentiment in the home.

Families could also purchase mass-produced objects which conveyed pious sentiments.[9] Parian statues of praying children and of the young King David were inexpensive items probably placed in children's bedrooms. Ladies could carry their calling cards in silver cases decorated with steepled churches. Paperweights with Christian emblems such as the cross and crown reminded their users that earthly trials would be rewarded by heavenly glories. The everyday activities of eating and drinking assumed a special character when associated with religious characters, events, and ideas. Elegant teapots and sugar bowls made by the Jersey City Pottery company included the twelve apostles standing under gothic arches. Drinking glasses had verses etched on them from the hymn "Rock of Ages," the "Our Father," and the Psalms. A glass bread plate with "Give Us This Day Our Daily Bread" embossed on the rim showed one woman leading another to a cross on which was written "Simply To Thy Cross I Cling." Tin molds shaped chocolate and butter into a variety of crosses. By placing

Fig. 50. Wooden bracket for holding a Bible or prayer book. Mrs. C.S. Jones and Henry T. Williams, *Household Elegancies* (New York: Henry T. Williams, 1875), p. 97.

Christian symbols, pious sayings, and biblical figures on commonplace objects, family members lifted the mundane to a more spiritual level and at the same time made theological concepts concrete and visual.

The most important religious article in the Protestant home was the family Bible. Families did not merely read from Bibles, they displayed them royally in the parlor. Advice books explained how to construct marble and wood brackets on which to display the Bible.[10] One bracket, shaped like a Gothic window, was eighteen inches high and carved out of walnut. Table-cloths with gold-embroidered letters on purple velvet gave the tables the Bibles sat on an ecclesiastical look.[11] The Bibles themselves, especially toward the end of the century, were highly illustrated, sported leather covers and golden clasps, and contained elaborate family record pages. Collins, Perkins and Company's *The Holy Bible,* published in 1807, had only a simple page for registering births and deaths. When new pages had to be added, one family updated the Bible by adding colorful Gothic-style family record pages.[12] The text of the Scriptures compromised only a small portion of what actually was in the Sacred Book. Turn-of-the-century family Bibles contained biblical dictionaries; treatises on ancient coins, gems, trees, plants, flowers, manners, and customs; illuminated parables; temperance pledges; wedding certificates; and chronologies. By 1882, A.J. Holman's *The Holy Bible* could boast an overwhelming one hundred and ninety such additions.[13]

Family Bibles expanded and became encyclopedic while, at the same time, individual verses were taken out of their textual context and memorialized. Bible sayings could be stitched into samplers and hung on walls, made into book markers, or constructed into motto-cases.[14] Each day a different motto might be displayed on a wooden case which also held mail, a plant, or used newspapers. Women rendered biblical stories in needlework, to be framed and placed throughout the house. Young children played with puzzles that, when put together properly, showed Old and New Testament scenes. In 1897, W.M. Ford copyrighted his "Progressive Chautauqua Cards," which posed questions and gave answers concerning biblical people and events. Biblical toys, from miniature Noah's arks to magic-lantern slides illustrating the Ten Commandments, helped the family members enshrine the Scriptures in their memories.

By the end of the century, sandwiched among velvet swags and gilded picture frames were wax crosses, family Bibles, and religious paintings. Fashionable Protestants, filled with admiration for European painters like Raphael and Murillo, decorated their parlors with reproductions of the

Fig. 51. Frontispiece, *Pictorial Family Bible* (Philadelphia: A.J. Hoffman, [ca. 1900]).

Virgin Mary and Babe. Fascinated with French design and fashion even prompted advice-book writers to include instructions on how to make Marian shrines.[15] This fascination with Mary had little to do with Catholic belief but instead spoke to the Victorians' concern for domesticity, taste, and piety. In his 1880 article, "The Ethics of Home-Decoration," Presbyterian J.R. Miller summarized the effects that such art had on the minds of the family. While a country house with "neatly-painted palings . . . pleasant walks, lovely plants and beds of flowers" has a good moral influence, "the moral effect of interior home-decoration is still greater."[16] Merely believing was not enough. Christians must visually demonstrate their piety. They must make their homes sacred.

Family Worship and Moral Instruction

Since Victorian Americans considered the home as a sacred space, they felt comfortable in conducting religious activities there. Christenings, weddings, and funerals could take place either in the church or in the home. Before the practice of embalming was perfected in the 1880s, families and not undertakers had control of the dead body. In the days before the "funeral home" and the "living room," formal parlors functioned as the public space in which rites of passage could be legitimately conducted. Although the clergy were always involved in such rituals, families had greater involvement in creating the proper dramatic and religious setting for the event. The crepe-decked parlor, stuffed with fresh and dried flowers and presided over by men and women dressed in black, is almost emblematic of Victorian society.

While mourning rites have caught the imagination of contemporary cultural historians, advice-book writers in the nineteenth century found that other rituals more significantly expressed Christian piety and family continuity. Protestant ministers penned numerous books urging families to instill the proper Christian attitudes in their children and servants through formal and informal domestic worship. Two types of rituals were encouraged: group family worship led by the father, and individual instruction given by the mother. The father, as the head of the household, was to direct formal family worship. Since the Reformation, the father had been understood as "priest" to his family. Teaching from denominational catechisms, an activity that had been prominent among seventeenth- and eighteenth-century Protestants, had lost some of its popularity. Fathers instead were enjoined to lead the family in formal worship twice a day. Mid-nineteenth-

Fig. 52. Family prayer, ca. 1860–65. Courtesy of the National Archives, Washington, D.C., Photograph No. 165-CN-10907.

century engravings and photographs show the father gathering not only his family, but also the servants and even the family's pets, together for worship. The father then read from the Bible, commented on the day's reading, and perhaps led his family in singing a few hymns while mother played the parlor organ. Although family prayerbooks were available, ministers insisted that families merely needed to read from the Bible. Group prayer was an important way that the father expressed his patriarchal authority over his household. Formal family prayer, like formal church worship, was directed by men.

Ministers encouraged women to support their husbands' patriarchal religious activities but not to overshadow them. "The loving wife lights the lamp," wrote one clergyman, "lays the Bible by your side, and tells the little children to 'sit down and be still, while papa prays.' " [17] The mother's religious duties, in contrast to the father's, did not entail leading group worship. Women not only were expected to create a Christian home through proper childrearing and home decoration, but also they were to educate their children in piety and morality. This education was of an individual nature, because a mother understood the psychology of her child and thus could make religious percepts clear and palatable. While engravings show fathers performing family worship in groups, women are shown with one or two children reading from the Bible or talking with their children. "When I was a little child," a saved male related, "my mother used to bid me kneel beside her, and she placed her hand upon my head while she prayed." [18] Women were assumed to be experts in religion when it was equated with sentiments, feelings, and emotions. When religious authority, biblical knowledge, or family leadership was needed, men took control of domestic Christianity. Within the home, gender roles determined the religious activities of mothers and fathers.

Impact of Domestic Protestantism

From 1840 to 1900, Domestic Protestantism functioned to provide the appearance of a common, agreed-upon, Bible-based religion in a religious milieu rent by theological arguments, church splits over the issue of slavery, and growing secularism. While theologians debated the meaning of the Christian message, the ideology presented in domestic Protestantism assured families that religion could be simple, unchanging, and eternal. By eliminating denominational differences, home religion led American Protestants to believe that there was one set of foundational religious values. Families continued to attend their Presbyterian, Methodist, or Congregational churches, but they also believed that the generalized Christian spirit demonstrated in domestic religion was "true" Christianity. The "old-time religion" which Americans nostalgically wished for was the simple Christianity learned at their mother's knee, not at the preacher's pulpit. Domestic religion served as a unifying force among American Protestants who faced an endless numbers of churches, all claiming to be the one and only expression of true Christianity.

By emphasizing that the home—as a physical entity and as a set of relationships—shaped morality, ministers, reformers, and families helped to promote a consumer ethic. Building a good house and decorating it with tasteful and religious art was not perceived as the beginning of conspicuous consumption; it was a way to ensure the salvation of the family. Families invested their time and money purchasing, making, and displaying religious articles because they believed that the physical environment was crucial in producing good citizens and Christians. Even secular but tasteful art and furnishings would help instill proper values in the family. The consumption of domestic material goods—now affordable due to industrialization—was legitimized by its association with the home. Americans could indulge in consumerism without guilt.

It is important to recognize that the concern over the material aspect of home life—architecture, design, decoration—not only enabled Christian nurture but also demonstrated the Christian sensibilities of the family. The middle class of the nineteenth century did not merely hide in its castles, safe from the industrial world. Its members believed that their homes and families demonstrated their special character, morality, and spirituality. Consequently, they sought in a variety of cultural and social ways to prove this character to their neighbors and relatives, and politically to the world. The Victorian house was not a secluded refuge. Families filled it with symbols of status and piety which marked the household as distinct from the less-than-desirable Americans who populated tenements, farm shacks, and back alleys. Mainstream Protestants, by maintaining a proper Christian home, separated themselves from those they considered undesirable. John Hall, in his *A Christian Home: How to Make It and How to Maintain It* (1883), assumed that the "Mormon problem," with its "many wives for one man," and the "divorce problem" of "practical permission for many successive unions" would be solved once families established family worship and domestic piety.[19] Not only did a Christian home legitimate consumerism, but it also provided a means of blessing middle-class values and norms. Domestic Protestantism was not merely an individualized form of popular piety. The ideology promoted by secular and clerical writers helped to justify middle-class notions of gender, economics, and taste by presenting the Victorian home as eternal and God-given.

Twentieth-Century Domestic Protestantism: The Liberal-Moderate Response

Domestic Protestantism was created between 1830 and 1850, strongly promoted between 1850 and 1900, and radically changed during the first decades of the twentieth century. Between 1900 and 1930, parlor piety was pushed from the center of Protestant spirituality to its margins. It is not surprising that domestic Protestantism would evolve and change during a one-hundred-year period. What is especially significant, however, is that we can no longer trace one single stream of attitudes toward the Christian home. By the turn of the century, two forms of discourse on family and religious life can be discerned. Liberal/moderate Protestants loosened their previous insistence on the ability of the home to shape American society, rejected the patriarchal role of the father in family worship, and radically curtailed their promotion of explicitly religious activities in the home. At the same time, they set up a series of institutions and associations to examine the situation of the family and its relationship to Christian principles. Conservative Protestants, who rejected liberal attitudes toward biblical criticism and evolution, promoted a domestic Christianity in which the father acted as the spiritual and liturgical head of the family. These Christian ministers scorned the notion that societal ills could be solved by scientific analysis and continued the rhetoric of the previous century. For them, only a Christian home could solve the horrors of divorce, modern disbelief, and societal anarchy. Consequently, during the years 1900 to 1930, parlor piety came to reflect the general split in American Protestantism.

The evangelical consensus in American Protestantism had slowly begun to erode under the pressures of religious and social modernization of the late nineteenth century. By the 1920s, one group of Protestants who called themselves "modernists" accepted (for the most part) biblical criticism, biological evolution, and social scientific methodologies. While they believed that the Bible was inspired, they did not believe that it was literally true. For them the Bible served as a guide to morals and religion, not as a textbook on history and the laws of nature. Modernist ministers, and those lay people who attended their churches, asserted that scientific modes of knowledge—both in the hard sciences and in the social sciences—did not threaten the structure of religious belief or Christian ethics. Liberal/ moderate Protestantism thrived in urban centers and on the east and west coasts. From that vantage point, such Protestants saw America as an ethnically diverse, urbanized, industrial nation. Their "modern" perspective shaped their attitude toward the home and set them apart from more conservative Protestants.

Faced with a complicated industrial society, some liberal/moderate Protestant ministers attacked privatized, individualistic Christianity as a source of urban ills. Promoters of the "Social Gospel" movement sought to extend Christian ideals to the social and economic order. Like other reformers of the Progressive era, promoters of the Social Gospel were concerned with tenement laws, public health, temperance, and controlling the abuses of capitalism. According to these Protestants, it was "not a matter of getting individuals to heaven, but to transforming the life on earth into the harmony of heaven."[20] The Social Gospel movement, because of its prophetic insistence on social reform, remained unpopular with many Protestants. It did, however, encourage the growing awareness that social change demanded new forms of community response and action.

In 1912, under the guidance of Henry Sloan Coffin, Washington Gladden, and Walter Rauchenbusch, an interdenominational men's organization applied Social Gospel principles to a study of "Home Life." Comments on the role of the father in family worship took a back seat to the real problems of families: tenement overcrowding, high rents, low salaries, and worker exploitation. Ignoring the situation of middle-class homes, the study focused on the working class and the poor. "Space, light, air, privacy are natural rights," it asserted; "greed must be shamed. Exorbitant values and rents must be reduced. . . . The community must be forced to clear the way, by public improvement, for better private conditions. The pressure of moralized public sentiment must be brought to bear upon public officials, private real estate owners, legislators, and the guardians of ideals."[21] Under the impact of the Social Gospel, Protestants began to see that housing, substandard incomes, and child labor were the real threats to a proper home life.

Liberal/moderate Protestants also joined secular experts in questioning the family's ability to determine public morality. Social ills, rather than being remedied via the healing environment of home, appeared to cause the breakdown of the family itself. Examining the economic and sociological failings of industrial society, Social Gospel ministers saw how the greater social system determined the private structure of home life. By 1937, doctoral candidate Blanche Carrier could assert that "church leaders have been prepared, therefore, for the recognition that the home is both the product of the social order and the agent for the continuous infusion of the social heritage into the habits of the next generation."[22] A world war and an international economic depression had convinced many Protestants that a domestic Protestantism could not remedy the world's social and economic ills. *The Modern Family and the Church* boldly stated that the family "is regularly utilized, exploited, disrupted or despoiled as an incident in the climb to power or to wealth which are the obsessions of this ruthlessly competitive, individualistic age."[23] How could the home be the source of public morality if it was so greatly influenced by outside concerns? If religion was going to speak to the problems of the public world, according to liberal/moderate Protestantism, it had to move from the private space of the home and into the public space of politics and economics. Domestic religion could not solve the perceived crisis in the family or the greater crisis in the world. The family lost its place as an eternal, unchanging institution established by God to uphold the moral order of the community.

The Social Gospel movement within American Protestantism was short lived. Few ministers could maintain in their middle-class congregations a sustained concern for the working class and the poor. Personal piety, which released the individual from a general social concern, held strong appeal. Consequently, liberal/moderate Protestants still directed most of their attention to understanding the changes occurring in the middle-class family. Social scientists in 1889 had gathered enough statistics to prove that the United States had the highest divorce rate in the world. By 1924, sociologists could report the fact that one marriage out of every seven ended in divorce. At the same time, a declining birth rate cast into question the very future of the native-born, white, Protestant family. In 1850, women bore 5.42 children during their lives. By 1900, this number had declined to 3.6, and by 1933, there was an average of only 2.10 children per family. While more children were living to adulthood, the general impression was that the family was not as healthy as it had been a generation before. Fears of anarchism and a deteriorating urban environment motivated many middle-class families to flee to the suburbs, where they could safely preserve their domestic lifestyles.

Concern over the demise of the middle-class family, however, did not result in a flurry of advice books explaining how solve domestic problems by religious means. Liberal/moderate Protestant leaders, following general American trends, looked to professional sociologists, social scientists, and medical experts to explain not only what was wrong with the home but how to improve it. G. Stanley Hall in 1890 had already posited the outlines of a psychology of child development and, by the 1930s, the American Home Economics Association (1908), the American Child Health Association (1909), and the national Council of Parent Education (1924) could all present their "scientific" perspectives on family life. Protestant churches established their own commissions to investigate family life, including the Federal Council of Churches' Committee on Marriage and the Home

(1927) and the International Council of Religious Education's program "Education for Christian Family Life" (1931). Ministers and parents no longer were experts on domestic religious life. Committees and scientific studies existed to inform middle-class Americans how to establish a healthy and pious home.

Consequently, with uninhibited directedness, a 1934 Presbyterian bulletin remarked that "parenthood is too grave and exacting a responsibility to be faced without some specific and reliable training."[24] Parenthood did not come naturally as a God-given gift but had to be learned from experts. Regina Westcott Wieman's book, *The Modern Family and the Church* (1937), aptly summarizes this trend. Devoid of any mention of family worship or pious rhetoric on the sacred character of the home, Wieman's bibliography shows her reliance on specialized journals, federal reports on unemployment, and books such as Arnold Gesell's *Guidance of the Mental Growth in Infant and Child* (1930) and John Dewey's *Human Nature and Conduct* (1922). The "crisis" in American family life was to be remedied not by specifically religious means but by applying insights gained from sociology, psychology, educational philosophy, and medicine.

"Modern" and "scientific" notions of the family shaped the way advice-book writers understood how religion should be presented to children. Proponents of the "modern" Sunday school were the first to alter their views on the religious training of children. As early as 1919, the general secretary of the Religious Education Association, Henry Frederick Cope, combined new ideas about childhood with liberal attitudes toward the Bible. The Sunday school teacher "is no longer content with producing a boy or a girl who can pass any sort of intellectual tests regarding the history and literature in the Bible," he explained. The real purpose of Sunday schools was to "develop boys and girls who can pass the tests that the schools, the street, business, social relations and daily work put on them."[25] The Bible should be used as a means toward an end; it was one tool in moral development. Modern Sunday schools departed from the "uniform" Sunday school lessons set up by a disciple of evangelist Dwight L. Moody in 1872 and sought more efficient ways to instill Christian beliefs and values.

Cope's attitude toward the religious training of children emphasized adult understanding of the psychology of the child and encouraged teachers to allow individual expression among children. Christian principles were to be developed in a subtle, indirect manner. "The teacher does not teach the Bible," Cope wrote, "he teaches persons."[26] This shift from seeing religious education as a means to "teach the Bible" to viewing it as a way of developing the person was not a radical innovation. What Cope and other supporters of the modern Sunday school did was to give institutional credence to the ways that mothers had been told to educate their children in Christian piety. Throughout the nineteenth century, mothers were expected to provide informal instruction geared to the age and aptitude of their children. "Modern" religious education validated Victorian maternal instruction and devalued paternal domestic preaching. Authority no longer rested with the power of the father to interpret and convey biblical messages to his family. By the early twentieth century, both fathers and mothers were expected to train their children in religious matters by using the models employed by women in the nineteenth century.

Experts in religious education no longer praised the Victorian father when he acted as prophet, priest, and king. Writers on domestic Protestantism now held up the "democratic" family as the ideal. In 1934, George Walter Fiske included a chapter on "Maintaining a Home Democracy" in his book *Problems of the Christian Family Life To-Day*. In the chapter, he described the problems of a Russian Orthodox Jewish family whose children refused to give obeisance to their father by handing over their weekly paychecks. Rather than praising the strength of the Jewish father for asserting his right as head of the household, Fiske chided the father's un-American attitudes. Undemocratic Jewish families are then contrasted with Christian families who solve problems through family councils. "The Christian family must be a true democracy." Fiske concludes, "in which every member's personal rights are respected, including the children's."[27] Following in the tradition of other writers, Fiske uses domestic Protestantism to separate the virtuous Christian from the unvirtuous non-Christian. His anti-Semitism notwithstanding, Fiske continued the trend toward legitimizing changes in American family life by associating it with the "true" religion of Christianity.

Those liberal and moderate Protestants who continued to promote formal family worship recognized that older patterns had to be radically modified. In 1923, Presbyterian Harold McAfee Robinson published a short work entitled *How to Conduct Family Worship*. Although most Victorian writers condemned long sessions of family prayer, Robinson was unique in explaining that it only had to last between six and ten minutes.[28] Everyone could have a part in the service which should vary daily. Following the general American trend to shape family life around children's needs, Robinson argued that music, Bible reading, and prayer must be adapted to the needs

Fig. 53. Mother reading Bible stories to her children. A.W. Beaven, "Parents as Teachers of Christian Living," *International Journal of Religious Education* (April 1931):11. Photo by Underwood and Underwood.

of the youngest child. A Presbyterian guide insisted that "all the elements of family worship . . . can be introduced in ten minutes without destroying the spirit of reverence by confusion and haste."[29] Gone was the attitude that the father should offer sophisticated supplications and prayers to God for his family. Now the child was the central focus of abbreviated family devotions. A short grace before meals and the attendance at children's bedtime prayers by one of the parents became the remnants of longer family devotions.

Domestic Protestantism and the Fundamentalist Response

The large urban churches of liberal/moderate Protestants were well funded, had direct contact with influential political figures, and set the character of American theological education. They continued to be important culturally and socially in the early twentieth century, just as they had been throughout the nineteenth century. What had changed, however, was what framed this Protestant establishment. By the 1930s, immigrant religious groups, particularly Roman Catholics and Jews, exerted their own weight in the political and cultural spheres. Catholic Alfred E. Smith's 1928 presidential candidacy symbolized the end of Protestant domination of politics. America was no longer a "Christian" (read: white, Protestant, Anglo-Saxon) nation. Catholics and Jews challenged the liberal/moderate Protestant hegemony from without, while conservative Protestants threatened it from within.

Not all Protestants felt comfortable accepting biblical criticism, evolution, and social-scientific insights. Conservative Protestants rejected theological liberalism and the passing of what they understood as Puritan moralism. By 1910, some of these people had put their ideas down in a booklet called "The Fundamentals." In contrast to "modernists," these "fundamentalists" believed that the Bible was literally true and without error, that the world was heading quickly to its end with the Second Coming of Christ, and that modern lifestyles were sinful and must be replaced by proper Christian living. Some conservative Protestants remained in their denominations as Methodists, Baptists, or Presbyterians but became outspoken proponents of fundamentalist Christianity. Others joined new denominations such as the Church of the Nazarene, founded in 1908, or the Assemblies of God, founded in 1914. The liberal Protestant journal *Christian Century* reported in 1925 that "there is a wedge of division into almost every one of the older and greater religious bodies. This is the wedge of fundamentalism."[30] This wedge not only would separate Protestants theologically, it would divide them in their attitudes toward home and domestic religion.

While there was, and still is, great variety among conservative Protestants—some are Pentecostals, others are Evangelical; some are black, others are white; some live in cities, others in rural areas—all would agree on crucial role that the family plays in defining Christian living. For conservative Protestants, the family serves as the last stronghold in a world threatened by secular values, government interference, and Communism. A Presbyterian pamphlet, this time written by a conservative pastor, explained that the "family altar is a bulwark against the world. It is one occasion where the world is shut out, and where ills and wrongs and temptations cannot enter."[31] Even more than for the Victorians of the last century, for this author the home was a refuge from an evil and incomprehensible world. As moderate/liberal Protestants looked to the public world to help them understand the situation of the family, conservative/fundamentalist Protestants looked to a protected family to make sense out of the chaotic world.

A revitalized Christian family would be able to conquer the pressing social chaos. Not only would the divorce problem be solved, according to one 1905 evangelistic tract, but "family worship should be maintained for the sake of the nation . . . Family worship has more to do with the future American greatness than the tariff or the Philippines."[32] A 1915 encyclopedia of religious education in effect rejected the Social Gospel assumption that society shaped family life and asserted that "the character of the nation is fashioned, in quality, after the character of the product of its family. The home life is the lining of the world's life. If it is kept pure and wholesome, all life will be made purer and the world better."[33] The more the public world of government, education, business, and media was perceived as alien, the more conservative Protestants sought to preserve the family as the last bastion of true Christian virtues.

Crucial to the preservation of traditional family life and home worship was the reiteration of the father's role in directing domestic religion. "I do not know a more sacred institution than the home," wrote Robert Speer in 1912, "nor any priesthood higher than that of the Christian father as he sits at the head of the table with his family gathered around him."[34] The editors of the Presbyterian encyclopedia concurred, asserting that "family worship, as a rule, should be conducted by the father as patriarch of the home."[35] Although even conservative ministers condemned the stately and formal worship of former times, the father should still be the leader of the religious life of his family. As late as 1937, the pastor of a Dutch Reformed church in New York City imagined that Jesus came from a family with several children, in which Joseph, not Mary, read aloud from the Bible to his family.[36] Conservative Protestants rejected as secular and un-Christian the ideas that women were equal to men and that the family should be run as a democracy, with children having a say in domestic decisions. Women could produce religious handicrafts and informally instruct their children in righteousness, but they must not lead the family in either its spiritual or worldly endeavors. Children would be treated with love and discipline, but they must submit to the authority of the father.

In 1919, a "World Conference on Christian Fundamentals" was held in Philadelphia. Twenty-five addresses from noted conservative Protestants upheld the inspired and inerrant nature of the Scripture and asserted the continued importance of the Trinity, the Virgin Birth, Heaven, Hell, and Original Sin. In addition, the conference reported on the state of Christian education, the religious press, Bible conferences, and missionary societies. In a section on prayer, we can clearly see the conservative perspective on parlor piety:

> There is in my heart a profound conviction that if we should somehow bring to pass a revival of the family altar in the world we would have a world revival of Christianity. . . . A boy is not going out of the home wherein he has knelt before Almighty God and heard a believing father take the name of his Christ in adoration and praise, day after day, through eighteen years, he is not going out of that home into the halls of some college to be quickly moved away from his faith by some half-baked scientist. He is not going out to besmirch his morals, after his mother has had around him with her own arms the arms of her God and has breathed into his soul the breath of faith and prayer.[37]

For the World Conference on Christian Fundamentals, the secular threat to the family especially threatened men and boys. If true Christianity—a Christianity free from modern skepticism—was to survive, it would need the support of families where the father led his family in prayer and the mother provided individual moral instruction. Only then, when a boy could hear "a believing father take the name of his Christ in adoration and praise, day after day" could the boy be safe from "half-baked" scientists who sought to tarnish his faith. Conservative Protestants, who rejected

The KING'S BUSINESS

☙ THE BIBLE FAMILY MAGAGZINE ❧

"FOR EVER, O LORD, THY WORD IS SETTLED IN HEAVEN"– PSALM 119:89

VOL. 16   AUG. 1925   NO. 8

GOD BLESS
OUR HOME

HONORING GOD IN THE HOME
RE-ESTABLISH THE OLD-FASHIONED FAMILY WORSHIP AND LET THE WORD OF GOD SETTLE ALL OUR PROBLEMS

Fig. 54. Father leading the family in worship. Note the similarity of this representation of fundamentalist family worship in 1925 to the illustration of domestic devotions in 1860–65. *The King's Business,* Aug. 1925, cover page.

trends in biblical criticism and science, promoted a particular type of domestic religion and family life to help counter threats to church and nation.

By 1930, liberal and conservative attitudes toward the family were different enough that we can no longer speak of a "parlor piety" which united
Protestants from various denominations. While liberal Protestants might
have lost some of the radical perspectives of the Social Gospel movement,
they did not turn away from using social-scientific methods to help them
understand home life, nor refrain from setting up interdenominational organizations to administer and promote their family policy. Conservative
Protestants continued the Victorian perspective that the home was the
source of public morality and that men and women each had unique roles
within that environment. The ramifications of the fundamentalist decision
to promote the divinized home, according to historian Betty DeBerg, reinforced "the sexual and social conventions of the separate spheres and
[served] to attack woman's movement outside her sphere into paid employment, social reform, electoral politics, and higher education."[38] Fundamentalist ministers sought to reclaim American Protestantism for men and
masculinity by limiting women's role within the church and expanding it
within the home. Fundamentalists and modernists both respected the importance of the home, but each group had its own perspective on the source
of domestic problems and on the solution to those problems. Domestic
piety no longer avoided denominational and theological differences and indeed was merely one more topic over which Protestants could disagree.

Changing Attitude toward Domestic Design

While the division of American Protestants into conservative and liberal
camps certainly influenced domestic religion, we must not overlook the importance of general cultural changes in hastening the decline of parlor
piety. In the last chapter of Katherine Grier's *Culture and Comfort: People,
Parlors, and Upholstery,* she describes the weakening of the parlor as a "a
central location for symbols."[39] Although "parlor" piety did not happen
solely in the parlor, the evolution of the parlor into the living room had
important consequences for domestic religion. During the early twentieth
century, the house was portrayed less as a "sacred hearth" and more as an
efficient, sanitary, technologically innovative space in which scientific
values and rational planning produced people capable of negotiating modern society.

Although mid-nineteenth-century housing reformers such as Catharine Beecher perceived the home as a workplace for women, it was not until the end of the century that the discourse about housekeeping became "professionalized." In the 1890s, newly established home economics departments encouraged college women to consider their "household engineering" and "home management" as equal in importance to male occupations. One woman's prizewinning 1899 essay likened "the home to a business where a hierarchy was necessary, meetings were a spur to good rapport, and the 'purchasing agent' was a specially trained worker."[40] The decline of the servant class meant that more middle-class women were doing their own scrubbing, cooking, and laundry. Since servants typically had carried out hard domestic work, technological innovations did not necessarily lessen housework for middle-class women. More than relieving the burden of housework, electrical appliances, hot-air heat, and handcranked washing machines lent a respectable air of "science" to the domestic environment. The housework which middle-class women did could be described as sophisticated because it utilized innovate technology and was conducted by a skilled professional.

The scientific values and rational planning of home economists filtered into the popular consciousness via countless women's magazines and government pamphlets. Obviously, most women did not have the resources to fully follow these sources' guidelines. During the Depression, even middle-class women found that their efficient housekeeping could not keep their families fed and housed. However, by introducing such descriptions as "scientific," "rational," and "efficient" as positive characteristics for the household, home economists unconsciously "de-converted" the home. Where did religion fit into a domestic rhetoric in which the home was described as a factory and the mother as the "purchasing agent"?

The "modernizing" of the home also occurred in the areas of design and decoration. In the decades beginning in 1910 and 1920, decorative-arts critics praised trends toward simplicity and naturalness in domestic architecture and interior design. The Arts and Crafts movement, which began in the late nineteenth century, had been popularized in the early twentieth. Mail-order catalogues sold mass-produced goods which reflected the simple forms and honest expression of the handmade Arts and Crafts furniture. Homes and furnishings were to be convenient, pleasurable, and comfortable but, perhaps more importantly, easily cleaned and simple. The knickknacks, books, live plants, ceramics, fancy needlework, and photograph albums of the former era served only to clutter the home, collecting dust and creating a false sense of the family's social status. The advice now given to the American public showed how interior decorating could present an "honest" picture of the family. "Homes which cannot free themselves from the clutter of trivial and futile objects," commented one critic in 1916, "are mute declarations of the insincerity of their creator's pretensions to good taste and refinement in other directions."[41] Homes not only should be functional, sparse, and informal, they also should reflect the real-life interests and character of the family.

The formality of Victorian life, with its elaborate codes of social etiquette, also came to an end after the First World War. With the popularization of more informal means of social interaction and the eventual proliferation of telephones, the parlor no longer served a social need. Houses with fewer rooms, no formal parlor, and open-floor plans did not provide the formal setting for father-led family prayers. Churches and funeral homes provided the air of dignity need for rites of passage. The informality of domestic relations meant that whatever religious activities went on in the home would have to be equally informal. A brief prayer at the kitchen table before eating fit more closely with modern family social rituals than structured family prayer.

The combination of simplicity and honesty in home design and domestic rituals meant that those men and women who were sensitive to prevailing fashion could legitimately desacralize their homes. Family Bibles which were never read but were set prominently on decorative tables could be put up in the attic, along with the needlework Bible scenes, carved wooden prayer-book holders, and wax crosses. The "modern" way of home design asked furnishings to be functional, not inspirational. Explicit evidence of religious beliefs did not have to be displayed in the parlor along with other evidence of cultural refinement and family memory. People could still be religious, but they need not demonstrate their beliefs visually in the symbolic space of the home. At the very most, religious pictures and sayings would be relegated to the private space of children's bedrooms. The "honest" home did not have to display publicly religious objects produced a generation before—objects with the rich patterns, bright colors, complex designs, and visual detail that modern designers detested.

As American home life became less theatrical, more informal, and supposedly more "sincere," domestic religious activities seemed more and more out-of-place. It would not be until the 1950s, with a renewed social and cultural preoccupation with family and home life, that liberal/

moderate Protestant ministers would once again actively advocate domestic Christianity. Even then, advice books urged parents to conduct relaxed and inclusive family worship. Children, not mothers, would make religious objects for special holidays and for their own bedrooms. Conservative Christians, ridiculed in the public media and among established Protestants, made little impact on general cultural trends before the 1970s. When this group became more powerful economically and more visible culturally, their forms of Christian home decorating came to reflect middle-class taste. Parlor piety, which flourished in the nineteenth century and helped Protestants transcend denominational differences, by the twentieth century had become a powerful clue to the various factions of religious life in America.

Notes

1. Catharine Beecher and Harriet Beecher Stowe, *The American Woman's Home, Or, Principles of Domestic Science* (New York: J.B. Ford and Co., 1869), 455–58. The discussion of domestic Protestantism is drawn from Colleen McDannell, *The Christian Home in Victorian America, 1840–1900* (Bloomington: Indiana Univ. Press, 1986).

2. Horace Bushnell, *Christian Nurture* (1888; rptd. New Haven, Conn.: Yale Univ. Press, 1967), 12.

3. William Ranlett, *The Architect* (New York: W.H. Graham, 1847), 3.

4. Ibid.

5. Orson S. Fowler, *The Octagon House: A Home For All* (1853; rptd. New York: Dover 1973), 11.

6. Henry W. Cleaveland, William Backus, and Samuel Backus, *Village and Farm Cottages* (1856; rptd. New York: American Life Foundation, 1982), 2.

7. Oliver Smith, *The Domestic Architect* (Buffalo: Derby and Co., 1852), iv.

8. Mrs. C.S. Jones and Henry T. Williams, *Household Elegancies* (New York: Henry T. Williams, 1875), 181.

9. These articles may be found at the Ryan Memorial Library, Archives and Historical Collections, St. Charles Seminary, Philadelphia.

10. Williams and Jones, *Household Elegancies*, 97.

11. Henry T. Williams and Mrs. C.S. Jones, *Beautiful Homes* (New York: H.T. Williams, 1878), 200–201.

12. This Bible is located in the Rare Books Room, Logan Public Library, Philadelphia.

13. *Pictorial Family Bible* (Philadelphia: A.J. Hoffman, n.d. [ca. 1900]).

14. These articles may be found at the Ryan Memorial Library, Archives and Historical Collections, St. Charles Seminary, Philadelphia.

15. Henry T. Williams and Mrs. C.S. Jones, *Ladies' Fancy Work* (New York: H.T. Williams, 1877), 151.

16. J.R. Miller, *Weekday Religion* (Philadelphia: Presbyterian Board of Publication, 1880), 269.

17. Davis Newton, *Apples of Gold in Pictures of Silver* (New York: Published by Author, 1869), 346.

18. John Power, *Discourses on Domestic Piety* (Cincinnati: Swormstedt and Power, 1851), 73–74.

19. John Hall, *A Christian Home: How to Make It and How to Maintain It* (Philadelphia: American Sunday School Union, 1883), 57.

20. Walter Rauschenbusch, as cited in Martin E. Marty, *Modern American Religion: The Irony of It All, 1893–1919* (Chicago: Univ. of Chicago Press, 1986), 288.

21. *Messages of the Men and Religion Movement* (New York: Funk and Wagnalls, 1912), 40. For a discussion of the relationship between this male organization and the Social Gospel Movement, see Gail Bederman, "'The Women Have Had Charge of the Church Work Long Enough': The Men and Religion Forward Movement of 1911–1912 and the Masculinization of Middle-Class Protestantism," *American Quarterly* 41 (Sept. 1989): 432–65.

22. Blanche Carrier, *Church Education for Family Life* (New York: Harper & Bros., 1937), 21.

23. Regina Wescott Wieman, *The Modern Family and the Church* (New York: Harper & Bros., 1937), 5.

24. Carrier, *Church Education,* 12, citing *Christian Education in the Family,* bulletin no. 3 (Philadelphia: Board of Christian Education of the Presbyterian Church in the USA, n.d. [ca. 1934]).

25. Henry Frederick Cope, *The School in the Modern Church* (New York: George H. Doran, 1919), 89.

26. Ibid., 90.

27. George Walter Fiske, *Problems of Christian Family Life To-Day* (Philadelphia: Westminster Press, 1934), 26.

28. Harold McAfee Robinson, *How to Conduct Family Worship* (Philadelphia: Presbyterian Board of Publication and Sabbath School Work), n.p.

29. *Christian Education in the Family,* bulletin no. 3, p. 20.

30. *Christian Century,* 30 July 1925.

31. James Grier, *The Family Altar* (Pittsburg, Pa.: Presbyterian Board of Publication and Bible School Work, n.d. [ca. 1920]), n.p.

32. James Vance, "Family Worship" (N.p.: Committee on Evangelistic Work, 1905), 13.

33. John T. McFarland and Benjamin S. Winchester, eds., *The Encyclopedia of Sunday Schools and Religious Education* (New York: Thomas Nelson and Sons, 1915), 1167.

34. Robert E. Speer, *The Church in the House* (East Northfield, Mass.: The Bookstore, 1912), 5.

35. McFarland and Winchester, *Encyclopedia of Sunday Schools,* 1168.

36. W. Melmoth Bomar, *I Went to Church in New York* (New York: Graymont Publishers, 1937), 115–17.

37. *God Hath Spoken* (Philadelphia: Bible Conference Committee, 1919), 51f.

38. The fundamentalist move to divinize the home and reinforce declining Victorian sex roles is perceptively discussed in Betty DeBerg, *Ungodly Women: Gender and the First Wave of American Fundamentalism* (Minneapolis: Fortress Press, 1990), 148.

39. Katherine C. Grier, *Culture and Comfort: People, Parlors, and Upholstery, 1850–1930* (Amherst: Univ. of Massachusetts Press, 1988), 300.

40. Gwendolyn Wright, *Moralism and the Model Home: Domestic Architecture and Cultural Conflict in Chicago, 1873–1913* (Chicago: Univ. of Chicago Press, 1980), 135.

41. Katherine Grier, *Culture and Comfort,* 291.

CHAPTER EIGHT

Gardens of Change

Patricia M. Tice

Dramatic change marked the design of the domestic landscape during the late nineteenth and early twentieth centuries. Just as household reformers and designers grew dissatisfied with the rigid formality of the Victorian parlor, so landscape architects and gardeners began casting a critical eye toward the formal garden, the "outdoor parlor." In response to a broader cultural trend, household and garden designers alike reshaped and restated nineteenth-century ideas, aesthetics, and visions to suit twentieth-century life. The parlor emerged as the more casual living room. The garden evolved from a space which had often emphasized a formal and distant relationship between architecture and landscape into a more integral union between nature and that which was constructed. Between late Victorian design and twentieth-century reform—whether indoors or out—lay a wide middle ground in which many people combined some aspects of the new with the familiar practices of the past.

Both professionals and amateurs had developed a tremendous interest in gardening during the late nineteenth and early twentieth centuries. According to census records, the number of persons listing their occupations as gardeners, seedsmen, and nurserymen nearly tripled between 1890 and 1920, as gardening emerged as another arena for the expanding consumer culture.[1] More and more Americans gained employment—and added leisure time—in nonagrarian enterprise during this period; yet, ironically, their move into cities and crowded towns prompted many to take up the garden hoe as a hobby, in a burst of newfound enthusiasm for the soil. As journalist and amateur gardener Charles Dudley Warner frankly admitted, writing from his Hartford, Connecticut, home, "Hoeing in the garden on a bright, soft May day, when you are not obliged to, is nearly equal to the delight of going trouting. Blessed be agriculture! if one does not have too much of it."[2]

This avocational interest in gardening owed much to earlier nineteenth-century developments. Landscape architect Andrew Jackson Downing had promoted the pastime in the 1840s, through his book *The Theory and Practice of Landscape Gardening* and his articles for *The Horticulturist,* a popular magazine he edited. Horticultural societies by the dozens were organized between the 1820s and 1860s. Together with the post–Civil War Grange movement, they distributed information about gardening and later spawned informally organized garden clubs that focused more specifically upon the domestic landscape than upon the cultivation of field crops. Before World War I, many of these clubs formed state and national associations, such as the Garden Club of America, founded in 1913.

Mail-Order Seed Businesses

Still other factors accounted for the increasing popularity of gardening, such as the production of low-cost seeds. Before the Civil War, most seed houses were small, unspecialized enterprises. In 1850, *The Horticulturist* advised the amateur home gardener to cultivate plants that were easy to grow or easy to propagate:

phlox drumondi	crocus
candy tuft	sweet pea
sweet alyssum	lupine
pansy	oleander
globe amaranth	snowball
china aster	flowering currant
forsythia	bridal wreath
althea	balsam
honeysuckle	waxberry
spirea	hardy rose
lilac	ten week stock
peony	arbor vitae
chrysanthemum	morning glory[3]

According to an 1877 history of Monroe County New York, soon to become a major seed-producing area,

> But few flower seeds were grown in America for market, and these were the common-onest kinds, such as could be produced with little care and skill. American seedsmen imported their finest sorts mainly from France

and Germany, a few from England, while Holland supplied not only the bulbs commonly known as Holland bulbs, but most of our lilies.[4]

By the 1860s, large seed houses began more extensive and scientific production of garden seeds that could be mass-marketed at relatively low prices. Not only did seed houses provide gardeners with less expensive plant materials, they gradually offered a greater variety as well. Englishman James Vick began this trend when he founded his seed house in Rochester, New York, in 1861. After several unsuccessful harvests, Vick traveled to Europe to study meteorology and cultivation techniques used by European seed companies. Upon his return, he established extensive trial grounds and began developing a business based upon the accepted components of late-nineteenth-century industrial organization—a commitment to large-scale production, the use of power-driven machine tools, division of labor within a factory system, and a departmentalized management system. By 1877, Vick's seed farm encompassed more than one hundred acres, conveniently located near a branch of the New York Central Railroad. He maintained his own printery, an art studio staffed with engravers, a bindery, and a box-making factory. Vick's five-story office building featured a retail store for seeds and garden furnishings, including "all garden requisites and adornments, such as baskets, vases, lawn-mowers, lawn-tents, aquariums, seats, etc., etc."[5]

Like many other businessmen of his time, Vick spared no expense when it came to advertising. The *History of Monroe County* reported:

> The immense amount of business done may be understood by a few facts: . . . Over three thousand reams of printing paper are used each year for catalogues, weighing two hundred thousand pounds, and the simple postage for sending these catalogues by mail is *thirteen thousand dollars*. Millions of bags and boxes are also manufactured in the establishment, requiring hundreds of reams of paper and scores of tons of pasteboards.[6]

Once Vick and such competitors as D.M. Ferry of Detroit, Michigan, and Comstock-Ferry of Wethersfield, Connecticut, distributed their products through the United States postal system, "seeds were placed within the reach of the masses, and a new era was entered upon in the culture of flowers."[7] By 1886, the average consumer was able to order a wide variety of garden seeds from catalogs for only five cents a packet; nursery plants, always a more expensive commodity because they required special care and handling, ranged from twenty-five cents for common plants such as geraniums to three dollars for more unfamiliar plants such as azaleas and fanleaf palms.[8]

Continued improvements in transportation also spurred the growth of gardening in the late nineteenth century. Railroad construction accelerated after the Civil War and facilitated the distribution of seeds, catalogs, and other gardening supplies. Improvements in printing stimulated a plethora of horticultural catalogs, journals, periodicals, and books. Consumers became conversant with some of the fundamental practices of gardening.

Popular interest in gardening also developed as a reaction to concerns about urban life. By the late nineteenth century, many physicians recommended fresh air and outdoor exercise such as gardening as a tonic for the nervous decline and physical debility that many Americans associated with the stress of city life and industrialization. Increased leisure time, ready cash, and interest in the outdoors allowed many manufacturers to cultivate and reap a new crop of consumers—home gardeners.

New Technology for the Victorian Garden

By the turn of the century, no matter what style, scale, or form a garden may have assumed, manufacturers, nurserymen, and seedsmen offered a wide array of specialized goods guaranteed to meet all of its needs. Reflecting the industrial expansion of the period, the New York City Henderson Nursery unabashedly promised "everything for the garden" in its 1911 catalog. Materials developed in the nineteenth century were applied to gardening and enhanced this diversity. Rubber atomizers misted plants; metal screen covers, replaced in the 1920s by waxed paper covers, protected them from insects. Rakes with wire tines provided a finer, more precise alternative to cast-iron tools. Manufacturers also designed new types of tools to satisfy the unique needs of urban and suburban gardeners: digging and weeding implements with short handles were ideally suited to small garden plots. As municipal water companies offered water under pressure to their city and town customers, new types of gardening tools—lawn sprinklers, garden hoses, nozzles, and hose carts—found their way into middle-class garden sheds. Other goods awaited the spread of public water supplies. Although late-nineteenth-century venders, such as the Boston hardware firm Smith and Winchester, advertised lawn sprinklers as early as 1890, these garden tools were not in widespread use until the twentieth century.[9]

Commercially processed fertilizers and insecticides also became commonly available by the 1870s. Many consumers welcomed these new products as a scientific triumph over the caprices of nature, one that allowed the gardener to control the garden's yield while protecting it from insect infestation. Peruvian guano and other manures, plaster, bone, and chemical compounds were neatly bottled and marketed for town and city gardeners. Nurseryman Peter Henderson complained that more than fifty different types of fertilizers were on the market in New York City in 1886. Some gardeners continued to produce their own homemade remedies for sick plants, including soap and water or "tobacco tea," made by infusing tobacco in water, which was then applied to an infested plant. Many, however, chose to purchase commercial preparations. As a curative for insect-ridden plants, most gardening supply houses offered customers a selection of Paris green, London purple, and powdered pyrethrum, a poisonous evergreen. These were liberally dusted on the affected plants using either inexpensive tin shakers or more expensive and more efficient dusting bellows.

The Late Victorian Garden

A chromolithograph published in New York's *Scipioville Nursery* trade catalog around 1890 illustrated an ideal ornamental garden design that many late-nineteenth-century horticulturists, nurserymen, and seedsmen advocated. In this formally organized landscape, the work areas—stables, as well as dooryards where laundry hung and livestock roamed—were separated and screened from the public front portion of the property, much the same way that the hall separated the kitchen and other nonpublic areas of the house from guests. Because the house was viewed by many landscape architects, among them Elias Long, as having "crowning importance," the structure dominated the property and was separated from ornamental plantings, which were placed at a distance from the house so they could be viewed from the porch and parlor windows.[10] Only a vine clinging to one side of the house hinted at a blending of nature with architecture. The lawn, planted with contrasting specimen plants gathered from around the world, formed a botanical anthology, a representative sampling of the vegetable kingdom, in the same way that many late-nineteenth-century American parlors contained displays of collections of objects. Whether composed of fans, dolls, postage stamps, coins, or selected plants, these collections in and out of the house attested to their owners' awareness of cultural trends, as well as their personal interests, tastes, and wealth.

Fig.55. Chromolithograph, ca. 1890. Published in the New York *Scipioville Nursery* trade catalog, this picture illustrates an idealized late nineteenth-century garden, characterized by an intricate design, specimen plants, and garden ornaments. Courtesy of the Strong Museum, Rochester, N.Y.

Carpet beds, intricately shaped beds in the forms of scrolls, crescents, stars, and circles, massed with brightly hued annuals, also were key elements of the late-nineteenth-century garden. Large estates and public gardens often featured *parterres,* garden beds planted in complex geometric patterns. Like specimen plants, carpet beds and *parterres* generally were planted away from the house to enhance window views, and great emphasis and value were placed upon plant materials which, like parlor furnishings of the day, offered richness, diversity, and contrasts of color, texture, shape, and scale. Variegated plants called "fancy leaf" plants were extremely popular at this time, as were other vibrantly toned flowers. *Vick's Home Floriculture,* published in 1890, compiled a list of bedding plants recommended precisely because they made "a brilliant show"—crimson, yellow, and purple coleus, cannas, caladiums, feverfew, tuber begonias, salvia, heliotrope, verbena, and geraniums. "The geranium stands at the head of the list," wrote author Eben Rexford, "A garden without at least one bed of geraniums is seldom seen now-a-days."[11] Potted exotics, such as yucca, aloe, and fan-leaf palm, were also placed outdoors in mild weather, for gardeners prized not only their unusually shaped leaves and textures but also their association with romantic, distant places. Affluent gardeners, such as Naomi Richardson of Oswego, New York, patronized nurseries for such plants, paying three dollars each for a fan-leaf palm and a rubber plant in the 1880s. At the same time, she paid her maid Kate two dollars and fifty cents for six days of hard physical labor.[12]

Those endowed with more patience and perseverance than means, however, also were able to participate in this same gardening craze for exotic specimen plants by purchasing inexpensive seeds and roots. Most large seedhouses, such as the Maule Seedhouse of Philadelphia, Pennsylvania, offered special packaged collections of seeds, roots, and grafts at bonus prices. Typically, each collection, which contained ten to fifteen varieties of plants, sold for one dollar.[13] Gardeners also continued the old practice of saving seeds and sharing them with family and neighbors. In addition, horticultural societies, gardening clubs, and granges frequently sponsored seed exchanges among their members and with other societies and clubs.

Most late nineteenth- and early-twentieth-century gardeners were content to leave house foundations unplanted to improve drainage and ventilation and to prevent infestation. Window boxes and vines, on the other hand, were common adornments to the home at this time; they added another layer of detailed decoration to the domestic exterior. Horticulturist Eben Rexford in 1890 noted with pleasure the "increasing popularity of the window box" and urged gardeners to "be sure and have at least one window box."[14] He recommended morning glories, nasturtiums, pansies, petunias, heliotrope, ferns, geraniums, yellow and crimson coleus, and fancy caladiums as suitable materials for the window box. As for vines, Rexford declared, "No house is what it ought to be, in the sense of the beautiful, without some vine trained about its windows. Perhaps the most popular of all climbing plants just at present," he continued, "is the Clematis," particularly esteemed for its profuse blooms, rapid growth, and rich colors.[15] Dutchman's pipe, honeysuckle, trumpet vine, and wisteria were also commonly cultivated at this time. Like the window-box garden, these vines maintained their popularity throughout the first half of the twentieth century, when gardeners, facing new demands upon their time, increasingly valued low-maintenance gardens.

Many gardeners ornamented their gardens during warm weather with decorative displays of houseplants, grouped on small tables and stands which were either purchased or made at home. Directions for rustic-work

Fig. 56. This unidentified New York residence, photographed in 1899, depicts the liberal use of vines, vases, and variegated plants. Courtesy of the Strong Museum, Rochester, N.Y.

furnishings, made by applying bark and twigs to metal or wooden containers, appeared frequently in household advice books and in popular periodicals. Gypsy stands, composed of a tripod that supported a painted, plant-filled pot, were popular ornaments placed outside working-class and lower-middle-class homes, much to the dismay of horticulturists. "I do really hope that no reader of this book ever had the 'Gypsy Kettle' craze," Rexford remarked. "If she or he has, I trust that they have recovered from it long ago. . . . The sight of a dinner-pot painted a fiery red, and dangling from three sticks, with a poor, down-hearted little plant in it, has often made me feel like committing trespass."[16] More affluent homeowners purchased classical statuary and vases, with which they decorated their "outdoor parlor" (as landscape gardeners often called the garden) in the same way that they adorned their indoor parlor. While classical vases were universally acknowledged to be a joy forever, the "gazing globe," a bright, shiny glass ball mounted on a pedestal; and sentimental subjects such as "Out in the Rain" captivated upper-middle-class gardeners. "Out in the Rain," costing $125 in 1894, was based upon a terra-cotta figure of two children holding an umbrella, which had been shown at Philadelphia's Centennial Exhibition in 1876.[17] The piece was so popular that many manufacturers, such as E.T. Barnum of Detroit and James Fiske Iron Works of New York, produced life-size renditions advertised to serve both as fountains or as lawn ornaments, should plumbing be unavailable. A menagerie of cast-iron stags, hounds, and other animals were also priced to suit a variety of purses. E.T. Barnum in 1894 listed its casting of a stag for $85, as well as smaller, less detailed castings of "wide awake rabbits" for $1.98.[18]

Although people from all economic backgrounds often chose simply to move serviceable tables and chairs out into the garden or porch, manufacturers tempted gardeners with an increasing array of furnishings designed especially for garden use. Industrial textile innovations brought furnishings such as hammocks and camp chairs into widespread use. Consumers with average incomes quickly accepted rope, grass, and canvas hammocks, priced between $1.25 and $2.25. More elaborate hammocks made from highly figured cottons were sold with the additional options of fringe, matching cushions, and side draperies called valances, which made them closely resemble their parlor counterpart, the upholstered lounge or couch. Hammock chairs, also called camp or deck chairs, provided soft, form-fitting comfort. So did furniture made of wicker (woven rush, reed, rattan, raffia, cane, willow, or grasses), long a favorite choice for the garden because it was lightweight, moderate in cost, durable, and a cooling open-weave construction. Moreover, as author Gervase Wheeler had observed in 1852, wicker offered "that greatest of all luxuries—an easy seat and a springy back."[19]

Rustic furniture continued to please Americans as it had since the mid-nineteenth century. Made from branches, roots, logs, and twigs, this furniture literally celebrated nature and outdoor living. Gardeners and landscape architects alike esteemed it for its seemingly artless qualities, its harmony with the natural surroundings, and its democratic appeal: all nature lovers could either buy or make rustic furniture.

Cast-iron chairs and benches also had been manufactured for use in gardens and cemeteries since the mid-nineteenth century. Whereas fragile wicker and textile furnishings have tended to perish, cast-iron furniture has survived in numbers perhaps disproportionate to its actual use. This furniture consistently remained expensive throughout the nineteenth century; as salaries rose, so too did the price of cast-iron settees and chairs. In 1894, E.T. Barnum sold a fern-pattern settee for eighteen dollars, the equivalent of an average week's wage for a skilled tradesman. That same eighteen dollars could have purchased a five-piece living room suite—a settee, rocking chair, armchair, and two side chairs—from the 1893 Montgomery Ward catalog. Large foundries continued to produce cast-iron garden furniture during the 1890s in the same naturalistic patterns (such as the ivy, grape, and fern designs), as well as in Gothic and rustic patterns which had been introduced around the mid-nineteenth century. A number of firms, such as the James Fiske Iron Works, continued to offer these furnishings through the 1940s.

Inventors, designers, and manufacturers experimented with furniture made from steel wire, which could be rolled, bent, and formed into fancy furnishings and plant stands. Introduced shortly after the Civil War, wire garden furniture was most popular between the 1890s and the First World War. Lightweight and less rigid than cast-iron goods, wire furnishings were slightly less expensive and far less durable.

The outdoor parlor usually was well separated from the rest of the world by a fence, made of cast iron, wrought iron, or wood. Fences were considered essential to protect cultivated areas from intruders of all kinds, to distinguish further between public and private property, and to help deter the spread of weeds. So common were the latter that landscape architect Elias Long observed that "nearly all the best places have some sort of fence or guard."[20] Most landscape and garden authorities preferred iron or wood fences to hedges and walls because the widely spaced palings of these fences merely veiled the house and gardens—much as fashionable lace curtains veiled the parlor windows. Both sorts of barriers allowed bypassers a tantalizingly obscure glimpse inside the grounds or parlor, while permitting its residents a carefully filtered view of the outside world.

The Craftsman Gardens

While the formal decorative style was at its height in the late nineteenth century, already under way were significant changes in the form and function of the American home, changes which affected both the domestic interior and the landscape throughout the twentieth century. As many interior decorators and architects began endorsing the more casually designed and furnished "living room," as opposed to the formal parlor, so also many professional and amateur gardeners began taking an interest in less structured "wild gardens" composed of ferns and wildflowers rather than hybrids and exotic plant materials.

Two English landscape architects, William Robinson and Gertrude

Fig. 57. House of Catherine Walter, 215 Flint Street, Rochester, N.Y. The protective fence, hammock, and plant-laden porch were common features of the average late-nineteenth-century garden. Courtesy of the Strong Museum, Rochester, N.Y.

Jekyll, more clearly articulated the principles of the design reform movement that changed the way many Americans viewed their gardens. Robinson and Jekyll criticized the complicated and highly structured garden designs of their day, the carpet beds, *parterres,* and straight ribbon borders— annuals strung along a walk or garden bed. They also rejected highly ornate garden furniture, ornaments, and contrasting exotic and hybrid plant materials that many found so endearing; design reformers perceived them to be garish and discordant. Jekyll, in particular, turned to the English cottage garden for romantic inspiration. "Not infrequently," she observed, "in passing along a country road, with eye alert to note the beauties that are so often presented by little wayside cottage gardens, something is seen that may well serve as a lesson in better planning. The lesson is generally one that teaches greater simplicity—the doing of one thing at a time; the avoidance of overmuch detail."[21] Like many contemporary household reformers who advocated an uncluttered interior, Jekyll urged gardeners to exercise similar restraint in the garden. "The possession of a quantity of plants, however good the plants may be themselves and however ample their number, does not make a garden; it only makes a *collection*. Having got the plants, the great thing is to use them with careful selection and definite intention."[22] Accordingly, Jekyll designed what appeared to be much simplified plans—although, arguably, these gardens required just as much care as carpet beds. Massing drifts of harmoniously toned perennial plants and shrubs in borders, she created "soul-satisfying pictures—a treasure of well-set jewels."[23] Imitating small cottage gardens where land was at a premium, she grouped plants and vines around house foundations and other built structures to better unite nature with architecture. Although more than willing to include exotic and hybrid plant materials when they were called for, Jekyll delighted in using plant materials indigenous to a locale.

Jekyll's concepts of garden design appealed to many Americans who were troubled by the social ills of industrialization and modernization. Alice Morse Earle, a staunch New Englander and trumpeter of the colonial past, echoed Gertrude Jekyll's denunciation of harshly colored hybrids, particularly those with vivid magenta colors. "It has come to be in textile products a stamp and symbol of vulgarity," Earle observed, "through the forceful brilliancy of our modern aniline dyes."[24] Those who espoused the ideals of the Arts and Crafts movement, a broad-based reform aimed at improving the living conditions of the average American, also found merit in this simplified concept of garden design. Like Robinson and Jekyll, furniture designer Gustav Stickley rejected the ornate aesthetics of nineteenth-century design, seeking inspiration for the future by looking to the pre-industrial past. Beginning in 1902, Stickley's *The Craftsman* magazine regularly featured articles on the new approach to gardening. "A Craftsman house should be surrounded by grounds that embody the Craftsman principles of utility, economy of effort, and beauty," *The Craftsman* commented. "Gardens must be planned in such a way as to require the minimum amount of care and stand the maximum amount of neglect."[25] Economy of effort was particularly important to many middle-class Americans, who, faced with the decreasing number of domestic servants, began to take on more and more household chores themselves.

In 1908, Grace Tabor, the gardening editor for *Woman's Home Companion* and a contributor to *The Craftsman,* contrasted the old and new styles of gardening with a graphic rendering of a landscape before and after renovations. The "before" illustration, labeled as a "mistake in landscaping," was typical of the formal landscaping style of the late nineteenth century. "The first and most glaring fault," wrote Tabor, ". . . is the entire absence of any sense of spaciousness" created by planting too many types of

ART IN ORNAMENTAL GARDENING

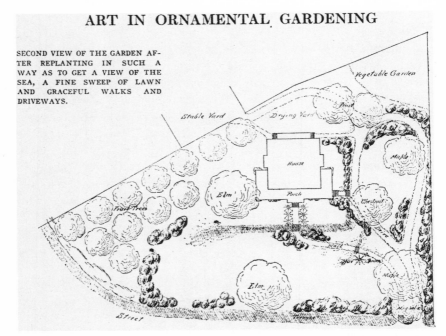

SECOND VIEW OF THE GARDEN AF-
TER REPLANTING IN SUCH A
WAY AS TO GET A VIEW OF THE
SEA, A FINE SWEEP OF LAWN
AND GRACEFUL WALKS AND
DRIVEWAYS.

Fig. 58. Like many other garden designers, Grace Tabor proposed simpler, less complicated garden plans for twentieth-century homes. *The Craftsman,* Aug. 1905. Courtesy of the Strong Museum, Rochester, N.Y.

trees, shrubs, and other plant materials.[26] The property sported a circular carpet bed which "was only bare earth until July. Then coleus and petunias filled the space; later, salvia appeared, making a color combination too dreadful for words." In the closed-in lawn, Tabor reported, "there stands a foolish urn, which is neither decorative nor useful." Her solution was to relate the house, lawns, and driveway to each other by introducing a gently curving driveway which emphasized the natural slope of the land. She eliminated many plantings to create unbroken stretches of lawn and a vista. Crimson rambler roses planted throughout the property provided a unified color scheme. Climbing roses, particularly the crimson rambler rose and the Dorothy Perkins rose, became favorite choices for gardeners throughout the early twentieth century because they were hardy and required a minimum of care—an important consideration for the average American gardener. Climbing roses were also viewed as choice planting materials because they could be trained over porches and doorways, literally uniting the garden with the dwelling.

CRAFTSMAN HOUSE. SERIES OF 1905. NUMBER VIII. EXTERIOR VIEW.

CRAFTSMAN HOUSE. SERIES OF 1905. NUMBER VIII. THE REAR PORCH

Fig. 59. "Let the garden surge up to and splash against your house, caressing it, as it were, as the sea washes against the shore." "A Craftsman's House," *The Craftsman,* Aug. 1905. Courtesy of the Strong Museum, Rochester, N.Y.

The desire to integrate house and garden led many architects, designers, and gardeners to introduce plantings around the house's foundations, in a manner recalling the cottage gardens Jekyll praised. "Let the garden surge up to and splash against your house, caressing it, as it were, as the sea washes against the shore," counseled *The Craftsman* in 1911. "Let garden and house float together, in one harmonious whole, the one finding completion in the other."[27] When planted around foundations, shrubbery subtly blended the house and landscape together, obscuring any separation. In the interest of beauty and utility, ground covers such as Japanese spurge came into common use because they provided a low-maintenance planting for foundations and garden beds and reduced weeding time. Foundation gardens were also a practical option for many Americans who could afford only small properties and therefore had only limited space for gardening.

Whereas previously fences had been standard garden fixtures, many early-twentieth-century gardening advisors favored open-grounds planning, in which one suburban lawn rolled into the next. Not only did this create an unobscured view of the neighborhood, but it also eliminated the time-consuming chore of trimming grass growing around fences. Some landscape architects, harking back to the hedgerows of the early nineteenth century, added living walls of privet, box, and arbor vitae kept clipped at a low two- or three-foot height so as not to clutter the landscape or deprive the enclosed property of light.

While some early-twentieth-century landscape architects and gardeners, such as C. A. Byers, professed that "no set of rules for gardening can be devised since each garden must be developed in accordance with the possibilities of the locality," most nevertheless agreed that the color schemes of the garden were best when they were restrained.[28] "One color, in a single border creation, is far better and prettier than half a dozen colors," Byers observed; ". . . there is always more danger in having too many colors in any flower plot than too few."[29] Colleague Vivian Burnett concurred, adding that the color scheme of the garden should always be in harmony with the colors of the roof, walls, and other structural elements of the house.[30]

Economy of effort was a fundamental principle of Craftsman gardens. In 1910, *The Craftsman* reported, "What are known as hardy herbaceous plants are the most popular ones now, and justly so. They are the best ones because they mean the smallest amount of trouble, and because they are likely to survive the largest amount of neglect."[31]

Evergreens of all descriptions thus became favorite choices of many con-

Fig. 60. Illustration from trade catalog, D. Hill Nursery, Dundee, Ill., 1931. Foundation plantings of evergreens and ground covers had been the low-maintenance choice of gardeners since the 1920s. Courtesy of the Strong Museum, Rochester, N.Y.

sumers. Not only were these materials hardy and easily cultivated; they also were associated with invigorating mountain and lake resorts which symbolized a healthful environment at a time when many Americans were concerned about the spread of contagious disease. Evergreens which filtered and purified the air were as sensible as they were beautiful—a fitting addition to the American home.

With practicality the watchword, many landscape architects and contributors to *The Craftsman* agreed that garden ornaments needed to be chosen with extreme care. "The past generation, vaguely realizing the value of the contrast of substantial forms with the variety of color and vegetation, stationed cast-iron dogs, elves, deer and settees over lawns and about the shrubbery," charged *The Craftsman* in 1909, "which was neither practical or useful." Terra-cotta pots and sundials, on the other hand, contrasted and "were beautiful things of their kind . . . [they] belong [in the garden] by right of long association and of use; none of the gardens in which they are would be complete without them. Yet a job lot of marble importations dumped into an American backyard would never constitute the furniture for a successful garden in this country."[32] Truly useful structures—latticework, arbors, and pergolas (colonnades with cross-timbers on top to support vines) provided an interesting degree of ornamentation to the garden while synthesizing nature and architecture. Arbors and trellises, painted white or green or left to weather, further connected nature with the built environment.

Even the most ideal outdoor spot, however, had to be adapted to human comfort. While a variety of outdoor furnishings were manufactured throughout the first quarter of the twentieth century, most household advisors agreed upon the three best choices for the American garden. "No matter how formal or naturalistic the garden may be," *The Craftsman* mused, "there is one kind of furniture that always seems to be in keeping—perhaps because it combines somewhat rustic materials with a certain simple dignity of design. And that is the hickory furniture."[33] The hickory furniture cited was manufactured by the Old Hickory Furniture Company of Martinsville, Indiana. This well-established producer of rustic-style furniture marketed a variety of porch and garden suites, benches, tables, lawn swings, and other articles in their bid to "furnish the great outdoors."[34] *The Home Magazine* in 1923 also favored rustic hickory furnishings, which it claimed added "the precisely right tone. . . . The curved arms of the hickory rocking chair and settee give almost irresistible invitation to sink into the cushion covered seats."[35] *The Home Magazine* judged wicker and reed furniture stripped of its nineteenth-century ornament, to be "light and cool" and "the most appropriate porch furniture."[36] *The Craftsman* concurred, asserting that "willow chairs and settles seem to belong naturally to life in the garden."[37] Both publications further allowed that "plenty of hammocks" or "a canvas porch swing with padded seat and back and a liberal supply of pillows" provided the additional comfort that living in a modern Eden demanded.

The late nineteenth and early twentieth centuries witnessed significant change and development in gardening practices and styles. Popularly priced mail-order seeds allowed consumers to cultivate a wide variety of useful and ornamental plants. Tool manufacturers and iron foundries, celebrating newly realized manufacturing capabilities, developed new lines of tools for the suburban tiller of the soil, while other manufacturers and designers continually experimented with new materials from which to create garden furnishings and ornaments. While fashions came and went in the garden, much as they did inside the house, one thing remained constant. That was the timeless satisfaction and pleasure that gardening offered those who undertook it as a pastime. As Charles Dudley Warner reflected after tending his own garden plot, "It is not simply beets and potatoes and corn and string beans that one raises in his well-hoed garden: it is the average of human life."[38]

Notes

1. U.S., Bureau of the Census, *Historical Statistics of the United States, Colonial Times to 1970* (Washington, D.C.: U.S. Government Printing Office, 1975), 145.

2. Charles Dudley Warner, *The Complete Writings of Charles Dudley Warner* (Hartford, Conn.: American Publishing Co., 1904), 18.

3. *The Horticulturist* 3 (Mar. 1850):153.

4. W.H. McIntosh, *A History of Monroe County, New York* (Philadelphia: Everts, Ensign, and Everts, 1877), 113–16.

5. Ibid., 115.

6. Ibid., 115.

7. Ibid., 114.

8. *Maule's Seed Catalogue for 1891* (Philadelphia, 1891), 94. Naomi Richardson, Oswego, N.Y., unpublished diaries, 2 Apr. 1885; private collection.

9. *Illustrated Catalogue, Smith and Winchester* (Boston, 1890), 160.

10. Elias Long, *Ornamental Gardening for Americans* (New York: Orange Judd Co., 1885), 166.

11. Eben Rexford, *Vick's Home Floriculture* (Rochester, N.Y.: James Vick, 1890), 173.

12. Naomi Richardson, diary, Apr. 2 1885

13. Maule, *Seed Catalogue,* 94.

14. Rexford, *Home Floriculture,* 43.

15. Ibid., 45.

16. Ibid., 213.

17. *E.T. Barnum Wire and Iron Goods* (Detroit, Mich., 1894), 11.

18. Ibid., 10.

19. Gervase Wheeler, *Rural Homes* (New York, 1852), cited in Richard Saunders, *Collection and Restoring Wicker Furniture* (New York: Crown, 1976), 16.

20. Long, *Ornamental Gardening,* 237.

21. Gertrude Jekyll, *Colour Schemes for the Flower Garden* (Boston: Little, Brown, 1988), 140.

22. Ibid., 17.

23. Ibid., 18.

24. Alice Morse Earle, *Old Time Gardens Newly Set Forth* (New York: Macmillan, 1902), 176.

25. Vivian Burnett, "Craftsman Gardens for Craftsman Homes," *The Craftsman* 18 (Apr. 1910):46.

26. Grace Tabor, "Art in Ornamental Gardening," *The Craftsman* (1908):36–37.

27. "The Individuality of American Gardens," *The Craftsman* (Aug. 1911):61.

28. C.A. Byers, "The Proper Consideration of Lawns and Gardens," *The Craftsman* (Apr. 1907):107.

29. Ibid., 108.

30. Burnett, "Craftsman Gardens," 51.

31. Ibid., 52.

32. "New Use of Concrete for Garden Ornaments," *The Craftsman* 16 (Aug. 1909):586.

33. "Furniture for Garden Life," *The Craftsman* 25 (Mar. 1914):606.

34. *Old Hickory Porch and Garden Furniture* (Martinsville, Ind.: Old Hickory Chair Co., 1928), 1.

35. "Porches and Porch Life," *Home Annual Supplement to Woman's Weekly,* 1923, 15.

36. "Furniture for Garden Life," 606.

37. "Porches and Porch Life," 15.

38. Warner, *Complete Writings,* 18.

PART III

KEEPING HOUSE

CHAPTER NINE

Coal Stoves and Clean Sinks: Housework between 1890 and 1930

Ruth Schwartz Cowan

In the forty years between 1890 and 1930, the equipment with which housework was done underwent a veritable industrial revolution.[1] The phrase "Industrial Revolution" rarely conjures up images of domestic appliances; pictures of railroads and factories come to most peoples' minds faster than images of washing machines and bathrooms. Nonetheless, the washing machine and the bathroom are as much products of industrialization as the railroad and the factory—and they are just as full of social portents. Before we examine those portents, however, it will be helpful to learn something about the industrial revolution in the home, about the changes in the two great technological systems—the fuel system and the water system—that occurred between 1890 and 1930 and that forever marked the practices and the attitudes that characterize housework in the United States.

The wood- or coal-burning cast-iron stove was replaced by a gas (or oil) range, which meant that the chores of hauling fuel, carrying out ashes, "blacking" the stove (to prevent rust), and manipulating the draft vents were all eliminated; indeed, beginning around 1915, most gas ranges had thermostats which could automatically regulate the temperature of an oven. Electric lighting replaced oil and gas lamps, which meant that no-one had to clean a black residue off the lamp globes again (walls stayed cleaner, too). As soon as a household installed electric wiring for lights, it could also consider purchasing electric appliances. The first of these (around 1880) was the household fan. After the fan came the electric iron (around 1905) and then the thermostatically controlled electric iron (about 1925; earlier versions had had to be unplugged when they got too hot), both of which replaced the aptly named "sad iron"—a very heavy but very simple tool that was kept hot by its own little coal-burning stove. As electric manufacturers learned to build fractional horsepower motors cheaply, the fan and the iron were followed quickly (just before and after World War I) by the vacuum cleaner, the electric sewing machine (which replaced the treadle machine), the electric (but not automatic) washing machine, and (after 1925) the electric refrigerator. In 1941, according to the Bureau of Labor Statistics, 80 percent of all residences in the United States were wired for electricity, 79 percent of the housekeeping families in the United States had electric irons, 52 percent had power washing machines, a similar percentage had refrigerators, and 47 percent had vacuum cleaners.[2] Thus, in many American homes metal washboards and wooden tubs had been replaced by electrically driven agitators and wringers; rugs were being vacuumed on the floor instead of being carried outside and beaten; and the services of icemen had been dispensed with, along with melting trays that repeatedly had to be dumped.

In addition, and just as significantly, by 1930, hot and cold running water systems had become the norm in middle-class housing and even in housing for the urban poor (the rural poor had to wait, in some instances until after World War II). "Hot and cold running water systems" are complex technologies (as anyone knows who has had to wait to get a plumber to fix one), and a brief consideration of their several parts will indicate, by implication, what a profound difference they can make in housework. The system begins with a *water source* (which may be operated by a municipality, a utility company, or an individual household); it also includes *pipes* to conduct water into more than one room of a house, *devices for heating* some of the water *and distributing* it, specialized *containers* for holding some of the water (water closets, sinks, bathtubs, shower stalls), and finally *drains, pipes, and sewers* for removing "used" water.

Between 1900 and 1930, small electric and gasoline motors became available to run water pumps in rural homes. Gas and electric companies began to lower the price and promote the sale of self-sufficient water heaters. New technologies were introduced in the manufacture of sanitary fixtures (ceramic finishes over metal bases), which both lowered the price and eased the maintenance of bathroom and kitchen furnishings. New processes (particularly a technique for alloying zinc with steel) lowered the price of plumbing pipes, and monopolistic organization in the pipe industry allowed plumbing systems to become standardized. By the advent of the Depression, the majority of American households had stopped using an outdoor privy, children had stopped carrying buckets of water, and housewives had stopped boiling laundry on their stoves.

Like all revolutions, the industrial revolution in the home had a profound effect on people, in this case on the people who do housework: housewives and domestic servants. In order to describe and to understand that effect, however, we must distinguish two great classes of housewives—those who were, for want of a better term, middle-class; and those who were poor.

In statistical terms, it is hard for historians to calculate precisely how many people belonged in each of those two categories in the early decades of the twentieth century; the census did not then ask people about their incomes (while it is difficult to remember this, such information was once considered very private), and there was no income tax from which the information could be derived indirectly. Nonetheless, from very partial information historians who specialize in such matters have concluded that before World War II roughly two-thirds of the population lived *below* what was then considered the standard of "health and decency."[3]

The fabled "prosperity" of the 1920s was more apparent than real and more intermittent than continuous for the families of industrial workers, small farmers, day laborers, and skilled craftsmen—the bulk of the American population. Helen and Robert Lynd calculated, for example, that in Muncie, Indiana, in 1924, $1,920.87 was required to achieve "health and decency" for a family of five (the estimate included the costs of rent, food, fuel, clothing, insurance, union dues, and other such items) and that somewhere between 70 percent and 88 percent of all the households in town in that year failed to attain it.[4] Similarly, in 1926, in Zanesville, Ohio, 70 percent of all families had incomes below $2,000.[5] The Brookings Institution attempted a nationwide survey in 1929, when the "boom" had been "booming" for more than a decade, and calculated, a little more optimistically, that 59 percent of the nation's families did not earn enough (all sources of income being considered) to live decently. Needless to say, that figure went up, rather than down, during the next decade.[6]

Both middle-class and poor housewives benefitted from the industrial revolution in their homes, but the pattern of benefits was different for each group and for the various members within their families.

Servants, Services, Standards: The Middle Class

We happen to know a good deal about what happened to middle-class housewives during the early decades of this century, thanks to the patient inquiries of home economists. Home economists began to professionalize in the first decade of this century; the *Journal of Home Economics,* the leading professional publication, has appeared continuously since 1908. In the profession's early years, one of the methodologies that home economists used extensively was time study, a technique they borrowed from management specialists such as Frederick W. Taylor and Frank Gilbreth. (Frank Gilbreth, in fact, was the husband of Lillian Gilbreth, one of the leading home economists and management authorities of her day; their life together is described in *Cheaper by the Dozen* and other books by their children.) Home economists wanted to know how much time housewives spent on their work and how the time was divided among tasks. They sometimes went into people's homes and followed a housewife with a stopwatch ("participant observation"), or they prepared complex blank schedules and asked housewives to fill them in regularly during the day or just before retiring ("retrospective" analysis); or they might time themselves, or their students, doing the work in a home, or they might time someone doing the work in a laboratory. Occasionally they even studied the human energy expended on a task by hooking the worker up to a basal metabolism machine and studying, for example, the difference between sweeping a floor with a broom and vacuuming it.[7]

Most of the housewives studied by home economists were of the middle class: faculty wives in the communities that had university schools of home economics, or members of community groups such as the Parent-Teacher Association, the League of Women Voters, or the American Association of University Women—women who, when approached, would be willing to participate in such an experimental study. In the early 1970s, a sociologist at the University of Michigan, Joann Vanek, reanalyzed hundreds of the time studies which had appeared over the decades in the *Journal of Home Economics* and came to a conclusion that some home economists had recognized even earlier: an average middle-class housewife in 1940 spent more (that's right, *more*) time doing housework than her mother (assuming that her mother had also been middle-class) had been spending in 1910.[8]

In the face of all the changes that had occurred in the equipment with which housework was done, how could that have been true? The answer to that question has three components. First, the number of domestic servants had declined. Second, the number of commercial services provided to households also had declined. Third, standards for housework had risen. We shall briefly consider each of these components.

Between 1900 and 1920, the number of households in the United States rose from 15.9 million to 24.4 million; at the same time, the number of domestic servants counted by the census dropped from 1.6 million to 1.4 million. This meant that the ratio of households to servants almost doubled in those twenty years, rising from 9.9 to 17.4. Between 1920 and 1930, the ratio's increase was even more precipitous, because the Immigration Restriction Acts of the mid-1920s closed the door on the nation's prime supply of servants: single women who had recently immigrated. The employment of a servant had been, since early in the nineteenth century, the single most significant indicator of middle-class status; indeed, the income that the Lynds calculated for a family of five to live at a minimum standard of decency included the wages of a domestic servant.[9] Those servants were not idle status symbols; without modern household equipment, it took the labor of at least two adult women to maintain a family at a decent standard of living. Put simply, what happened in middle-class families between 1900 and 1940, approximately, was that they replaced their living servants with nonliving ones. Indeed, many advertisers used precisely this inducement to sell their products. "Our vacuum cleaner," an ad might say, "is more reliable than your Annie. All you need to do is plug it in. It never asks for a raise, calls in sick, or gets drunk." Someone had to run the vacuum cleaner, of course; someone had to operate the new washing machine and run all the clothes through the wringer; someone also had to be cooking in front of that lovely gas range. As servants disappeared, that "someone" increasingly became the middle-class housewife herself.

Between 1900 and 1940, the extent to which a middle-class housewife could rely on the services of commercial agencies also declined. The middle-class housewife of 1900 was, essentially, a manager—one might even say a contractor. She supervised the work of some people whom she employed directly and of other people to whom she subcontracted part of "her" work. Some of her laundry might be done by a laundress, but some of it might be "sent" to a commercial laundry ("sent" is in quotes here, because the laundry often provided pickup and delivery services). Retailers regularly came to her house: the grocer, the baker, the butcher, the coal man, the ice man all delivered. Seamstresses came in for the day, or sometimes for the week, to help get seasonal clothes in order. The doctor made house calls.

By 1940, much of this commercial service was gone. The steam laundry, although not yet completely dead, was in the process of dying, killed by the electric washing machine. The grocer, the baker, and the butcher no longer could afford to deliver, struggling as they were to compete with the supermarket and to survive the Depression. The seamstress had been displaced

Fig. 61. Lux soap advertisement. This advertisement illustrates the middle-class pattern of doing laundry with servants. *Ladies' Home Journal,* 1918. Courtesy of Lever Brothers.

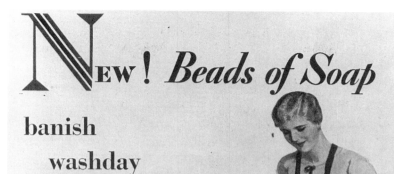

Fig. 62. Supersuds advertisement. This advertisement illustrates the change that the washing machine wrought (no servant). *Ladies' Home Journal,* 1928. Courtesy of Colgate-Palmolive Co.

Fig. 63. Elmont, N.Y., date unknown. This photograph illustrates the way some groceries were delivered in the first decade of this century. Courtesy of the Nassau County Museum, Hempstead, N.Y.

by ready-made clothes for women and children. The doctor had gotten a car but had also figured out that he could see many more patients if he stayed in his office. As a result, the middle-class housewife ceased to be a manager and became, instead, a worker—the person who provided transportation services for goods and people, the person who traveled to shops and stood in line to obtain the things that once had been brought to her mother's doorstep. Such activities weren't arduous work, but they certainly were work, and they certainly took time. Hence, they accounted for part of the increase in the time spent in housework by middle-class women.

Finally, standards had risen. The housewife of 1940 was expected to spend much more time with her children than her mother had spent— playing with them on the living room floor, taking them to playgrounds, providing nurturance and education at all hours of the day and night. This was work that, if it was done at all, servants once had been delegated to do. "I accommodate my entire life to my little girl," one Muncie housewife reported to the Lynds in 1924. "She takes three music lessons a week and I practice with her forty minutes a day."

"My mother never stepped inside the school building as far as I can remember," another woman reported, "but now there are never ten days that go by without my either visiting the children's school or getting in touch with their teacher. I have given up church work and club work since the children came."

"I put on roller skates with the boys and pass a football with them," said a third, "and my mother back East thinks it's scandalous."[10]

Cleanliness standards had risen as well. People began changing two sheets a week instead of just one. Men stopped wearing detachable collars and cuffs, so the whole shirt had to be laundered after it was worn. The new germ theory convinced people that bathrooms and kitchens had to be kept scrupulously clean in order to prevent disease. The advent of information about vitamins convinced them that every meal had to be balanced. In these years the classic American standard of living was taking shape— three square meals a day, scrupulous cleanliness of persons and places, compulsive attention to preventive medicine, concern with every child's psychological and physical development. But at every step along the way, there was more work for middle-class housewives to do in their homes.

Bills, Babies, Better Futures: The Poor

For poor housewives, the pattern of change was somewhat different—and, unfortunately, we know less about it. Home economists did not routinely ask poor housewives to do time budget studies, and, as a consequence, we cannot know whether, on the whole, this group of women was spending more or less time on its work in the years between 1890 and 1940. On the other hand, home economists and others (particularly social reformers) did routinely worry about the money budgets of the poor and about their housing conditions, and this means that we can learn something at least about the equipment with which poor housewives did their work. Several sociologists became interested in interviewing poor housewives in the years after 1900 (in the tradition of what has come to be called "community studies," beginning with Margaret Byington's sympathetic portrait of Homestead, Pennsylvania, and ending, for the period of time of interest for this paper, with Margaret Hagood's investigation, *Mothers of the South*). As a result, we also know something—albeit not in enormous depth—about the attitudes that poor housewives brought to their work.[11]

Fig. 64. Homestead, Pennsylvania, ca. 1910. A typical poor urban housewife and some of her tools and living conditions. Photograph by Lewis Hine. From Margaret Byington, *Homestead: The Households of a Mill Town* (New York: Russell Sage Foundation, 1910).

Between 1910 and 1940, poor urban (but not rural) housewives were beginning to benefit from some of the amenities that already had become standard for their middle-class contemporaries. The hard-pressed house-wife of this period was not investing in luxuries (although some conservative critics accused her of this); but when times were good, she and her husband were trying to create for themselves and their children the standard of living to which more prosperous families had already become accustomed. With the help of building and loan associations, they were trying to buy their own houses; in Zanesville, Ohio, for example, in 1926, 79.9 percent of the households owned their own home, despite the fact that 70 percent of them earned less than two thousand dollars a year.[12]. These houses were neither spacious nor elegant, but they might well have been wired for electricity (73.7 percent in Zanesville) and outfitted with running water (90 percent), a bathroom with indoor toilet and tub (60 percent), piped gas (96 percent), a gas range (89.6 percent), a telephone (69 percent), and even a car (48 percent).[13]

Fig. 65. Livermore, Calif., 1972. A typical California suburban kitchen, early 1970s. One might think of the woman depicted as being the granddaughter of the woman in figure 64. Photograph by Bill Owens. Bill Owens, *Suburbia* (San Francisco: Straight Arrow Books, 1972). Courtesy of Bill Owens.

From the point of view of those who had known the discomfort of poverty in their youth, these amenities were not so much amenities as basic decencies too long withheld. To own one's own home meant to be out from under the thumb of a landlord who could evict a family; to have electric lights meant an end to eyestrain, kerosene explosions, and the need to clean lamps; to have running water, an end to exhausting labor; to have a toilet, an end to the discomfort of a privy on a snowy night and to typhoid fever in the summer.

In the period after the First World War, the diffusion of these amenities combined with increasingly prevalent public health measures—purification and inspection of milk, water treatment plants, sewers for poor neighborhoods (the rich had long had them), diphtheria inoculations, certification of meat and poultry, regular refuse collection—to give this generation a higher standard of living higher (or rather a lower standard of death and illness) than their parents had had.[14]

On the other hand, the poor housewife still had burdensome and mind-numbing chores to perform. Although she might have entered the twentieth century in terms of amenities, she had not entered it in terms of birth control; until the 1950s, the poor continued to bear more children than the rich—and nothing increases the burden of housework more than the presence of children, especially small ones. When there are eight or nine mouths to feed, cooking is a difficult enterprise, even if it can be done at a gas range; and the drudgery of laundry, especially if there are diapers, is not greatly eased when the hot water comes out of a tap rather than a pot.

Nor could the poor housewife be certain of having access to amenities when they might be needed most. The washing machine, the car, and the living-room furniture all were likely to have been bought on an installment plan; the house carried a mortgage; and the utility companies presented their bills monthly. Thus, in bad times, when her husband was out of work or disabled and she was forced into the labor market—precisely the time when she most needed her washing machine to do the laundry or her car to reduce trips to the market—the family was more than likely to fall behind in its payments. As a result, the electricity might be turned off or the car repossessed. The Lynds described the technological conditions of working-class homes in Muncie as, under the best conditions, a "crazy quilt": "A single home may be operated in the twentieth century when it comes to ownership of an automobile and vacuum cleaner, while its lack of a bathtub may throw it back into another era and its lack of sewer connection . . . put it on par with life in the Middle Ages."[15] This quilt must have been even crazier when conditions were not the best; no small part of the horror of the Depression was the reality of eviction and repossession.

The widespread popularity (and the cheap price) of women's magazines made the possibility of a middle-class standard of living ever obvious to the poor housewife; her own experience of the crazy quilt did the same. What such housewives seem (judging from their words and their behavior) to have perceived very clearly was that, if they could be released from the burden of intermittent market labor and if they could get access to decent housing and a bare minimum of appliances, they and their families too could manage to achieve a middle-class standard of living. Keeping house might be a long day's work, but it would be a productive day; the children would, on the whole, stay healthy and go off to school reasonably well dressed, rested, and fed, and the husband would go off to work the same way. And if the kids could make it through school, there was a possibility that some of them could make it into white-collar work, secure in the knowledge that Mom and Dad could provide a bath more than once a week (white-collar workers could not smell of sweat and keep their jobs) and that the laundry too would be done (we call desk jobs "white-collar" for good reason). From the perspective of the poor housewife in the early decades of this century, housework was not just work; when it could be performed productively, it was a ticket to a better future for her family.

Thus the middle-class woman and the poorer woman, although performing the same work, often with the same tools, brought very different attitudes to their work. The middle-class woman may well have resented finding herself with burdens that her mother had not had; to the poorer woman, full responsibility for cooking and cleaning, nursing and tutoring, laundering and sewing, was not a burden at all, but—under the best of conditions, and with more than a little luck—a source of considerable pride and emotional gratification. Housework is, after all, work, and work can mean many different things to many different people, depending on the conditions under which it is done, the attitudes that people bring to it, and the character of what they produce. It is small wonder that, in the next generation, the daughters of middle-class women became desirous of liberation, while the daughters of poorer women (even those who had finally made it into the middle classes) remained happy to be doing housework.

Notes

1. The argument presented in this chapter is derived from my book, Ruth Schwartz Cowan, *More Work for Mother: The Ironies of Household Technology from the Open Hearth to the Microwave* (New York: Basic Books, 1983).

2. "Prices, and Cost and Standards of Living," *Monthly Labor Review* 61 (Dec. 1945):1220–21.

3. See James T. Patterson, *America's Struggle Against Poverty, 1900–1980* (Cambridge, Mass.: Harvard Univ. Press, 1981), ch. 1, for a summary of literature on this issue.

4. Robert S. Lynd and Helen Merrill Lynd, *Middletown: A Study in American Culture* (New York: Harcourt, Brace, 1929), 84.

5. R.O. Eastman, Inc., *Zanesville, Ohio, and Thirty-six Other American Cities* (New York: Literary Digest, 1927), 52.

6. For 1929 data, see Maurice Leven, Harold G. Moulton, and Clark Warburton, *America's Capacity to Consume* (Washington, D.C.: Brookings Institution, 1934), 54. For the impact of the Depression, see U.S., National Resources Committee, *Consumer Incomes in the United States: Their Distribution in 1935–36* (Washington, D.C.: U.S. Government Printing Office, 1938).

7. For information on time studies, see U.S., Department of Agriculture, Agri-

cultural Research Administration, Bureau of Human Nutrition and Home Economics, *Time Costs of Homemaking, A Study of 1500 Rural and Urban Households* (mimeo., 1944); U.S., President's Conference on Home Building and Home Ownership, *Household Management and Kitchens*, Reports of the Conference, vol. 9 (Washington, D.C., 1932); Joann Vanek, "Keeping Busy: Time Spent in Housework, United States, 1920–1970" (Ph.D. diss., Univ. of Michigan, 1973); and Joann Vanek, "Time Spent in Housework," *Scientific American* 231 (Nov. 1974):116–25.

8. Vanek, "Keeping Busy."

9. Robert Lynd and Helen Lynd, *Middletown*, 84, 518.

10. Remarks made by various housewives of the "business class," as quoted in ibid., 146–48.

11. Margaret F. Byington, *Homestead: The Households of a Mill Town* (New York: Russell Sage Foundation, 1910); Margaret J. Hagood, *Mothers of the South: Portraiture of the White Tenant Farm Woman* (Chapel Hill: Univ. of North Carolina Press, 1939). See also Robert Coit Chapin, *The Standard of Living Among Workingmen's Families in New York City* (New York: Russell Sage Foundation, 1909).

12. R.O. Eastman, Inc., *Zanesville*, 52.

13. Ibid., 43, 55, 91.

14. The data and interpretations in this paragraph are taken from George Rosen, *Preventive Medicine in the United States, 1900–1975* (New York: Science History Publications, 1975), *passim*.

15. Robert Lynd and Helen Lynd, *Middletown*, 174–75.

CHAPTER TEN

Conduits and Conduct: Home Utilities in Victorian America, 1876–1915

Thomas J. Schlereth

Between the 1876 Centennial World's Fair at Philadelphia and the 1915 Panama-Pacific International Exposition in San Francisco, the middle-class house became increasingly connected to a growing maze of pipes, wires, ducts, cables, conduits, and mains. Each disappeared into a wall or into the ground and joined an elaborate network that spread beyond the house. Residents greeted these new home utilities with both enthusiasm and anxiety. Such technologies simultaneously made everyday life easier and more complicated.

While the new forms of utilities—heat, light, power, sewerage—altered home life, the change was uneven as to pace and place. The wealthy secured such services before the poor, city residents before farm families, and, to an extent, easterners before southerners and westerners. Another pattern characterized the utilities' evolution. Devices such as improved septic tanks or efficient windmills, first installed by independent homeowners on their own grounds, usually had to be abandoned once population density increased around them. Such property owners connected (or were coerced to connect) to centralized services such as a district sewerage system or a municipal waterworks. Public services thus replaced private labor. Water, heat, light, and sewerage became commodities to be purchased rather than to be made or maintained at home.

In this brief overview of certain changes in home utilities in the era 1876–1915, we shall survey three topics. First, we shall look at how two of life's necessities, water and waste, came in and out of the house; second, let us trace what impact new methods of heating and lighting had upon American residential behavior; and, third, let us assess what role these changing technologies played in the development and use of a new interior space, the American bathroom.

Water and Waste

In the 1870s, the tasks of lugging fresh water into the home and carrying dirty water and liquid refuse out were accepted facets of the daily routines of most American women and children. Late-nineteenth-century rural householders got water by multiple means: buckets were filled at water courses, cisterns, and rain barrels; and kitchen pumps were located over farmhouse wells or connected to tanks maintained by windmills. Urbanites secured water from barrels filled by water-hauling carts; from street hydrants in tenement courtyards or water taps in a tenement hallway; or through a house plumbing system connected to public water mains.

Municipal waterworks owed their existence more to public health alarms than to consumer water demands. Widespread yellow fever epidemics of the 1790s forced Philadelphia into pioneering the country's first major public water supply system. Other large cities followed Philadelphia's lead, so that by the 1876 Centennial, most cities over ten thousand population had some kind of municipal water supply to some of their neighborhoods. In 1915, similar service reached communities of five thousand.[1]

Rural towns dug city wells or hired tank wagons to deliver bulk water to the storage barrels of households contracting for their service. Other communities constructed hilltop reservoirs to dispatch water, via gravity, through wood, iron, and steel pipes. The water tower, usually the community's tallest public structure and frequently emblazoned with the community's name and population, loomed as one of small-town America's most visible icons. Homer Croy, writing of a Missouri town in *West of the Water Tower* (1923), notes: "The tower was a town character; the city revolved around it almost as much as the court house, or around the square. Picnic parties were held at its base; boys climbed up the little iron ladder, which seemed to reach to infinity, as high as courage lasted, and scratched a chalk mark on the red brick; then the next boy tried to raise it."[2] Town photographers made the same ascent to snap panoramic views.

Unlike small-town or big-city folk, most farm families got their water on their own, from springs, creeks, or rivers. Wells were dug and redug, some of Brobdingnagian proportions. One farmer in 1889 had to put down a four hundred-foot shaft on Cliff Table, Nebraska, to get a home water supply. Windmills, if they could be afforded, alleviated some of the backbreaking labor of water procurement.

Municipal concern for a water supply did not necessarily entail responsibility for water disposal. Sewerage and garbage collection lagged behind water provision. Before the 1850s, no American city had sewers adequate to remove human waste from houses. In the 1880s, however urban areas began constructing sewerage systems, although most were largely for storm water collection.[3] City ordinances usually forbade people to dump wastes in them, but many urbanites did. Some homeowners contracted with scavengers (night soil men) or farmers to collect wastes from privy vaults; others dumped waste in the backyard, the front street, or vacant lots. Adoption of the water closet, first installed in urban dwellings, further exacerbated the problem.[4]

Heat and Light

Throughout the nineteenth century, Americans experimented with different ways to heat their homes. In 1800, Benjamin Thompson (later Count Rumford) proposed that if the fireplace's two functions—heating and cooking—were separated, each would have a greater thermal capacity and use fuel more efficiently. Patents for cast-iron parlor stoves, baseburners, (figure 66) and kitchen ranges proliferated, beginning in the 1840s. Made in small foundries such as the Dubuque Stove Company in Iowa or Dowagiac Round Oak Stove Company in Michigan, house stoves came in all shapes, styles, and sizes, simple or elaborate, and often enhanced by the personal innovations of individual craftsmen. At the 1915 Panama-Pacific Exposition, one could still see displays of box, cannon, globe, or "pot-bellied" stoves, with all manner of flues, campers, and grates.[5]

No matter what model or brand, heating stoves demanded three tasks of the homeowner: getting the fuel, tending the fire, and removing the ash. While some of the more complicated (and more expensive) stoves came equipped with "automatic" self-feeding mechanisms, most heating stoves demanded continual fuel hauling, monitoring and maintenance. Even the so-called "self-tenders" tended themselves only between hopper fillings.

In frontier communities, almost anything combustible was burned to keep warm. Homesteaders on the western Texas Plains in the 1880s used mesquite, shinnery (a dwarf oak), corncobs, and cow chips. Euphemistically called "surface coal" and "grassoline," dried cow manure provided a cheap, abundant, and fairly efficient, although slightly odorous, fuel. Even after railroads brought coal to this region, some settlers continued to maintain a chip shed.[6] Urban dwellers fueled their stoves and later their furnaces mostly with coal. So did American industry. Coal ton-

Fig. 66. Formal parlor, Lucien Warner residence, St. Paul, Minn., 1890. Courtesy of Minnesota Historical Society.

nage increased from 15.2 million in 1870 to 127.8 million in 1920, making the mining of both hard and soft coal vital to the national economy. Entire towns, such as Carltonville, Illinois, or Connelsville, Pennsylvania, owed their existence to King Coal.[7]

Only the middle class could afford a central furnace in the late nineteenth century. Workers and their families usually made do with some variety of a room baseburner. "Start your fire in the fall," claimed the 1908 Sears, Roebuck catalog about its Acme Sunburst model, "fill the magazine at the top once or twice a day . . . regulate the draft . . . shake down the fire . . . remove the ashes occasionally, and the stove does the rest."[8] But every house stove, no matter what its cost or claims, had its problems: cracked pipes, inadequate dampers, poor drafts, smoky flues. Stoves too airtight produced stuffy rooms and headaches; others leaked carbon monoxide, creating hazardous breathing. Almost all sucked up a room's available moisture, resulting in dry skin and cracked plaster.

Despite their many stoves (over 7,000 models patented by 1910), most

Americans living through winters north of the Ohio or Missouri rivers endured cold from mid-November to mid-April. Families resigned themselves to awakening to chilly mornings after nights spent sleeping in unheated attics and second-floor bedchambers. As Alice LaCasse, a New Hampshire cotton worker, recalled: "We had a big stove in the kitchen and three grills in the ceiling, so that in the winter a little bit of heat went up to the second floor, but hardly any at all reached the third and fourth floors."[9] To counteract the cold, some heated iron ingots, ceramic "bed bricks," and soapstones to serve as bedwarmers. Those whose familial status determined that they slept in the upper stories (usually children and adolescents) devised a simple daily routine in order to cope: undress by the stove at night and dash upstairs; in the morning, bolt as quickly as possible back to the stove to dress again.

Central heating, largely a middle-class comfort (figure 67) that was enjoyed only by some working-class families after World War I, transformed the American home by both cluttering it and enlarging it. Cast-iron radiators, developed in the 1890s, and brass floor registers complicated interior decoration on the first and, later, upper stories.[10] The cellar expanded into a basement. Typically an ill-ventilated hole in the ground with stone walls and an earthen floor, the cellar had been used only for storing items unaffected by dampness. Basements, on the other hand, were larger, drier, cleaner spaces, often walled in Portland cement rather than stone. Reached from a stair in the kitchen as well as from outside, they increasingly housed the numerous home technologies that delivered creature comforts to the widening middle class. By 1915, in addition to the ungainly octopus of the massive coal furnace, with its labyrinth of pipes (if hot water heat) or cylindrical ducts (if hot air heat) squeezing through walls and floors, one might also find a hot water heater, a washing machine, and laundry tubs, plus a welter of cast-iron, lead, and tile pipes which clung to basement walls and hung from floor joists.

While central heating eliminated the necessity of a large baseburner on the first floor or the luxury of separate stoves in individual rooms, it did not banish the traditional hearth. The turn-of-the-century middle-class residence, whether designed in a historical or a "modern" style, often retained the fireplace's symbolic function even when it did not need its utilitarian one.

Artificial lighting drastically altered everyday life in the postbellum American house. Slowly, by means of new fuels (gas and petroleum), power sources (electricity), and a myriad of lighting devices, the daily natural

Fig. 67. Advertisement, Williamson Underfeed Furnaces and Boilers. *McClure's Magazine,* 1914.

cycle of light and darkness ceased to condition human activities. Rural families lit their homes by traditional methods, such as tallow candles, floating tapers (in assorted greases), and oil lamps that burned lard, whale, cottonseed, and castor oils, turpentine, or camphor. Kerosene, a petroleum derivative, came into wide use after the discovery of oil in Titusville, Pennsylvania, in 1859. "Kero" reigned as the country's most important refined product, with gasoline viewed as only a petroleum by-product until the expanded use of the internal combustion engine. Sold at country stores, town oil dealers, and urban lumberyards, kerosene lit the lamps (figure 66) of the homes of the working class.[11] Innovations took place on every element of kero lamps—burners, wicks, and chimneys—throughout the nineteenth century. Their result: more light for less fuel. In the 1870s, kerosene lamps burned at six to twenty candlepower; by the 1910s, advertisers claimed sixty to eighty.

The care and feeding of kerosene lamps meant their daily filling, wiping, and wick trimming; weekly washing of the chimneys and shades; and periodic rewicking and dismantling for a thorough cleaning with a soda cleanser. Despite their operational demands, fire hazards, odor, and soot, kerosene lamps (like coal stoves) fostered living in a space defined by a specific light or a heat source. Immigrant memoirs and rural autobiographies of the period often reflect on the family closeness generated by a room's central stove or center lamp.[12] Central heating and electrical lighting slowly tended to disperse such family circles. Centrifugal privacy replaced centripetal intimacy.

Gaslight offered an alternative to the dirts and demands of kerosene illumination—if the homeowner could afford its installation and if his home was located close to its supply. While manufactured gas (rather than natural gas) lit Rembrandt Peale's Baltimore Museum as early as 1816, its use in the homes of the American wealthy came in the Victorian era, giving the period one of its romantic (but unrepresentative) sobriquets as "The Gaslight Era." The mansions of a city's elite (who often capitalized the private or municipal gasworks) sported elaborate multilight chandeliers, ornamented with porcelain and glass shades.

Most Americans, however, initially experienced gaslights in public rather than private places. Main streets, fashionable residential thoroughfares, and sometimes suburban streets (in Cincinnati, Clifton's streets have been gaslit since 1853) first received gas illumination. So, too, did fashionable bars, department stores, and government buildings. Gaslighting could also be found in some schools, hospital, and factories.[13]

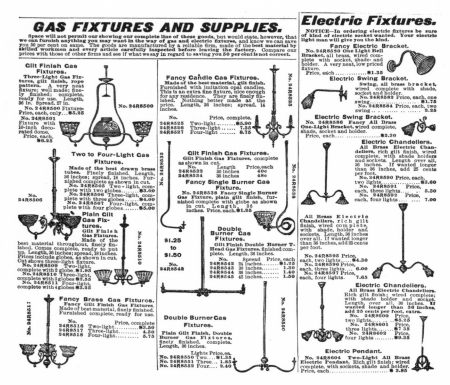

Fig. 68. Combined advertisement featuring both gas and electric fixtures and supplies. *Sears, Roebuck Catalog,* 1902.

Thomas Edison's innovations in perfecting an incandescent lightbulb in 1879 and developing a delivery system (generators, fixtures, lamp sockets, wiring, meters) opened the "energy wars" (figure 68) of the late nineteenth century. In the competition for the residential lighting market, gas eventually lost to electricity. Gas, however, entered the home to fuel machines that did other everyday work. By the turn of the twentieth century, gas stoves, ranges, water heaters, and furnaces had appeared, frequently being sold by the gas companies themselves or manufactured by their subsidiaries. In 1899, roughly 75 percent of the gas being produced nationwide was used for illumination (industrial processes consumed the largest part of the remainder); in 1919, only 21 percent was being used for illumination, while domestic gas consumption for heating had climbed to 54 percent. Two years after Edison opened the world's first central generating station (near New York's Wall Street) in 1882, five hundred New York homes and several thousand businesses used his electric lamps, wire, switches, and sockets. In 1907, 8 percent of the country's residences were wired for electricity, a figure that grew to 34.7 percent by 1920.[14]

Many Americans, however, got their first sense of the Edison "system" and its elaborate network of conduits and cables at the World's Columbian Exposition in Chicago—the first world's fair to have a separate building completely devoted to electricity. Here, for example, in the "All-Electric Home," were portents of the household's future: electric stoves, hot plates, washing and ironing machines, dishwashers, carpet sweepers, electric doorbells, phonographs, fire alarms, and innumerable lighting devices.[15] The fair's massive dynamos symbolized to Henry Adams a new energy force whose application in everyday life seemed unlimited.[16]

Electrical power appeared to have many advantages: a more regular light, no soot, no need to ventilate. Not all homeowners were convinced. Many feared electricity's unknown consequences. For example, in the 1880s, one architect claimed that its use for residential lighting caused freckles. Other critics blamed it for fires, explosions, or electrocution. Families who put in electricity usually had their residences wired first only for lights. In a home being converted from gas, the same fixtures and conduits were often recycled. Hence the first electric lights hung from the center of a room's ceiling or as wall sconces. Portable lamps plugging into outlets were available as early as the 1880s but were not in wide use until house wiring became less expensive in the decade after 1910.[17] As with the gas companies, electric power manufacturers such as Consolidated Edison of Chicago sold customers both electric service and electric servants (figure 69) in their neighborhood retailing of appliances.[18]

New lighting and heating options oriented the home differently to the surrounding community. One secured kerosene or other fuel oils at a store or had them delivered periodically. Gas and electricity, however, involved no contact with a merchant or deliveryman. One need not converse with meter readers (a new occupation in Victorian America), only pay bills by mail. Lighting artifacts fueled by the competing energies affected the use of space in the home. Oil lamps and, once a house had ample outlets, electric lamps were portable; gas fixtures were not, a restriction to which furniture had to be adapted.

Electricity altered life at home in another significant way with Alexander Graham Bell's application of it to what he called "an improvement of the telegraph." Here I only note that the telephone gave rise to a new occupation for women, the "Hello Central" operative, and also a new occupation for men, the electrical engineer. This invention changed the ways Americans conversed, advertised, shopped, and even courted. It also marked, as one Bell biographer has put it, the final technological "conquest of solitude."[19]

The American Standard Bathroom

Not until World War I did the bathroom evolve into a special area containing a tub, sink, and toilet. In the Centennial year, only wealthy homes had bathrooms, that is, prescribed places for bathing. If a home also had an indoor toilet, it likely was located in a closet or other storage area. Sink, stool, and tub migrated to the bathroom from elsewhere inside or outside the home. The sink originated as a wash bowl and pitcher set in individual bedchambers; the stool replaced the outdoor privy or the indoor chamberpot; the tub derived from the portable tin-plated or wooden tubs of the kitchen. The bathroom itself traveled about the house, being located in basements, kitchens, utility rooms, and, sometimes, the smallest bedchamber. Since it required a constant water supply, house remodelers and new home designers kept it close to the building's plumbing system. Like other artifacts in the nineteenth century's age of patented furniture, the bathroom's components—for example, the tub—underwent continual and sometimes imaginative experimentation.

Nineteenth-century Americans attended to their daily necessities in outdoor privies. The more fastidious called the privy's "a house of office," a "necessary house," or simply "the necessary"; most folks knew it as the outhouse. If there were separate outhouses for men and women, as there were behind worker apartments, a crescent on the door signified women, a sun indicated men. Behaviors and beliefs surrounding privies made them favorite subjects of everyday humor and folklore. Outhouse jokes were common. Stories of falling through the outhouse hole and of attacks from below by spiders, snakes, and bees were legion. Stealing, moving, or tipping over of outhouses became a Halloween ritual. When the Rockefeller Sanitary Commission (1909), U.S. Public Health Service (1912), and various state bureaus of health attempted to impose a "sanitary privy" or to have indoor plumbing installed in farm homes, such groups often encountered resistance from those who saw no need for "one of them newfangled white crock-flushers."[20]

The indoor chamberpot, used at night by those not wishing to journey sixty yards in dark or inclement weather, came in assorted shapes and sizes.

Fig. 69. Electrical appliance salesmen, Consolidated Edison Co., Chicago suburbs, ca. 1910. Photograph courtesy of Commonwealth Edison.

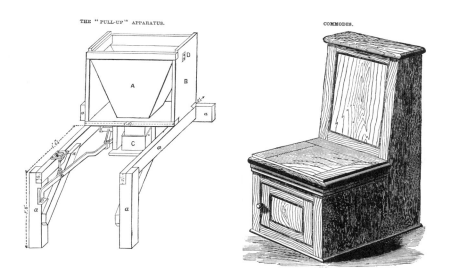

Fig. 70. Two toilet arrangements: a) Schematic drawing of Waring earth closet, 1869; b) Wood Commode earth closet design, 1869. Catharine E. Beecher and Harriet Beecher Stowe, *The American Woman's Home,* 1869, figures 68 and 67.

Usually kept under the bed, the pot or "potty" (for children) required daily cleaning. Pots encased in wooden boxes to disguise their purpose assumed names such as *chaise percée* or commode. American males often used British terms such as Cousin John or Jake to refer to a privy or a chamberpot.

Women found using the outhouse especially distasteful. Understandably, one of the early advocates of indoor plumbing was Catharine Beecher, who, in her household manuals, offered detailed advice about the two major sanitation systems advocated by those who sought to bring the outhouse into the main house. Beecher first (1849) endorsed the earth closet (figure 70), a system of human waste disposal advocated by sanitary reformer George Waring.[21] The earth system operated on a principle of dropping dry earth on human waste in order to induce rapid fermentation without the generation of noxious gases. The simplest form of earth closet was a wooden commode equipped with a back hopper filled with earth. Waring's model, movable to any room, required no water supply and no expensive jangle of pipes and fittings, as the rival water closet systems did. Waring (and his imitators) argued that the treated wastes could be recycled as fertilizer for gardens and farms. Impressed by this aspect of the Waring system, Horace Greeley claimed, "I think that America will be worth 25 percent more a hundred years hence than it would have been without it."[22]

Waring's approach, however, proved unfeasible in big cities, since the large quantities of treated waste had to be hauled away. Also the opportunity to be rid of wastes instantly, as in the water closet, had its appeal. Thus, despite concern over which bowls, traps, or vents to buy or what precautions to take to prevent the dreaded sewer gas, the technology that flushed wastes out of sight through a network of invisible pipes to either a municipal sewer or an underground cesspool proved the most attractive option for most middle-class Americans in dealing with one of life's necessities.[23]

Sears, Roebuck, which had offered few plumbing furnishings a decade earlier, by 1910 sold separately or as a suite bathtubs with claw feet, toilet "closets," and "lavatories." The white trio of tub (with canvas shower-curtain optional), toilet, and sink (freestanding or wall-hanging), aligned along a wall and compressed into an average of forty-eight square feet, became a distinct architectural form.[24] Unlike their migratory predecessors, these fixtures were permanently attached to networks of water and waste. The fixtures came in standard sizes, with standard fittings, many made by a plumbing manufacturer appropriately named American Standard (figure 71). Edward and Clarence Scott improved upon commercially prepared

Fig. 71. Advertisement, Standard Guaranteed Plumbing Fixtures, Standard Sanitary Manufacturing Co. *McClure's Magazine*, 1914.

toilet paper (which sold in bulky packages of five sheets) by selling toilet "tissue" that came in small perforated rolls. Its whiteness matched the other standardized bathroom fixtures.

Conduits and Conduct

In a number of ways, the emergence of the American bathroom epitomizes several of the implications of the new home utilities of the period 1876–1915. Leaving aside the telephone (which seems only to have entered this private space via the contemporary hotel or motel), the bathroom illustrates the impact of all the new techniques for providing water and waste, heat and light. The cultural and social ramifications of this household material culture were many. In summary, I see them as five.

First, as I noted above, the new techniques changed a home's relationship to its surrounding neighborhood and altered the physical landscape, above and below its surface. A household no longer depended upon itself for many of life's necessities. While once largely self-sufficient, the household's "modern" interconnections with the new utilities made it dependent upon others. Now forces beyond its domestic circle dictated the quantity and quality, cost and availability, of several of its vital life-support systems.

To create this new landscape of telephone line, water main, sewer, and power cable required political and economic decisions by governmental and corporate enterprises, both of which assumed greater control over the home residence's shape, structure, and placement, via zoning ordinances, fire regulations, and building codes. Power had its politics.

The new utilities accustomed Americans to think of "systems" as a metaphor for modern life. Introduced to the idea by the railroad companies (the Pennsylvania System) and their related corporations (the Pullman System), they hooked up to or plugged into the Edison or Bell System.

American householders did so as consumers. As noted earlier, instead of being the products of the homeowners, heat, light, and water became commodities to be purchased elsewhere. Utility commodities begat other commodities, as successive waves of new domestic appliances invaded every room of the house. Once one had gas or electric light, advertisers assured consumers, it was vital to secure gas or electric heat. Once power outlets were installed throughout the house, a panoply of power vacuum cleaners, refrigerators, sewing machines, and radios eventually followed.

While their promoters promised efficient, trouble-free services, sewers plugged, mains leaked, power lines shorted, and appliances broke. Hence, in addition to the initial installers of home utilities, other individuals performing new occupations increasingly entered the house. We know little about these early service people. As with real estate agents (about whom we also need additional scholarship), repair or service personnel—how companies recruited, trained, or used them—remain another important topic on the twentieth-century house history agenda.

A final, and perhaps the most important, ramification of the new utilities for everyday life at home was their gradual but increasingly widespread homogenization of the domestic environment. Pioneered first in American hotels and skyscraper office buildings, the new systems of heating, cooling, lighting, and waste removal blurred outside/inside differences, obscuring nature's temperature and climate; they also eradicated nature's time, replacing the natural rhythms of day and night (sunrise, high noon, sunset) with mechanical impulses of the electric light and electric clock.

The new utilities provided many modern conveniences and comforts, but such modern conduits also had modern consequences. At the flick of a switch, the twist of a dial, the turn of a valve, the push of a button, everyday life at home in 1876–1915 became more controlled, quantified, and standardized.

Notes

1. Nelson M. Blake, *Water for the Cities* (Syracuse, N.Y.: Univ. of Syracuse Press, 1956); F. E. Turneature and H.L. Russell, *Public Water Supplies,* 3d (New York: Wiley, 1924), 9.

2. Homer Croy, *West of the Water Tower* (New York: Harper and Row, 1923).

3. Joel A. Tarr and Francis C. McMichael, "The Evolution of Wastewater Technology and the Development of State Regulation: A Retrospective Assessment," in *Retrospective Technology Assessment,* ed. Joel A. Tarr (San Francisco: San Francisco Press, 1977), 165–90.

4. Lawrence H. Larsen, "Nineteenth-Century Street Sanitation: A Study in Filth and Frustration," *Wisconsin Magazine of History* 52 (Spring 1969):239–47; Joel A. Tarr, "From City to Farm: Urban Wastes and the American Farmer," *Agricultural History* 49 (Oct. 1975):598–612.

5. Susan Strasser, *Never Done: A History of American Housework* (New York: Pantheon, 1982), 51–58; also see Catharine E. Beecher and Harriet Beecher Stowe, *The American Woman's Home, or, Principles of Domestic Science* (New York: J.B. Ford & Co., 1869), 66–83, 360–66, 419–32. Tammis Kane Groft, *Cast with Style: Nineteenth-Century Cast-Iron Stoves from the Albany Area* (Albany, N.Y.: Albany Institute of History and Art, 1981); Josephine Pierce, *Fire on the Hearth: The Evo-*

lution and Romance of the Heating Stove (Springfield, Mass.: Pond-Eckberg Co., 1951).

6. Deborah J. Hoskins, "Brought, Bought, and Borrowed: Material Culture on the Oklahoma Farming Frontier, 1889–1907," in *Home on the Range,* ed. John R. Wunder (Westport, Conn.: Greenwood, 1986), 121–36.

7. U.S., Department of Commerce, Bureau of the Census, *Historical Statistics of the United States, Colonial Times To 1970* (Washington, D.C.: U.S. Government Printing Office, 1975), 580.

8. Sears, Roebuck & Co., *1908 Catalog No. 117,* ed. Joseph J. Schroeder, Jr. (Chicago: Follett, 1969), 159, 613. Also see Henry J. Kaufmann, *The American Fireplace: Chimneys, Mantlepieces, Fireplaces, and Accessories* (Nashville, Tenn.: Thomas Nelson, 1972).

9. Tamara K. Hareven and Randolph Lagenbach, *Amoskeag: Life and Work in an American Factory-City* (New York: Pantheon, 1978), 258; Walter Hough, *Collection of Heating and Lighting Utensils in the U.S. National Museum* (Washington, D.C.: U.S. Government Printing Office, 1928).

10. Robert Bruegmann, "Central Heating and Forced Ventilation: Origins and Effects on Architectural Design," *Journal of the Society of Architectural Historians* 37, no. 3 (Oct. 1978):143–60; David Handlin, *The American Home: Architecture and Society, 1815–1915* (Boston: Little, Brown, 1979), 479; Eugene S. Ferguson, "An Historical Sketch of Central Heating, 1800–1860," in *Building Early America,* ed. Charles E. Peterson (Radnor, Pa.: Chilton Book Co., 1976), 165–85.

11. Katherine C. Grier, *The Popular Illuminator: Domestic Lighting in the Kerosene Era, 1860–1900* (Rochester, N.Y.: Strong Museum, 1986), 3–9; Harold F. Williamson and Arnold R. Daum, *The Age of Illumination, 1859–1899,* vol. 1 of *The American Petroleum Industry* (Westport, Conn.: Greenwood, 1981), 55–60, 521–25; also see Catherine M. Thuro, *Oil Lamps: The Kerosene Era in North America* (Des Moines, Iowa: Wallace-Homestead Book Co., 1976).

12. Albert Eide Parr, "Heating, Lighting, Plumbing and Human Relations," *Landscape* 19, no. 1 (Winter 1970):28–29; William T. O'Dea, *The Social History of Lighting* (London: Routledge and Paul, 1958).

13. Louis Stotz and Alexander Jamison, *History of the Gas Industry* (New York: Stettiner Bros., 1938), 4–16; Denys P. Myers, *Gas Lighting in America: A Guide for Historic Preservation* (Washington, D.C.: U.S. Department of the Interior, 1978), 115–24; Loris S. Russell, "Early Nineteenth-Century Lighting," in *Building Early America,* ed. Charles E. Peterson (Radnor, Pa.: Chilton Book Co., 1976), 186–201.

14. Thomas Parke Hughes, "Thomas Alva Edison and the Rise of Electricity," in *Technology in America,* ed. Carroll W. Pursell, Jr. (Cambridge, Mass.: MIT Press, 1981), 123–25. The industrial backdrop for this discussion can be found in Harold Passer, *The Electrical Manufacturers, 1875–1900* (Cambridge, Mass.: MIT Press,

1953); and Thomas P. Hughes, *Networks of Power: Electrification in Western Society, 1880–1930* (Baltimore: Johns Hopkins Univ. Press, 1983).

15. J.P. Barrett, *Electricity at the Columbian Exposition* (Chicago: Exposition Press, 1894); Hughes, *Networks of Power*, 82–83. Henry B. Cox, "Plain and Fancy: Incandescence Becomes a Household Word!", *Nineteenth Century* 6, no. 3 (Autumn 1980):49–51.

16. Henry Adams, "The Dynamo and the Virgin," ch. 15 in Henry Adams, *The Education of Henry Adams, An Autobiography*, Sentry ed. (Boston: Houghton Mifflin, 1961), 379–90.

17. Fred E.H. Schroeder, "More Small Things Forgotten: Domestic Electric Plugs and Receptacles, 1881–1931," *Technology and Culture* 29, no. 3 (July 1986):525–43; Bernard S. Finn and Robert Friedel, *Edison: Lighting a Revolution: The Beginning of Electric Power* (Washington, D.C.: Smithsonian Institution, 1979).

18. Harold L. Platt, "Samuel Insull and the Electric City," *Chicago History* 15, no. 1 (Spring 1986):20–35.

19. For more extended discussion of the telephone's impact on residential behavior, see Thomas J. Schlereth, *Victorian America: Transformations of Everyday Life, 1876–1915* (New York: Harper & Row, 1991), ch. 5. Also Robert V. Bruce, *Bell: Alexander Graham Bell and the Conquest of Solitude* (Boston: Little, Brown, 1973); John Brooks, *Telephone: The First Hundred Years* (New York: Harper & Row, 1975).

20. Philip R. Seitz, "The Privy Problem: Rural-Urban Conflicts and Sanitary Reform" (paper presented at the American Studies Association National Meeting, Minneapolis, Minn., Nov. 1984):12–18. Lawrence Wright, *Clean and Decent: The Fascinating History of the Bathroom and Water Closet and of Sundry Habits, Fashions, and Accessories of the Toilet, Principally in Great Britain, France, and America* (New York: Viking, 1960).

21. Beecher and Stowe, *American Woman's Home*, 403–18; George E. Waring, *Earth Closets: How to Make Them and How to Use Them* (New York: Tribune Association, 1868).

22. Quoted in Handlin, *American Home*, 463.

23. Martha Van Rensselaer, "Home Sanitation," *Chautauquan Magazine*, 34 (Nov. 1901):183–91; Jon A. Peterson, "The Impact of Sanitary Reform upon American Urban Planning, 1840–1890," *Journal of Social History* 13 (Fall 1979):83–101. May N. Stone, "The Plumbing Paradox: American Attitudes Toward Late-Nineteenth-Century Domestic Sanitary Arrangements," *Winterthur Portfolio* 14, no. 3 (Autumn 1979):283–309.

24. Siegfried Giedion, *Mechanization Takes Command: A Contribution to Anonymous History* (New York: Norton, 1948), 682–706; Ruth Schwartz Cowan, *More Work for Mother: The Ironies of Household Technology from the Open Hearth to the Microwave* (New York: Basic Books, 1983), 87–88.

CHAPTER ELEVEN

Modernizing Domestic Service

Daniel E. Sutherland

"To fail to apprehend the tendency of one's age, and to fail to adapt the conditions of an industry to it is to leave that industry ill adjusted and belated." These words, written in 1895 by social reformer Jane Addams, were meant as an indictment of the anachronistic economic and social status of America's household workers. Indeed, the founder of Hull House went on to insist that the conditions of service were "tinged with feudalism." She was right, and this aura of medievalism had become more apparent and less tolerable as the nineteenth century strained toward the twentieth. Workers performed the same work in much the same way in 1890 as they had in 1800. They worked twelve-hour days, six to seven days a week, in return for low wages, cramped living quarters, and paltry food. Even more galling was the low esteem in which servants were held by employers and the general public. Americans associated domestic service with serfdom, indentured servitude, even slavery. They identified household workers as "servants" and treated them accordingly.[1]

The years 1890–1930 witnessed a conscious effort to address this dismal situation by reforming, or "modernizing," domestic service. Current historical wisdom divides the history of domestic service in the United States into five chronological periods: (1) 1607–1776, (2) 1776–1850, (3) 1850–1900, (4) 1900–1930, (5) 1930–1990. The legitimacy of this periodization may be questioned. For instance, the year 1865, marking the end of slavery in the South, seems a necessary dividing line for one of these phases. Similarly, the conclusion of the fifth phase is rather capricious, for no historian has seriously explored the years beyond 1945. Thus a slight expansion of the fourth phase seems justified when seeking to capture the moment when domestic service escaped its medieval heritage. While complex, this momentous event may best be explained by exploring three distinct trends: alterations in household technology and architecture, a new relationship between employers and servants, and a new relationship among household workers. One should hesitate before attributing a sudden or conclusive revolution to these changes. Some aspects of domestic service remained unaltered, and others would change only gradually after 1930. Nevertheless, the era represents a time of transition, during which domestic service was nudged in a distinctly "modern" direction.[2]

The New Technology

The most visible changes came in the form of improved household technology. Some improvements, related to new systems of heating, plumbing, lighting, and sanitation, were intended to make life more convenient for middle-class families. Servants, however, also benefitted, insofar as water heaters, flush toilets, and central heating made housework easier. Such conveniences had become standard in most middle-class homes by the turn of the century, but many other technological improvements—machines and gadgets that would eventually ease the burden of housework—gained acceptance more slowly. Important innovations such as cooking stoves, washing machines, and carpet sweepers had been in use for decades, but many early machines remained crude, unreliable, and expensive. Most scholars believe that the decade of the 1920s proved to be the turning point in mechanization of the home.[3]

New technology made it possible to modernize domestic service in two quite different ways. On the one hand, machines promised to reduce household drudgery for servants. On the other hand, as some people began to question the logic of having both machines and servants, the possibility of *replacing* servants with machines drew increasing attention. Reasons for having both servants and machines varied. Some householders shrank from operating the machines themselves. One woman, upon receiving her mail-order vacuum cleaner in 1912, discovered it to be so "clumsy of construction" and so "awkward to handle" that two people were required to operate it. Many women, especially those with children or obligations outside their homes, did not have time for housework, not even with so-called labor-saving conveniences. Still other people seemed loathe to relinquish their servants because of the social status associated with employing household help. "The keeping of servants," admitted one gentleman in 1929, "is of course in the main a device for impressing one's neighbors and guests."[4]

Yet many Americans had become so frustrated by the "servant problems" (I use the plural to suggest the point of view of both employers and domestics) that ridding the home of servants seemed the only sure means of

Fig. 72. Ivory soap advertisement. Although the servant in this advertisement for
Ivory Soap wears a pleasant expression, she is engaged in messy, strenuous work
that her employer wishes to avoid. *Ladies' Home Journal* 16 (May 1899), inside
front cover.

reforming household labor. Statistically, at least, the old system of domestic service did seem to be crumbling. Between 1870 and 1910, even as the number of servants increased, the number of families employing servants declined. In 1870, one domestic was available to every eight American families; by 1910, it was down to one in twelve. By 1920, the ratio had dropped to one in sixteen, a number that held fairly stable for the next decade. Yet this apparent decline in the demand for servants became complicated when, between 1910 and 1920, the number of people willing to work as servants also declined. That number rose again during the 1920s, but the proportion of servants in the total work force continued to decline until the Great Depression.[5]

An intriguing debate developed over whether machines had *replaced* servants or merely *filled the void* created by their voluntary departure. "The first step in this process of modernizing the home has been taken blindly and even reluctantly," submitted a supporter of the latter premise in 1910. "Had anyone dared to predict, twenty years ago, that the exit of the servant girl by one door would be followed by the entrance of an army of cleaners and wash-machines through the other door, he would have been laughed into oblivion. But today it is almost an accomplished fact."

"We used to have a woman come in by the day," confirmed one gentleman. "When she stopped coming, we just purchased a vacuum cleaner for $120, which the woman folks now prefer to outside help. . . . We have also a motor-operated washing-machine, two electric sad-irons, and one gas iron!"[6]

Other people believed that a growing desire to escape the trials of acquiring and directing household workers *"had an immediate effect in stimulating the demand for kitchen appliances."* A New England woman claimed in 1912, "I never hesitate to spend money for any labor-saving device." Her reasons clearly suggested a desire to rid her home of servants. "In the last year," she explained, "I have kept no maid . . . and have enjoyed the year more than any previous one." Machines also allowed employers unwilling to forego all assistance to hire parttime rather than fulltime help. "A laundress and cleaning-woman give two or three days a week," explained an observer of this process, "and by the aid of the vacuum-cleaner, the power-washer, and the electric flat-iron, her work is made easier and her accomplishments much more than doubled." By the early 1920s, one commentator predicted that mechanization of the home meant "the passing of the servant in the house." A few years later, another observer boldly declared, "The future household servant will be the neighborhood electrician and mechanic, summoned for emergencies when fixtures get out of order."[7]

Evidence of both trends may be seen in the changing roles played by servants in magazine advertisements. Before World War I, when household technology remained somewhat primitive, pictorial ads for vacuum cleaners, washing machines, and other innovations frequently displayed smiling servants operating the new gadgets. This imagery changed in the postwar years, as ads began to stress the possibility of replacing household help with machines. Housewives increasingly operated the machines themselves, thus suggesting the ease with which the machines could be handled and hinting at the secret of a servant-free home. Meanwhile, servants slowly disappeared from the ads, and when they did appear, it was more often in a decorative role. Instead of being the prime operators of the new technology, they stood in the background or performed simple tasks, such as pushing a tea cart or replacing a window shade. They became less necessary in a practical sense and more obviously important as status symbols, as means of conveying an image of a chic, affluent household.[8]

Still, not everyone viewed the machines as harbingers of a new day. Some employers simply ignored the innovations. "Perhaps there is an old worn-out can-opener or none at all," complained one domestic in 1912, "knives that are not sharp, no sleeve-board for ironing—little things that could be bought at the ten-cent store. When I ask if I can have a new one, the answer is, 'Well, we [the family] have used that one' or 'done without it,' as the case may be, 'for the last forty years.'" Similarly, this same worker complained, "They [employers] will not hire the washing done if they can get the girl to do it. They say, 'Really, if the girl does not do the washing, I would not have anything for her to do.'" In other words, why buy a washing machine? The largest number of employers taking this stance lived in the South. Sales of household machines of all varieties in the South lagged far behind those in the rest of the country. At the same time the ratio of servants per family remained the highest in the nation. The explanation of these regional differences lies partly in the southern tradition of hiring help, but also, and perhaps more to the point, in the lower wages paid to southern domestics. Servants were simply cheaper than machines.[9]

In all parts of the country, servants themselves sometimes resisted machines. Older domestic workers simply preferred the old ways, even when new technologies saved work. "Somehow," marveled one employer, "servants and washing-machines do not seem to get along well together. . . . The majority . . . do not like them at all, and generally contrive to get

Fig. 73. This advertisement illustrates the bright promise that mechanical innovations held out to housekeepers who wished to rid themselves of both servants and household drudgery. Notice, however, the servant in the upper left, which shows that some people wished to make use of both servants and machines. *Literary Digest* 39 (27 Sept. 1909):977.

them out of order after using them for a few weeks." Some employers attributed this to the dull-wittedness of their employees; more perceptive people realized that many servants feared the machines as tools in a conspiracy to force *more* work from them. Servants complained that the new machines seldom shortened workdays. One domestic explained that she and two coworkers daily cleaned the eighteen rooms of the employer's house, but that she alone washed and ironed all the linen, about three hundred pieces a week. "I have easy washing," she explained, "because I don't wash with my hands; the machine washes alone, I only cover the linen with soap and put 5 pieces into the machine at once." However, it took fifteen minutes to wash each load, so fifteen hours were required to do the lot. She then needed four days, working from 6 a.m. to 8 p.m., to iron the clothes. "I do nothing but iron for those four days,' she moaned. "Recent investigation," insisted an observer in 1915, "[shows that] labor saving utensils have greatly facilitated housework, yet housekeeping is still accompanied with much dissatisfaction on the part of the employer and employee."[10]

Technological changes outside the home also helped to modernize domestic service. Toward the end of the nineteenth century, Americans began to delegate a growing share of their household chores to people outside the home. The trend became clear by World War I and firmly entrenched by the end of the 1920s. Commercial bakeries, laundries, and restaurants, and prepared foods reflected the most popular of these trends. Besides lightening the burden of household labor for workers, such changes provided yet another temptation for American families to eliminate servants. "Except in those communities where unskilled domestic labor is plentiful and cheap," summarized a government report, "each year sees more and more old-fashioned washerwomen supplanted by steam-laundering operatives, one of whom can accomplish as much with the aid of machinery as several women at home by means of the old back-breaking methods." On a more positive note, the creation of commercial laundries and bakeries provided alternative employment opportunities for men and women who sought to escape service. Thus the number of women working in steam laundries increased by nearly 150,000 between 1920 and 1930; the number of restaurants and cafe waitresses rose by 98 percent, to 231,973.[11]

Changes in architecture also helped to modernize domestic labor. Nineteenth-century middle-class homes had been designed so that each room served a specific narrowly-defined function. Moreover, because such homes generally required live-in domestics, architects had provided space-consuming "service" areas, including servants' quarters and inordinately

Fig. 74. Advertisement. Not everyone ate commercially-prepared bread at the turn of the century, so servants still performed the ancient task of baking. *Ladies' Home Journal* 16 (Aug. 1899), inside front cover.

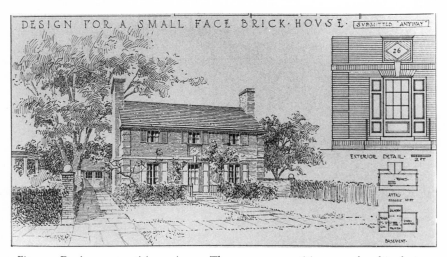

Fig. 75. Design competition winner. The 1919 competition won by this design called for, among other things, "a house which could be run without servants." *Architectural Forum* 31 (Nov. 1919):175–76.

large kitchens, pantries, and storerooms. With service areas deliberately separated from family living areas by a maze of halls, stairways, and partitions, the average home had become a housekeeping nightmare. During the early twentieth century, such mazes appeared less frequently, and middle-class houses generally became smaller, less cluttered, and easier to care for. Economic depressions in the mid-1890s and in the early twentieth century, rising construction costs and interest rates, changes in architectural tastes, and a desire to create "servantless" homes led architects such as Frank Lloyd Wright to produce single-story "ranchers," bungalows, and similarly compact, easy-to-care-for homes. "Our house is arranged on all one floor," boasted one gentleman of his new home in 1912, "and all unnecessary rooms and partitions are eliminated. Our efforts are directed towards keeping down the accumulation of 'things,' so that we will not be crowded, and dusting and cleaning will be simplified." Rather than employ servants, his family invested in the latest electrical appliances.[12]

Growing numbers of people fled their traditional, detached, single-family dwellings entirely. For decades past, some Americans, mostly bachelors and newlyweds, had preferred to live in boarding houses, hotels, and apartments, to avoid the expense of home ownership and the servant problems. But multistory apartment buildings became particularly numerous in the early twentieth century, and so joined with bungalows, duplexes, and other types of shrinking households to simplify housekeeping and provide families with a way to escape dependence on domestic help. While 61 percent of all Americans resided in single-family dwellings in 1900, by 1940 only 42 percent did so. Meanwhile, the number of people living in dwellings designed for five or more families increased from 6 percent to nearly 20 percent. "These [family hotels] are inhabited by people who could afford to 'keep house,'" wrote a feminist reformer in 1898. "But they do not want to keep house. They are tired of keeping house. It is difficult to keep house, the servant problem is so trying." In the 1920s, another commentator confirmed the effect of the servant problems on American living patterns: "The tendency is to desert private housekeeping for public housekeeping enterprises."[13]

The Growth of Live-Out Service

The impact of technological and architectural changes on housework led to a second modernizing influence: a new relationship between employers and servants. The legacy of feudalism had derived most noticeably from the unique and complex bonds between master and servant. Traditionally, this relationship, reminiscent of that between medieval apprentices and their "masters," had been defended as beneficial for both worker and householder. It supposedly imbued employers with a sense of responsibility for their domestics' health, happiness, education, appearance, and moral development. Workers, it was assumed, would repay employer benevolence with efficient, devoted service. Alas, the success of such arrangements rested largely on the unpredictable basis of personality. Where "good" masters and servants were coupled, the alliance could be a blessing to both, with bonds of mutual respect and affection being forged. But even the best employers tended to be condescending at times, and so long as workers were thought of as "servants" their positions remained less than enviable.

As the physical burdens of housework declined, and as growing numbers of workers outside of service enjoyed businesslike relations with their employers, the pressure grew to supplant traditional master-servant bonds with an "employer-employee" relationship. The pressure became particularly intense in the second and third decades of the twentieth century. The era's revolution in manners and morals, with its emphasis on individual freedom and self-expression, caused servants to resent more than ever the ways in which household service limited their lives, both socially and physically. On top of this, the labor demands of the Great War opened dozens of new occupations in factories, shops, and offices to working women. The competition for workers by these alternative employments forced the employers of domestics to grant concessions that would have been unheard of a generation earlier. Even if filling "service" positions as office cleaners, restaurant waitresses, or commercial laundry workers, women could escape the restrictions of household labor.[14]

Both employers and servants came to see live-out service, with workers returning to their own homes after a day's labor, as a plausible compromise. Employers, whether hiring someone to work fulltime or merely a couple of days a week, could escape the dictatorship of the proletariat; workers could escape the "slavery" of service. Employers would be spared the presence of "aliens" and "strangers" in their homes; employees would escape old feudal obligations and the social stigma that had always haunted live-in service. For instance, employers found it more difficult to convince daily and live-out workers to wear uniforms, which servants had always regarded as a "badge of servitude." Neat work clothes and perhaps an apron gained increasing acceptance. The process of hiring workers changed subtly, too. While employment offices (along with newspaper advertisements and recommendations from former employers) had always been important sources of servants, the shift toward live-out and daily workers made these offices even more practical as means of acquiring servants or filling places. Documenting the connection, one commentator observed in the mid-1920s that bureaus catering to the servant trade tended to be located in those parts of towns where "women occupied in domestic service lodged." Not coincidentally, many people stressed the need for more honest and efficient employment bureaus, believing that reliable agencies could lead the way in formalizing impartial contractual relations between employers and employees. Considering all of these changes, one commentator confidently insisted in 1919, "The servant problem is to be solved by eliminating the servant." He did not mean that American homeowners must do without domestic help, only that they should hire daily workers and treat them as "household assistants" rather than as "servants." Women's magazines such as the Ladies' Home Journal trumpeted the arrival of the new regime. Between 1900 and 1920, 16 percent fewer domestics came to live in. By 1945, live-in service had "virtually disappeared."[15]

However, once again, what logically might have been considered progress or modernization did not take everyone by storm. In a survey taken at the turn of the century, only 70 of 1,300 employers allowed their domestics to live out, and only 66 percent of those 70 people *approved* of live-out service. "Those who disapproved," stated the survey, "for the most part, based their disapproval either on the facilities for theft which were offered or on the fact that they did not want to dispense with the service of their employees during the evening." Somewhat surprisingly, only 27 percent of the 156 employees questioned wanted to live out. This may be explained in part by the refusal of employers to raise the wages of live-out servants, even though such workers incurred the added expense of room, board, and possibly laundry.[16]

Nearly a quarter-century later, 1,358 Baltimore domestics voiced their opinions on the subject. By this time, only about half expressed a willingness to live in fulltime, although another 8.5 percent were willing to live in parttime. Nearly 38 percent, however, clearly wished to live out (4.3 percent expressed no preference). Again, most of those still desiring to live in were influenced by the lack of wage adjustment. Age apparently played a role, too. Workers under eighteen or over forty most often chose to live in, while people between those ages chose to live out. Similarly, foreign-born workers preferred to live in more often than the native born. The decisive factor, however, appears to have been marital status. Sixty-three percent of single women wanted to live in. Clear figures are not provided for the preference of married women, but 64 percent of black women preferred to live out, and well over half of the black women were married (compared to a third of the whites). Other unmeasured considerations in this equation would be the quality of the living quarters and the degree of freedom allowed in the employers home. Similarly, one would have to know something of the quality of the quarters otherwise available to workers before being able to measure accurately the movement toward live-out service.[17]

The new employer-employee relationship also derived impetus from the changing racial and ethnic composition of domestic workers. After 1890, the characteristics of people willing to labor as domestics shifted rapidly. While native-born whites and foreign immigrants dominated outside the South for most of the century, blacks captured an ever-increasing share of service jobs in the latter part of the century. This happened largely because the new job opportunities outside of domestic service went to native-born whites rather than to the less skilled and less educated minorities. The number of black workers also proliferated as the post–World War I exodus of blacks from the South increased employment opportunities for black household workers, and as immigration restrictions reduced the availability of foreign-born servants. Thus, in 1900, 42.8 percent of all domes-

Fig. 76. By the 1920s, black employees were appearing more frequently in northern households, like this one in Wisconsin. Notice, too, that this worker wears a wedding ring, which suggests that she almost certainly "lives out." Courtesy of the State Historical Society of Wisconsin, Collection of Albert A. Johnson.

tics were native whites, 23 percent foreign-born, and 34 percent black. By 1930, blacks ranked first with 47.2 percent, with native whites sinking to 37.7 percent, and the foreign-born to 14.7 percent. This new racial balance helps to explain why growing numbers of white employers approved of live-out service. The general servant population had grown older, too (from an average of twenty-five years to an average of forty years), mostly because of new child labor laws and compulsory education. Servants in 1930 were also more likely to be married or divorced than in earlier years. The proportion of married servants nearly doubled between 1900 and 1920, from 33.5 percent to 64.2 percent. Again, the increase in married and divorced servants benefited from an increase in black domestics, over half of all married female servants being black.[18]

The growing dominance of middle-aged, black, and married domestics enlarged the number who favored live-out service. This may be one reason the tradition of live-out service had much earlier beginnings in the South, where black servants were far more likely than servants elsewhere to reside in their own homes. "In those days everybody had servants," recalled a southern employer born in 1897. "They were very cheap. And some people, if they'd had them a long time, had servants that lived on the place. But you could never get 'em to live there if they didn't already. They naturally wanted to go home with their own and have fun." Black washerwomen had the longest tradition of working out, going back to before the Civil War. Indeed, many laundresses arranged to work in their own homes. "My mother she washed and ironed in those days—at home," reported the daughter of a Mobile laundress. "She did their washing for about twenty years. She'd go get the clothes on a Monday and carry 'em back on Friday." The South, on the other hand, provides strong evidence that living out could not in itself eliminate the tradition of "master" and "servant," not when, as in the South, the issue was complicated by race.[19]

Employer-employee relations also changed as a result of the Progressive movement, which dominated the greater part of this era. Numerous Progressive reformers, such as Jane Addams, sought to convince employers that they should accept at least part of the blame for the servant problems. Pay workers fair wages, limit workdays to eight or ten hours, provide labor-saving machines, allow more freedom, and the whole image of domestic service would be transformed. The new image, they suggested, would attract a more capable class of workers. Joining the Progressive chorus came public statements by servants themselves. Articles and letters by domestics appeared in ladies' magazines and reform periodicals on an unprecedented scale after 1900. Their writings attested to the anger and frustration felt by domestics over working and living conditions and provided valuable insights into how they thought service ought to be modernized.[20]

Servant Unions

All this led to a third force modernizing service: a new relationship among the workers themselves. One of the chief grievances of servants, even in the early twentieth century, had been the isolation of service. Servants enjoyed little contact with one another or with anyone else, for that matter. Long workdays and few leisure hours traditionally had meant that live-in domestics spent most of their days alone in their employers' homes. "I had nobody to talk to," complained one servant; "it seemed to me that there was nothing in my life but dirty dishes to wash and a kitchen to clean up." A young Michigan girl reacted the same way: "I do not care how much hard work I have to do if I could have a little pleasure, but it is so lonesome hear [sic]."

"Ladies wonder how their girls can complain of lonliness [sic], in a house full of people," volunteered another domestic, "but oh! it is the worst kind of loneliness."

As late as 1911, a Polish immigrant (who upon taking a job in a house where two other women worked had claimed to be less lonely than in earlier jobs) could still lament, "I am in America and I do not even know whether it is America, only it seems to me as if there were only a single house in the whole world and nothing more, only walls and very few people."[21]

While not disappearing after 1890, isolation did become less formidable. The rising number of live-out workers, more leisure time for live-in workers, and better transportation and communication—especially the telephone—improved conditions. More extensive contact with the outside world and with each other produced the crowning modernizing touch: group solidarity, particularly as expressed in the formation of labor unions. One should not imagine that servants wholly succeeded in their organizational efforts; they have failed to do that even into the 1990s. Yet between 1890 and 1930 enough progress was made, and the idea of unionization was planted firmly enough, that the occupation was clearly affected by organizing efforts.

Many of the most successful efforts to organize domestics benefited from the assistance of existing labor unions and the encouragement of Progressive reformers. Still, the task was not an easy one. One historian believes that male-controlled unions offering help to domestics, such as the National Labor Union, Knights of Labor, American Federation of Labor (AFL), and Industrial Workers of the World (IWW), failed to work hard enough on behalf of female laborers. Similarly, Progressive reformers, who too often approached reform from the perspective of employers, failed to win the confidence of servants. In strictly practical terms, domestics lacked the sense of unity and purpose shared by people who struggled side by side in the same place under the same working conditions. Individual cooks and maids, scattered in scores of households throughout a neighborhood, found it difficult to associate with other workers. They were often defeated by this isolation and the timidity it bred.[22]

Some of the earliest "unions" of the 1890s followed more the tradition of labor clubs or benevolent societies. The Progressive Household Club, for example, founded and operated by Los Angeles domestics, offered a variety of services to its five hundred members. Workers owned a spacious clubhouse containing kitchen, laundry room, and recreational facilities. Here the club staged social and cultural activities, operated an employment service, provided low-rent rooms to unemployed members, and offered storage space for members' personal effects. Members financed their activities and facilities from dues, loans, and fees for club services.[23]

Other groups assumed a more militant tone. The American Servant Girls' Association, in Kansas City; the Domestic Servants' Union, in New York City; the Household Union, in Holyoke, Massachusetts; and the Servant Girls' Union, in Toledo, Ohio, were all organized during the late 1890s and early 1900s for the purpose of confronting local employers. The AFL sponsored ten domestic unions in San Diego and Los Angeles, California; Chicago; New Orleans; Houston, Denison, and Harrisburg, Texas; Glencoe, Illinois; Brunswick, Georgia; and Beaver Valley, Pennsylvania. The Hotel and Restaurant Employees Union (part of the AFL) sponsored domestic unions in ten southern cities. The IWW seems to have been the most active of all, with fairly large unions in Denver, Duluth, Seattle, Salt Lake City, Chicago, Cleveland, and Tulsa. Not a few organizations, however, grew spontaneously from reactions to local conditions. In Auburn, Alabama, for example, local cooks and housemaids formed a "club" and planned a strike or "general 'quitten',", as they called it, for more privileges and less work in 1905. One observer believed these workers possessed "a better understanding than . . . their white employers" of the need to organize.[24]

All of these organizations, however, were ineffective and short-lived. One of the earliest organizational efforts, the Working Women's Association of America (WWAA) was a grassroots movement founded by Chicago domestics in 1901 and assisted by the Women's International Union Label League and various Chicago social reformers, including Jane Addams. Within three months of its founding, the union had enrolled three hundred members and applied for membership in the AFL. Shortly thereafter, the WWAA prepared a manifesto demanding, on behalf of all Chicago domestics, shorter workdays, more free time, the right to entertain friends in their employers' kitchens, and the right to have a "business agent" represent them in disputes with employers. Members also hoped to set minimum wage levels, a step, they insisted, that would protect both employers and employees from unfair demands.

The manifesto drew a variety of responses. Employers and the general public regarded the union as a joke. Many workers agreed. Some domestics, fearing employer reprisals, doubting the union's ability to help them, or considering such protests improper for "servants," refused to join. "It's the rich in the parlor and the poor in the kitchen," one worker explained matter-of-factly, "and that's the way it's goin' to stay." Even workers who joined the union did so with widely differing views of what should be accomplished. Some members began plotting a domestic revolution in which they would dictate conditions of employment. More conservative workers wanted only to make household service a respectable profession and establish their right to collective bargaining.

Such divisions spelled disaster for the fledgling union. After an initial burst of enthusiastic support, the WWAA gained little headway. Its hundreds of members seemingly testified to the union's strength, yet they represented a tiny portion of Chicago's 35,000 female domestics. Signs of discord appeared among even dedicated members, as they bickered over nonessential issues and expended more energy in planning their Christmas dance than in trying to ratify their constitution. When only eight women attended a late October meeting—a mere eight months after the union's creation—no further meetings were scheduled.[25]

A later example of short-lived success may be seen in the Domestic Workers Industrial Union, IWW Local No. 113, in Denver. Founded in March 1916 by Jane Street, the union eventually enlisted 155 members (although only 83 were genuinely active). As membership grew, so too did the union's confidence. "We have the bulge on the rich women of Denver," insisted Street, "because they won't wash their own dishes. We can rule the women of Capitol hill through this failing of theirs." No general strike would be called to obtain their goals. Instead, workers would wear down employers through a war of attrition. The battle plan called for domestics to cause disarray and consternation to their employers' homes by leaving work undone, serving meals late, taking no "back talk," and insisting on "privileges for which they [had] been ask[ing] in vain." Meanwhile, the union established its own placement agency and accumulated an extensive card file on some 6,000 Denver employers. The file noted the wages these people paid their workers, the numbers of family members, the sizes of their houses, and so on. Then the union used the telephone systematically to raise wages. For example, two dozen workers would inquire by telephone about an advertised opening paying twenty dollars a week. They would insist on wages of thirty dollars. The harassed employer, eventually convinced that she could hire no-one for less than the larger amount, would cave in. Similar methods were used to shorten hours and increase benefits. However, the union died when the United States government declared the entire IWW—because of its antiwar activities—illegal under the Espionage Act of 1917.[26]

Numerous, defiantly similar local efforts were made to organize workers during the 1920s, but they made little impact. The triumph of this aspect of modernization was no nearer than the other two. As one observer noted on the issue of servants' unions in 1926, "The whole body of domestic employees might strike and industry would not be stagnated, transportation would go on just the same, trade would not be interfered with, and manufacture would know no difference." The world, in other words, simply felt no sense of urgency about the servant problems. Yet the early unions did accomplish two things at least. They prompted some employers to see that unions could serve a positive function, much like honest employment bureaus, by ensuring standards of efficiency and formalizing relations between employers and employees. Equally important, experience gained in these organizing experiments produced the first coordinated national effort to unite domestic workers and reform the medieval nature of domestic service.[27]

The National Committee on Employer-Employee Relationships, founded in 1928, represented a coalition of domestics, employers, reformers, philanthropists, organized labor, and the federal government (specifically, the Women's Bureau of the Department of Labor; the Department of Agriculture; and the Bureau of Home Economics). The committee sought to determine the grievances of household workers, discover what

Fig. 77. By 1930, many maids were more ornamental than necessary. This advertisement for Dupont window shades also suggests a certain freedom within the household, even to the point of standing on household furniture. *House Beautiful* 60 (Sept. 1926), facing p. 229.

was being done to solve them, and propose corrective measures. As coordinator of a national campaign to professionalize employer-employee relationships, its role was to supplement and direct volunteer agencies already at work. In April 1931, the committee announced a comprehensive proposal to modernize service. This "Magna Charta" for household workers, as one commentator christened it, urged employers to pay wages that would meet local costs of living for "independent women at a tolerable level," that is, wages capable of supporting live-out workers. Workers continuing to live in should be given their own rooms and "convenient access to modern bathroom facilities." Workdays should be limited to fifty-four hours per week for live-in workers and forty-eight hours per week for workers living out. Workers should enjoy at least one full day or two half-days off each week and one week's vacation each year.[28]

Marching beneath the committee's banner, workers and reformers continued to reshape employer-employee relationships into the 1930s. A "New Deal" for household workers was proclaimed, with Eleanor Roosevelt named honorary chairman of a National Council on Household Employment (NCHE), an expanded version of the committee. Inspired by the NCHE's lead, local and national agencies and societies investigated conditions in service. Joint organizations of employers and workers established local guidelines for employment. Placement agencies sponsored by universities, private and public employment offices, and philanthropic institutions insisted on written contracts to maintain standards of employment and worker efficiency. Mrs. Roosevelt joined the public debate and insisted that "businesslike" housekeeping would solve the nation's servant problems.[29]

Those were exciting times, and if domestic service had not been revolutionized, it had been altered. Opportunities for changing housework through technological and architectural innovations had been firmly laid down between 1890 and 1930, even if most domestics were only beginning to sense the possibility of concerted action to improve conditions of labor. True, the relationship between workers and employers had made only modest headway against the inertia of feudalism. One still encountered complaints that household work was "the least modernized, the most feudal of all work in the modern world." Even today, something of the old "master-servant" attitude adheres in the occupation. Yet something had happened to domestic service. "The servant problem is still unsolved," conceded one household advisor in 1929, but "the status of the household employee has changed." The change, admittedly, had been "gradual," but

Fig. 78. At household employment bureaus such as this one, prospective employers and employees could be interviewed and counseled about their respective responsibilities and rights. *Good Housekeeping* 81 (Sept. 1925):89.

it had also been "steady." One might say that the era had altered those aspects of service capable of being changed, and that it certainly had established the agenda for future reform.[30]

Notes

1. Jane Addams, "A Belated Industry," *American Journal of Sociology* 1 (Mar. 1896):550.

2. For historical periodization, see Donna L. Van Raaphorst, *Union Maids Not Wanted: Organizing Domestic Workers, 1879–1940* (New York: Praeger, 1988), 19. For the most current literature on domestic service in the U.S., see, in addition to Van Raaphorst, Helen C. Callahan, "Upstairs-Downstairs in Chicago, 1870–1907: The Glessner Household," *Chicago History* 6 (Winter 1977):195–209; Faye E. Dudden, *Serving Women: Household Service in Nineteenth-Century America* (Middleton, Conn.: Wesleyan Univ. Press, 1983); David M. Katzman, *Seven Days a Week: Women and Domestic Service in Industrializing America* (New York: Oxford Univ. Press, 1978); Elizabeth A. Perkins, "The Forgotten Victorians:

Louisville's Domestics Servants, 1880–1920," *Register of the Kentucky Historical Society* 85 (Spring 1987):111–37; Phyllis Palmer, *Domesticity and Dirt: Housewives and Domestic Servants, 1920–1945* (Philadelphia: Temple Univ. Press, 1989); Judith Rollins, *Between Women: Domestics and Their Employers* (Philadelphia: Temple Univ. Press, 1985); Daniel E. Sutherland, *Americans and Their Servants: Domestic Service in the United States, 1800–1920* (Baton Rouge: Louisiana State Univ. Press, 1981); Daniel E. Sutherland, "The Servant Problem: An Index to Antebellum Americanism," *Southern Studies* 18 (Winter 1979):488–503; Daniel E. Sutherland, "A Special Kind of Problem: The Response of Household Slaves and Their Masters to Freedom," *Southern Studies* 20 (Summer 1981):151–66; Susan Tucker, *Telling Memories Among Southern Women: Domestic Workers and Their Employers in the Segregated South* (Baton Rouge: Louisiana State Univ. Press, 1988).

3. Sutherland, *Americans and Their Servants*, 192–95; George T. Stigler, *Domestic Servants in the United States, 1900–1940* (New York: National Bureau of Economic Research, 1946), 24–25; Katzman, *Seven Days a Week*, 129–30; Ruth Schwartz Cowan, *More Work for Mother: The Ironies of Household Technology from the Open Hearth to the Microwave* (New York: Basic Books, 1963), 172–75.

4. Sutherland, *Americans and Their Servants*, 196–98; Robert M. Gay, "Help! Help!", *House Beautiful* 59 (Apr. 1929):452.

5. I.M. Rubinow and Daniel Durant, "The Depth and Breadth of the Servant Problem," *McClure's Magazine* 34 (Mar. 1910):576, 585; Van Raaphorst, *Union Maids Not Wanted*, 38–39; Mary V. Dempsey, *The Occupational Progress of Women, 1910–1930*, Bulletin of the Women's Bureau, no. 104 (Washington, D.C.: U.S. Government Printing Office, 1933), 29–30. For a different perspective on the numbers game, see Palmer, *Domesticity and Dirt*, 7–10.

6. Gay, "Help! Help!", 452; Rubinow and Durant, "The Depth and Breadth of the Servant Problem," 583; Martha Bensley Bruere, "The New Home-Making," *Outlook*, 16 Mar. 1912, p. 592.

7. Rubinow and Durant, "The Depth and Breadth of the Servant Problem," 583; Sutherland, *Americans and Their Servants*, 192, 196–98; Bruere, "The New Home-Making," 592; "The Passing of the Household Servant," *Literary Digest*, 8 July 1922, pp. 19–20; "To Save the Great American Home," *Literary Digest*, 2 Jan. 1926, p. 11.

8. Sutherland, *Americans and Their Servants*, 196–97; Susan Strasser, *Never Done: A History of American Housework* (New York: Pantheon, 1982), 78; Roland Marchand, *Advertising the American Dream: Making Way for Modernity, 1920–1940* (Berkeley: Univ. of California Press, 1985), 200–205; *House Beautiful* 60 (Sept. 1926):228.

9. "The Experiences of a Hired Girl," *Outlook*, 6 Apr. 1912, p. 779; George Rawick, ed., *The American Slave* (Westport, Conn.: Greenwood, 1972), ser. 1, vol.

6, pt. 2, p. 251; Tucker, *Telling Memories Among Southern Women,* 199; Katzman, *Seven Days a Week,* 130.

10. Sutherland, *Americans and Their Servants,* 198; Aleksandra Rembienska to parents, 20 Nov. 1911, in *The Polish Peasant in America,* ed. William I. Thomas and Florian Znaniecki, 5 vols. (New York: Knopf, 1927), I:779; Clara Helene Barker, *Wanted, A Young Woman to Do Housework* (New York: Moffat Yard, 1915), 2.

11. Stigler, *Domestic Servants in the United States,* 24, 28; Dempsey, *Occupational Progress of Women,* 29.

12. Sutherland, *Americans and Their Servants,* 188–90; Bruere, "The New Home-Making," 592. For a good summary of the new architectural trends, see Clifford Edward Clark, Jr., *The American Family Home, 1800–1960* (Chapel Hill: Univ. of North Carolina Press, 1986), 131–92.

13. Sutherland, *Americans and Their Servants,* 186–88; Stigler, *Domestic Servants in the United States,* 26–27; Charlotte Perkins Gilman, *Women and Economics: A Study of the Economic Relation Between Men and Women as a Factor in Social Evolution* (Boston: Small Maynard, 1898), 265–66; Edward Stratton Holloway, "Apartments and How to Furnish Them," *House Beautiful* 5 (Aug. 1924):130; "To Save the Great American Home," 11.

14. Sutherland, *Americans and Their Servants,* 185; Della Thompson Lutes, *A Home of Your Own* (Indianapolis, Ind.: Bobbs-Merrill, 1925), 294–95.

15. Francis A. Kellor, *Out of Work: A Study of Employment Agencies* (New York: Putnam, 1904), 152–78; Shelby M. Harrison, *Public Employment Offices: Their Purpose, Structure and Methods* (New York: Russell Sage, 1924), 30, 49–53; "Service Without Servants Brings a New Employer, a New Employee and a New Workshop," *Good Housekeeping* 81 (Sept. 1925):89, 220–21; "Assistants, Not Servants," *Life and Labor* 9 (Mar. 1919):56; Christine Frederick, "Suppose Our Servants Didn't Live with Us?", *Ladies' Home Journal* 31 (Oct. 1914):102; Christine Frederick, "Why Should Our Servants Live with Us?", *Ladies' Home Journal* 32 (Oct. 1915):47, 98; Rubinow and Durant, "The Depth and Breadth of the Servant Problem," 580, 584; Palmer, *Domesticity and Dirt,* xiii, 85.

16. Gail Laughlin, "Domestic Service," in *Report of the United States Industrial Commission on the Relations of Capital and Labor,* 19 vols. (Washington, D.C.: U.S. Government Printing Office, 1901), XIV:747, XIV;760–61.

17. Mary V. Robinson, *Domestic Workers and Their Employment Relations,* Bulletin of the Women's Bureau, no. 39 (Washington, D.C.: U.S. Government Printing Office, 1924), 30–34, 69–70.

18. Sutherland, *Americans and Their Servants,* 61–62; Van Raaphorst, *Union Maids Not Wanted,* 33–34, 39–45; Ethel M. Smith, "America's Domestic Servant Shortage," *Current History* 26 (May 1927):213–18; Stigler, *Domestic Servants in the United States,* 7; Katzman, *Seven Days a Week,* 72–81, 87.

19. Tucker, *Telling Memories Among Southern Women,* 118, 173–74, 202.

20. For the Progressive reform philosophy as it affected domestic service, see Sutherland, *Americans and Their Servants*, 163–81. A convenient listing of writings by servants may be found in the same book, 214–15.

21. Mary Anderson, *Woman at Work: The Autobiography of Mary Anderson* (Minneapolis: Univ. of Minnesota Press, 1951), 13–14; Anna to Margaret Scott, 1 Jan. and 25 Aug. 1886, Adrian [Mich.] Girls' Training School Records, Michigan State Archives, Lansing; Lucy M. Salmon, *Domestic Service* (New York: Macmillan, 1897), 151n; Aleksandra Rembienska to parents, 20 Nov. 1911, in Thomas and Znaniecki, *Polish Peasant in America*, I:779.

22. Van Raaphorst, *Union Maids Not Wanted*, 156–71; Sutherland, *Americans and Their Servants*, 136–37.

23. The club, like many similar ones, would collapse and revive on several occasions during the next two decades. See "A Servant's Union," *Harper's Bazar*, 2 June 1900, p. 319; Bertha H. Smith, "A Club for Maids," *Ladies' Home Journal* 33 (Feb. 1916):64; Helen E. Zuhlke, "What Household Workers Can Do," *Life and Labor* 5 (Dec. 1915):187–88.

24. Van Raaphorst, *Union Maids Not Wanted*, 172–74, 188–213; Walter L. Fleming, "The Servant Problem in a Black Belt Village," *Sewanee Review* 13 (Jan. 1905):15–16.

25. Sutherland, *Americans and Their Servants*, 134–37. However, Chicago maids did not give up. For a revival of their efforts, see "From Near and Far," *Life and Labor* 9 (Nov. 1919):303.

26. Van Raaphorst, *Union Maids Not Wanted*, 172–74, 189–92; Daniel T. Hobby, ed., "'We Have Got Results': A Document in the Organization of Domestics in the Progressive Era," *Labor History* 17 (Winter 1976):103–108.

27. Van Raaphorst, *Union Maids Not Wanted*, 213; Marguerite Mooers Marshall, "Why a Housewife Wants a Household Workers' Union," *Life and Labor* 10 (May 1920):135–36.

28. "Employer-Employee Relationships in the Home," *Journal of Home Economics* 21 (Feb. 1929):120–22; Mathilde C. Hader, "Conference on Employer-Employee Relationships in the Home," *Journal of Home Economics* 23 (July 1931):640–42; "Unionizing the 'Hired Girl,'" *Literary Digest*, 9 May 1931, p. 23; Hazel Kyrk, "The Household Worker," *American Federationist* 39 (Jan. 1932):33–39.

29. Ruth L. Frankel, "A New Deal for Household Workers," *Forecast* 50 (June 1934):251; Eleanor Roosevelt, "Servants," *Forum* 83 (Jan. 1930):24–28.

30. Kyrk, "The Household Worker," 33; Smith, "America's Domestic Service Shortage," 218; "Employer-Employee Relationships in the Home," *Good Housekeeping* 88 (Feb. 1929):104.

Contributors

DONNA BRADEN is curator at the Henry Ford Museum and Greenfield Village, a position she has held since 1977. She has a B.A. in anthropology, awarded with distinction in American history, from Ohio State University. She also completed a study program at the University of the Americas, in Puebla, Mexico, where she took courses in anthropology and cultural history. Her M.A. in Early American Culture is from the Winterthur Program in Early American Culture and the University of Delaware. Among her many publications is the book *Leisure and Entertainment in America* (Henry Ford Museum & Greenfield Village, 1988).

KARIN CALVERT is senior program officer for the National Faculty of the Humanities, Arts and Sciences—Southern Region. She has held teaching positions at the University of Pennsylvania, the University of Delaware, and the Mt. Silinda Institute and Teacher Training College in Zimbabwe. She received a B.S. from the State University College of New York at Brockport, an M.A. from the Winterthur Program in Early American Culture and the University of Delaware, and a Ph.D. from the University of Delaware in conjunction with the Henry Francis DuPont Winterthur Museum. Her numerous publications, consultations, and lectures cover topics such as the history of American childhood, material culture, fashions in eighteenth-century America, portraiture, and Christmas.

RUTH SCHWARTZ COWAN is professor of history and director of women's studies at the State University of New York at Stony Brook, where she has taught since 1967. A native of Brooklyn, she received an A.B. in zoology from Barnard College, an M.A. in history from the University of California at Berkeley, and a Ph.D. in history of science from Johns Hopkins University. An authority on the impact of technology on housework and home life, Professor Cowan has been awarded a number of grants and fellowships, has presented lectures throughout the United States, and has produced publications for a wide variety of scholarly journals. Her book *More Work for Mother: The Ironies of Household Technology from the Open Hearth to the Microwave* (Basic Books, 1983) was awarded the Dexter Prize, an annual prize for the best book on the history of technology.

ELIZABETH COLLINS CROMLEY is an architectural historian with a special interest in popular and vernacular American architecture. Since 1980, she has taught at the State University of New York at Buffalo, where she is currently associate professor of architectural history in the School of Architecture and Planning. She has a B.A. from the University of Pennsylvania and an M.A. from New York University's Institute of Fine Arts; was a graduate research fellow at the Institute for Architecture and Urban Studies; and received her Ph.D. in 1982 from the City University of New York Graduate School. Her book *Alone Together: A History of New York's Early Apartments* (Cornell University Press) was published in 1990. She was also the consultant editor for *The Elements of Style: A Practical Encyclopedia of Interior Architectural Details from 1485 to the Present* (Simon and Schuster, 1991).

JESSICA H. FOY has been curator of museum collections at the McFaddin-Ward House in Beaumont, Texas, since 1987. Previously, she worked for Old Salem, Inc., in Winston-Salem, North Carolina, as assistant in the curatorial and restoration departments. A native of western North Carolina, Ms. Foy received her B.A. in American studies and English from Salem College and her M.A. in history museum studies from the Cooperstown Graduate Program of the State University of New York at Oneonta. She is coauthor of *The McFaddin-Ward House: Lifestyle and Legacy in Oil-Boom Beaumont, Texas* (Texas State Historical Association, 1992).

KATHERINE CHRISTINE GRIER is assistant professor in the Department of History and program assistant at the Humanities Center at the University of Utah where she is the recipient of the George S. and Dolores Dore Eccles Fellowship for the project "Regarding Animals: Popular Thought about Animals and Animal-Human Interaction in the Nineteenth-Century American Household." She is also adjunct assistant professor in the university's Department of Architecture. Dr. Grier has a B.A. in politics from Princeton University, an M.A. in history museum studies from the Cooperstown Graduate Program of the State University of New York at Oneonta, and a Ph.D. from the Program in the History of American Civilization, Department of History, University of Delaware. Her book *Culture and Comfort: People, Parlors, and Upholstery, 1850–1930* (Strong Museum) was published in 1988.

LINDA MARKSON KRUGER now head, Art and Architecture Cataloging Team, Columbia University, has been with the University since 1979. Since January 1991, Dr. Kruger has been adjunct associate professor, Queens College of CUNY, Graduate School of Library and Information Science, where she teaches art librarianship and the history of books and printing. Dr. Kruger received a B.A. in English literature and European history from the University of Vermont, an M.A. in art history from Boston University, a certificate in advanced librarianship and an M.S. and doctorate in library science from Columbia University.

COLLEEN MCDANNELL holds the Sterling McMurrin Chair in Religious Studies at the University of Utah, where she is associate professor of history. Professor McDannell received a B.A. in religious studies from the University of Colorado, an M.A. in religious studies from the University of Denver, and a Ph.D. in religious studies from Temple University. Among her publications are two recent books: *Heaven: A History* (Yale University Press, 1988) and *The Christian Home in Victorian America, 1840–1900* (Indiana University Press, 1986).

THOMAS J. SCHLERETH is professor of American studies and director of graduate studies in American studies at the University of Notre Dame, where he teaches American cultural, urban, and architectural history, as well as material culture studies. He received his B.A. in history from the University of Notre Dame, his M.A. in history from the University of Wisconsin, and his doctorate in American and European intellectual history from the University of Iowa. Author of numerous publications, he has published over eighty articles in scholarly journals. Among his most recent books are *Cultural History and Material Culture* (University Press of Virginia, second edition, 1992) and *Victorian America: Transformations in Everyday Life, 1876–1915* (New York: Harper and Row, 1991), a Book-of-the-Month Club Selection.

DANIEL E. SUTHERLAND, professor of history at the University of Arkansas at Fayetteville, holds Ph.D., M.A., and B.A. degrees from Wayne

State University. His fields of specialization are nineteenth-century America, southern history, British history, and American literature. His book *The Confederate Carpetbaggers* (Louisiana State University Press, 1988) was a selection of the History Book Club and was nominated for the Pulitzer Prize. Among his other publications are *Americans and Their Servants: Domestic Service in the United States, 1800–1920* (LSU Press, 1981) and *Reminiscences of a Private: William E. Bevens of the First Arkansas* (University of Arkansas Press, 1992).

PATRICIA M. TICE is curator of furnishings at the Strong Museum, a position she has held since 1980. Ms. Tice received a B.A. in liberal studies from the University of Delaware and an M.A. in museum studies from the University of Michigan. She also studied English decorative arts at the Victoria and Albert Museum while a student at the University of London. She planned the exhibit "Gardening in America" and wrote an accompanying book, *Gardening in America* (Strong Museum, 1984). Since completing that project, she has continued her research into the subject of American gardening in the nineteenth and early twentieth centuries.

CANDACE M. VOLZ holds the positions of principal, decorative arts consultant, and historian with the firm Volz and Associates in Austin, Texas. She earned a B.S. in interior design at the University of Texas and an M.A. in museum studies from George Washington University. Ms. Volz has been historic interiors consultant to a number of organizations, including the National Society of the Colonial Dames in America (Neill-Cochran House, 1854); the Office of the Chancellor, Texas A&M University (Hirshfeld House, 1885); the Architect of the Texas State Capitol (Lieutenant Governor's Reception Rooms); the San Antonio Conservation Society (Steves Homestead, 1874); and the Texas Historical Commission (George Sealy Mansion, 1889), among others.

Index